From Seva to Cyberspace

From Seva to Cyberspace

The Many Faces of Volunteering in India

Femida Handy
Meenaz Kassam
Jillian Ingold
Bhagyashree Ranade

Los Angeles | London | New Delhi
Singapore | Washington DC | Melbourne

First published in 2011 by

SAGE Publications India Pvt Ltd
B1/I-1 Mohan Cooperative Industrial Area
Mathura Road, New Delhi 110044, India
www.sagepub.in

SAGE Publications Inc
2455 Teller Road
Thousand Oaks, California 91320, USA

SAGE Publications Ltd
1 Oliver's Yard
55 City Road
London EC1Y 1SP, United Kingdom

SAGE Publications Asia-Pacific Pte Ltd
3 Church Street
#10-04 Samsung Hub
Singapore 049483

Published by Vivek Mehra for SAGE Publications India Pvt Ltd, typeset in 10/12 pt Minion Pro by Diligent Typesetter, Delhi.

Library of Congress Cataloging-in-Publication Data

From Seva to cyberspace: the many faces of volunteering in India/Femida Handy... [et al.].
    p. cm.
    Includes bibliographical references and index.
    1. Voluntarism—India—History. 2. Non-governmental organizations—India—History. 3. Nonprofit organizations—India—History. I. Handy, Femida, 1949

HN690.Z9V644   361.3'70954—dc23   2011   2011034895

ISBN: 978-81-321-0698-2 (PB)

The SAGE Team: Gayatri Mishra, Shreya Chakraborti, Amrita Saha and Rajinder Kaur

To
all volunteers who make the world a better place.

Thank you for choosing a SAGE product!
If you have any comment, observation or feedback,
I would like to personally hear from you.

Please write to me at **contactceo@sagepub.in**

Vivek Mehra, Managing Director and CEO, SAGE India.

Bulk Sales

SAGE India offers special discounts
for purchase of books in bulk.
We also make available special imprints
and excerpts from our books on demand.

For orders and enquiries, write to us at

Marketing Department
SAGE Publications India Pvt Ltd
B1/I-1, Mohan Cooperative Industrial Area
Mathura Road, Post Bag 7
New Delhi 110044, India

E-mail us at **marketing@sagepub.in**

Subscribe to our mailing list
Write to **marketing@sagepub.in**

This book is also available as an e-book.

Contents

List of Tables and Figures

Tables

Figures

Foreword

I am delighted to write the foreword to this important book on volunteers in India. One of the authors was a college friend and thus it gives me great pleasure to see her academic work in many ways dovetailing my own passions. My work as a social activist, whether it is empowering female children in Mijwan, Azamgarh, through Mijwan Welfare Society, an NGO founded by my father Kaifi Azmi, or at Nivara Hakk, an NGO dealing with slum dwellers in Mumbai or with People Living with HIV/AIDS, would not be effective without the countless hours donated freely by volunteers. Volunteers are the lifeblood of social activism and care in India, without whom our efforts would be fruitless.

The volunteer sector has grown rapidly in India and assumes new forms in uncharted territories, and this book captures the changing nature of volunteering. The authors present various forms of volunteering and show how it rapidly draws in people of all ages, religions, educational and social backgrounds. Given the importance of the work volunteers carry out and the changing dynamics of what volunteerism entails, it is timely that we have a book that captures 'who is a volunteer' and draws out the key arenas in which volunteerism thrives. This is well presented within the framework of socioeconomic changes and technological transformations.

Helping others is not a new idea; however it has certainly changed and is often institutionalized in interesting ways from service clubs and corporate programs to internet volunteering and voluntourism. The importance of volunteering is elucidated in the book by outlining the dichotomy of the two faces of India—the gloss of the shiny *Incredible India* with its high-tech industries and pharmaceutical companies headed by billionaires and the well-heeled educated middle class consumers against a gloomy backdrop of pervasive poverty, hunger, and want. In the middle, we have thousands of NGOs and volunteers who attempt to bridge the gap and give dignity of life to the economically weaker sections of our society who hold out a helping hand to millions living in dire poverty.

This book is timely in that it is the first attempt to look at the phenomenon of volunteering in India where volunteers are taking on a critical role in bringing about the change required to bridge the dichotomy and make *Incredible India* an encompassing reality for all. It presents theories of why individuals volunteer and provides data, both from India and elsewhere, to back up these theories. However, it is when the authors write individual and organizational narratives that they are able to flesh out the numbers and give it a human touch. These interesting stories are based on real people and their experiences, and bring the book alive. This perspective of combining narratives with more straightforward academic writing finally makes this book satisfying and instructive.

SHABANA AZMI

Preface

In recent years, the cultures and traditions of India have been subject to increased attention. For example, the philosophy of the Vedantic scriptures and schools of yoga and meditation have affected the lives of people from a wide variety of backgrounds; Indian movies are enthusiastically received across the world; and charismatic Indian cricketers have captured the hearts of many sports fans. However, it is not only in the area of culture that India has been making an impact; entrepreneurs have also shaped India's image by helping to carve out an economic niche for the country through their efforts to encourage and facilitate the in-sourcing of manufacturing and services.

Cultural and economic globalization have accelerated India's opening up to the rest of the world, and the country's roughly trillion dollar economy is now touted as the fourth-largest in the world. Concurrent economic reforms have allowed for the expansion of trade, encouraged technological innovation, and brought about enormous changes in consumerism, employment, education, and training for many Indians. However, these changes have not brought an increase in the standard of living for all Indians, especially those living in rural areas and smaller cities, who have been left out of, or even been harmed by, this economic growth. Infrastructure has also not kept up with the needs of the poor, and there still exists a vast disparity in access to good public elementary education and primary health care. Not only the poor, but many women and members of low caste and minority groups continue to feel that social conservatism and prejudice have prevented them from fully benefiting from economic opportunities. Furthermore, despite great progress in many areas, there still exist some intractable social arrangements that give rise to systematic discrimination with inequitable distribution of social and economic opportunities by caste, gender, and religion.

The dichotomy between the two faces of India is perhaps nowhere better represented than in the contrast between travel commercials portraying the glories of "Incredible India" and the recent Academy

Award-winning movie Slum dog Millionaire. The former shows us the palatial hotels and royal experiences that often lure foreign tourists. The latter gives a graphic acknowledgement to the pervasive urban poverty of Mumbai, the very city hailed as an engine of growth and an instrument of globalization.

Eighty-one million urban Indians subsist below the poverty line (UNDP, 2009). Scholars such as Amartya Sen have argued that economic growth, though crucial for reducing poverty and improving the living standards of people, will not be enough unless it is accompanied by increases in the quality of life of the common people:

> The more conventional criteria of economic success (such as high growth rate, a sound balance of payments, and so forth) are to be valued only as means to deeper ends. It would be a mistake to see the development of education, healthcare, and other basic achievements only or primarily as expansions of "human resources"—the accumulation of "human capital"— as if people were just the means of production and not its ultimate end. The better of human life does not have to be justified by showing that a person with a better life is also a better producer. (Drèze & Sen, 1997, p. iii)

In a 2004 *TIMEasia* article, Alex Parry discusses the development of "two Indias," argued to have resulted from the uneven distribution of the fruits of India's economic development (Perry, 2004). "Fifty years ago in newly independent India, castes mixed in the street and overt displays of wealth were more than crass—they were suspicious," Perry writes, "[b] ut today rich and poor lead wholly separate lives. The rich shop in malls, patronize private schools and hospitals, and relax in gyms and spas. The poor live in slums, send their children to work, and can't afford health care." Perry argues that 60 years after Independence, Gandhi, who won the hearts of Indians from all backgrounds and classes through his appeals to simple and humble living, has become nothing but a sentimental symbol to many who now lust after a taste of the "finer things" in life. Although the Congress government has made bridging the gap between the "two Indias" a high priority, a number of prominent individuals such as columnist Swapan Dasgupta and Kingfisher beer baron Vijay Mallya have argued that the Mahatma's spirit of charity is all but dead, and that now "[t]here is no collective interest in India. Only vested interests" (Vijay Mallya, quoted in Perry, 2004).

While there may be some substance to such criticisms, Perry points out that a number of well-to-do Indians have undertaken major projects to promote the well-being of the country's poor. For example, manufacturing magnate Parmeshwar Godrej has helped to bring many Indian celebrities together in support of a national AIDS-awareness campaign, while Wipro head Azim Premji has spent millions on education projects. In this book we will profile many more Indian citizens who have used their wealth or their time to work toward the betterment of the country's needy. Our research indicates that the efforts of such individuals may reflect a change in India's style of development as well. Because reliance on government action for change is often futile, many middle- and upper-class Indians have taken on the task of providing for the poor by organizing at the grass-roots level, such as forming nongovernmental organizations (NGOs) to help women, children, the rural poor, minorities, and the other vulnerable populations. For example, in our previous book, we documented 20 women from Maharashtra who had seen the need and felt the desire to serve others, and left lucrative jobs to form NGOs to help the poor (Handy et al., 2006).

The media has not completely ignored those who work to help society. Every day, small and large newspapers publish the stories of individuals who have made a difference in the lives of others. For example, *India Today* published the stories of Kanta Krishen and her daughter from Chandigarh (Gill, 2009) and Ms Susan from Bangalore (Mehta & Kumar, 2009). Ms Krishen was featured for her efforts to launch a voluntary blood bank society. Her experience with community service started when she began volunteering at a local hospital in Chandigarh. She became aware that there was a shortage of blood, and wanted to do something to help ensure that there were sufficient voluntary donations, so that people would not be coerced into selling their blood. After spending decades trying to establish a blood bank, she finally achieved success in 2004. Ms Krishen is often referred to as the "mother of blood banks of India" and, together with her daughter Sarin, volunteers countless hours of her time educating people, organizing blood donation camps, and arranging activities to get others involved in their cause. The mother–daughter pair has also assisted with the building of blood banks across India.

Ms Susan represents a somewhat more controversial brand of volunteer. She started the "Consortium of Pub-going, Loose and Forward Women" as a tongue-in-cheek response to the right wing's attempts to ban the "pub culture," which allows the free mixing of men and women in public places. Using Internet resources such as Facebook and blogs, she mobilized over 39,000 people within 10 days to her cause. The volunteers responding to her call were women who felt their right to freedom of movement was being restricted. They helped her to carry out a rather innovative protest, which involved sending of pink underwear to members of a right-wing group. The success and publicity of her campaign led to the radical right-wing backing down from its attempts to ban women from going to pubs.

There are many other examples of Indians who contribute their time to volunteer and mobilize others to volunteer. Whether they do this as social activism with the aim of confronting social injustices, as a way of providing aid to the disadvantaged and vulnerable, or in response to a natural disaster, they all serve to make their communities and country better places to live.

Although many volunteers see their involvement as part of their obligations as citizens of India, others volunteer as a means of serving humanity or of satisfying their religious and spiritual duties. Indeed, all of the religions practiced by India's people—e.g., Hindus, Muslims, Christians, Sikhs, Jains, and Parsees—have basic tenets that promote helping the poor and vulnerable. These tenets require adherents to help others not only by giving money but by doing *seva*—direct service to others.

Seva can take many different forms, and although this book does not cover all of them, it does give the reader a glimpse of some of the ways in which Indians seek to bring about positive change in their society. The types of *seva* discussed here range from the traditional to the new. *Seva* is often done by individuals in and through organizations, and this remains the primary focus of the book. We recognize, however, that much of *seva* happens at the informal level, from person to person, and we provide examples of this type of service as well (see Chapter 2).

We often use the word "volunteering" to describe *seva* in order to avoid any misunderstanding that we are focused on service that stems from religious beliefs. Thus, because the word *seva* is used in everyday language in India to describe volunteering, regardless of its motivation, we use *seva* and "volunteering" interchangeably, recognizing that *seva* neither implies nor reflects purely religious motives for volunteering.

The Indian society presented in this book is different from that suggested in traditional global coverage. It explores India at the level of the individual, by narrating the stories of social activists, many of whom are increasingly Internet-savvy and dedicated to promoting issues such as health, environment, education, arts and culture, promoting the empowerment of the vulnerable, and disaster relief efforts. This book focuses on people and organizations working toward social, cultural, and economic development. We focus on unsung, grassroots heroes who strive to make India a better place to live by offering assistance through NGOs, service clubs, their place of employment, technology, or direct service.

We hope that by doing this we will give the reader a unique perspective on India that is essential for understanding the nature of the country's social fabric.

Who We Are

In order to truly understand the way people live, we recognize that one needs to live in India for many years. Yet, when one lives in India for many years, it is easy to forget how the rest of the world is organized and to take things around you for granted. Of the four authors of this book, one of us has lived her entire life in India and has the deepest understanding of how life is lived in this country. Another, born in the United States, specializes in India studies and its languages and has lived in India for several long stretches. The remaining two were born and raised in India, but have lived and worked in North America and the Middle East for many years. Thus, our first-hand experiences grounded in our formative years in India are balanced with an objectivity that comes from many years spent abroad. We have also made frequent trips to India to conduct interviews and collect materials for this book, and we have always kept our eyes and hearts open to new ways of understanding what is happening in the country.

We come from different disciplines: economics, development studies, sociology, and business. Hence, we each look at the world differently and have different assumptions about human behavior. This led to many late night discussions and debates, conference calls, and e-mails, and has deepened our understanding of the phenomenon we study.

Of course, we collected far more data and interesting narratives than we could use. So we debated which stories to share and which we should keep in our memories. Each story had merit, and the stories demonstrated the amazing capacity for selfless service that exists among the rich and poor, and the educated and uneducated. We saw the impact of hours freely given on both the giver and the cause or recipient. Although we dedicate this book to the millions of volunteers in India, we especially remember those whose stories do not appear in these pages. We thank them all for sharing their time and letting us into their busy lives to speak to us. They were funny, intelligent, and compassionate people with great insights into the lives of others and the poor. They wanted to make a difference. And they have. Together with the many uncounted and unrecognized volunteers, they have changed the landscape of development in India one hour at a time.

Acknowledgments

As with all books, this book would not have been possible without the help and support of many people. First and foremost, the many individuals who appear in our book and those who filled out surveys for us. They generously allowed us to survey them—interview, probe, and question them. They have incredibly busy lives, often working full-time and volunteering. Yet they graciously allowed us into their lives when we approached them for information. We hope that our words accurately capture their world of volunteering and the commitment they bring to the many causes for which they volunteer.... Old or young, they had a wealth of information to share, they gave us a glimpse of the many facets of volunteering that make up the social fabric of the country and represent the energy and imagination that feed the civil society in India.

Our editors at SAGE Publications, Rekha Natarajan and Gayatri Mishra wisely steered us in productive directions when we most needed it. We are also grateful to David Estrin who helped us with a careful and most intelligent review of our work, taking care of many details involved in writing this manuscript. We thank Adam in Toronto, Canada, for graciously keeping us caffeinated and fed as he served us in the restaurant where we wrote and revised many parts of the embryonic manuscript.

Our husbands, Ram, Mohammed, Wafadar, and Ajit, and our children provided the moral and emotional support which helped us persevere. They believed in this project, encouraged us from the very beginning, and tolerated our long absences as we conducted our research and spent many days together in India, Toronto, Dubai, and Philadelphia.

Introduction

This book is about volunteers in India. While studying NGOs in India for our previous book (Handy et al., 2006), we were struck by the number of people we encountered who volunteered to help the NGOs and other organizations achieve their mission and the interesting ways in which they did this. Some of these volunteers were teenagers, whereas others were in their 80s. Some volunteered in school, others at their workplace, and mostly during the time they carved out of their work and family responsibilities. We decided that one day we would return to do a book that portrayed the many different faces of volunteering in India.

As soon as our previous book had been published, and before other obligations overtook us, we approached our publishers about doing a volume on volunteers in India. We had done some preliminary research and found that although many countries systematically documented their volunteer labor force and scholars had produced multiple academic studies about volunteers, the topic was largely ignored in India.

The library at the University of Pennsylvania had a copy of on *Voluntary Work in India* by N. V. Lalitha (1975), which turned out to be the only systematic empirical studies of volunteers in India that we could find. There had been many interesting reports and Web sites that discuss volunteers, but finding national statistics on volunteer participation rates in India was difficult.

The Johns Hopkins Comparative Nonprofit Sector Project published an excellent in-depth study on the nonprofit/NGO scene in India—*Defining the Nonprofit Sector: India* by Siddhartha Sen (1993) but there was little attention given to volunteers. This Project's later publication, *Global Civil Society: Dimensions of the Nonprofit Sector* (Salamon & Sokolowski, & Associates, 2004), gave us the first statistics on the size of the civil sector in India. The study found that 2 percent of adults in India—16,490,000 persons engage in volunteering. The value of their work was estimated at US$1,356 million. From an organizational perspective, volunteers were found to be an important part of the labor requirements of the nonprofit sector. The findings suggest that volunteers in nonprofit organizations represent 0.8 percent of the economically active population—roughly 3,379,600 individuals. This number is even greater than that of the paid labor force in the sector, which represents 0.6 percent of the economically active population. The bulk of volunteers in India are reported to work in the social services (40 percent) and education and research (28 percent), followed by culture and recreation (21 percent), health (7 percent), and other (5 percent).

Because volunteering is a conscious decision, it is reasonable to ask why people choose to devote their time and energies in this way. Dr Rajesh Tandon and Dr S. S. Srivastava of PRIA ask these questions in the Indian context as a part of the comparative global study done in collaboration with the Institute for Policy Studies, Johns Hopkins University, Baltimore, USA. In their report, Tandon and Srivastava (2003) state that "[v]olunteering is 'alive and well' in India today" with nearly 10 million Indian households reported to have engaged regularly in volunteering in recent months. They found that volunteers came from all educational backgrounds, with nearly 25 percent having only a primary level of education or less. Likewise, volunteers were found to have come from all income groups, with nearly 33 percent coming from poor households. The majority (66 percent) of volunteers live in rural areas. These statistics suggest that volunteering is not only the purview of the rich and educated but widespread among all levels of society.

When asked what motivates volunteers to do unpaid work, they found that 88 percent reported "they offer value addition through volunteering"; 87 percent reported "a moral obligation to volunteer"; 82 percent reported that volunteering "broadens their life"; and 66 percent reported that volunteering "helps to advance their career" (Tandon & Srivastava, 2003, pp. 1–17). These motivations are very much in line with what we have found among volunteers throughout the world. There is a strong combination of altruistic and value-driven reasons to volunteer, as well a range of motivations that further their own personal interests. This complexity of motivations has been replicated and reported in much of the scholarly literature (e.g., Clary et al., 1998; Cnaan & Goldberg-Glen, 1991).

During the writing of this book in 2008, a unique event occurred that indicated to us that it was likely that there were many more volunteers and potential volunteers beyond those statistics, at least in large cities. One of India's largest newspapers, *The Times of India,* with the support of the United Nations Volunteers (UNV), ran a campaign called "Teach

India" to recruit teachers for the nearly 42 million children who did not have access to schools (UNV, 2008). The idea was to recruit volunteers in four large cities (Mumbai, Delhi, Kolkata, and Chennai) to volunteer two hours per week for a minimum of three months to teach underprivileged children and adults. This recruitment appeal, which ran in the newspaper for three weeks, attracted 150,000 responses and 83,500 applications, many of which were submitted by individuals who were first-time volunteers. This far surpassed the expectations of the organizers, and thus far, over 76,000 volunteers have been offered teaching opportunities. A high proportion of students and women applied, and a significant number of the applicants were highly educated and held full-time employment, with engineers making up the largest single group (UNV, 2008). One of the volunteers writes of his experience:

> Thus my colleagues and I at UNV help bridge the literacy gap by creating connections between those with a desire to teach the underprivileged and the NGOs that work with them. . . . It has opened people's eyes and made them realize that they have something to give back to society—in a sense; this has been education for the literate. . . . Taking people with different social, political, economic and educational backgrounds, the campaign has started breaking down stigmas and discrimination. Furthermore, it has engaged corporations and activated thinking about development and social activism. . . . "Teach India" demonstrates that citizens can be leaders and contribute to the country's development through volunteering; and it provides a platform to members of society who, irrespective of their personal and professional status, feel a strong desire to give back. (Immanuel, 2008)

The success of this appeal spurred us to continue with our study of volunteers. We believe that the active, voluntary participation of Indian citizens will help to make a difference in poverty reduction by increasing access to education and primary health care, as well as in other areas important for community betterment. We agree with Tocqueville, who, as early as 1840 suggested that voluntary associations help create and maintain a culture of citizenship and bring about a social solidarity among people who come together through their participation in voluntary projects (Bellah et al., 1985).

In this book we make the faces of volunteering in India visible both through individual stories and systematic study. We realize that in order to thoroughly explore the issue of volunteering in India or elsewhere, quantitative studies alone are insufficient. Although statistics are important in determining who the volunteers are, what they do, where they do it, and why they do it, we believe that qualitative data is perhaps even more important. It puts flesh on the bones. We adopt an approach similar to that used in our previous book, presenting narratives of volunteers and organizations that facilitate volunteering at the end of each chapter.

We begin with an overview of the history of volunteering in India, from its earliest appearances in premodern texts to its various present manifestations. We end the chapter by offering two narratives of volunteers in India who have made volunteering an integral part of their lives. We selected the narratives in an attempt to give the reader insights into two modes of volunteering prevalent in India: (*a*) the volunteer who works under the aegis of an organization, and (*b*) the volunteer who works on his or her own, without organizational backing. We refer to such individuals as "formal volunteers" and "informal volunteers," respectively.

In Chapter 2, having investigated the changing nature of volunteering from a historical perspective, we raise the fundamental question: "Who is a volunteer?" In this chapter we report on the results from an earlier study, examine the literature regarding the definition of a volunteer, and conclude that, because volunteering is essentially a social construct, it must be examined as such. We then investigate how people perceive "who is a volunteer" and report our findings for India, comparing our results with those of other countries to see if our proposed framework is robust across cultures.

Next, we turn our attention to three particular cohorts of Indian citizens. We acknowledge that volunteering may mean different things depending on which phase of life you are in. Thus, the three chapters examine volunteering at different stages of life. We consider young university students in Chapter 3. In Chapter 4, we discuss working adults who volunteer in the context of employer-supported programs. Finally, we look at retirees and seniors (i.e., "mature individuals") in Chapter 5. This last-named cohort has its own unique opportunities, including greater free time and less family responsibility, along with its own constraints, including potentially weaker health and energy levels.

For members of each group, we examine how they volunteer, the ways in which they choose to volunteer, and why they volunteer. For youth, we conducted our own survey to determine the profile of a typical volunteer, and examined volunteer motives. For the other two cohorts, we relied more on published literature and interviews with key informants. In all three chapters, we present narratives that give us an understanding of the many faces of volunteering while adding texture to the picture.

In Chapter 6, we examine religious volunteering. We do this because findings in India and elsewhere have shown that religion often motivates volunteering and philanthropy. Values of altruism, which encourage people to act selflessly for the good of others, form an important part of the teachings of all religions. Many religious believers see themselves as required by their faith to actualize their values through acts of charity and *seva*. We look at religious volunteering in the three largest religions of India and give narratives that offer an organizational, as well as a human, face to such volunteering.

In Chapter 7, we report on the different trends that can be found in India. This includes an upsurge in certain traditional forms of volunteering (e.g., service clubs), alongside newer forms of volunteering (e.g., cyberspace volunteers and "voluntourists"). Each of these trends is discussed briefly, followed by narratives that provide insight into the diversity and complexity of volunteering in India today.

In our concluding chapter, we raise the question of the value of volunteering. In part, because of its generally altruistic motivations, serving one's community without remuneration is often assumed to be worthwhile. But what exactly is its worth? How do we measure that worth? Here, we present some debates on these issues and conclude by exploring a social accounting system that has the potential to bring the contribution of the volunteers within an organization to the forefront. We calculate the worth of volunteering by using a value-added framework, and in this manner present the social accounts of a hypothetical NGO using volunteer labor.

This brings us back to the reason we took on this study. As mentioned previously, volunteers are active throughout India, with millions gladly contributing their time and energy for the betterment of their society. We want to portray them; we want their efforts recognized and encouraged. Although it would be impossible to give attention to all the volunteers and their unique contributions to society, we hope we will give the reader a glimpse of their lives through the narratives that follow each chapter. Volunteering, as we learned, is not a homogenous activity—far from it. It is kaleidoscopic in nature, and its forms and patterns are shaped and colored by human creativity and his urge to be compassionate.

1

A Brief History of Volunteering in India: When Did It Start?

Introduction

In this chapter, we will provide some background on the unique Indian context in which voluntary action takes place and the institutions that enable such action. This will allow the reader to better understand the specifics of the Indian environment as they relate to volunteering. With this in mind, we will provide a brief overview of the historical context in which volunteering took root in India and the institutions, individuals, and ideas that have shaped it into its present forms. We will also include a discussion of the religious impetus of volunteering and the spiritual and secular leaders who helped to bring about the voluntary action of citizens, through both mass movements and institutions. We will also examine the political and social atmosphere in which volunteerism has operated, focusing on the complex interplay between the centralizing tendencies of the Indian government and the grassroots and community-based efforts of NGOs. Finally, we will provide a brief overview of the environment in which voluntary organizations in India are operating today.

Throughout this book, we will discuss commonalities between volunteers in India and those residing elsewhere. These similarities are due to a wide variety of factors, such as similarities in human nature across cultures, the increasing interconnectedness of the peoples of the world, demographic parallels, and the global reach of many Indian institutions and organizations. Other findings, however, point to characteristics of volunteers and voluntary institutions that appear to stem from qualities and historical circumstances distinct to India and its cultures.

Early History

The concept of voluntary social action in India can be argued to date back as far as the *Rig Veda*, written around 1500 BCE.[1] The *Rig Veda* discusses voluntary action and devotes an entire chapter to the practice of charity (Ravichandran et al., 2006, p. 212; Sen, 1993, p. 3). With the exception of the few empires that were able to develop extensive public welfare systems, voluntary action was, by necessity, the main source of welfare in ancient India. Family and caste support mechanisms were supplemented by religious, trade, and other forms of solidarity, which encouraged assisting those in need (Sen, 1993, p. 3). Religious edicts, derived from Hindu and other sacred texts, promoted voluntary action. The doctrine of *Karma Yoga*, as laid out in the Bhagawad Gita,[2] is a good example of this. *Karma Yoga* teaches that "[an] action which is ordained, done by one undesirous of fruit, devoid of attachment, without love or hate, that is called pure" (Chinmayananda, n.d., XVIII, verse 23, as quoted in Lacy, 1965, p. 22). Acting according to one's duty and unencumbered by self-interest is said to lead to liberation from the cycle of rebirth by freeing the personality of the ego and from attachment to the fruits of one's actions (Chinmayananda, n.d., III, verse 7). The notion of charity is also prominent in Islam, the religion of over 13 percent of Indians. In addition to the obligatory almsgiving incumbent in the form of *zakat*, members of the Islamic community are also called upon to give supplementary, spontaneous alms (*sadaqah*). This may take the form of monetary donations or voluntary service. Mohamed Ariff (1991) argues that voluntary action has taken on a particularly significant role in countries in which Muslims are a minority. He notes that according to the doctrine of *fard qifayah*, those social duties that are obligatory in Islam must be performed somehow; if they are not performed by the state, they must be performed by members of society at large. As such, in a non-Islamic state, these responsibilities naturally fall to the Islamic voluntary sector (Ariff, 1991, p. 4). Other religions in India, such as Jainism, Sikhism, and Buddhism, also include teachings and edicts that encourage voluntary and charitable action (Sen, 1993, p. 3). For example, Ashoka, generally revered as one of the greatest rulers in Indian history, attempted to spread the ideals of *dhamma* across

---

[1] The *Rig Veda* is an ancient Indian collection of Vedic Sanskrit hymns. It is considered one of the four canonical sacred texts (*shruti*) of Hinduism.
[2] Another of the great sacred texts of Hinduism.

the subcontinent. These ideals emphasized tolerance, respect, and generosity toward others and were focused on "creating an attitude of mind in which the ethical behavior of one person toward another was primary" (Thapar, 2004).

It may be argued, however, that voluntary action, as we know it now, did not take on its more modern, institutionalized form until the early 19th century when Christian missionaries combined their efforts at propagating their faith with a range of voluntary charitable and social development initiatives, such as the building of schools, orphanages, and medical centers (Ravichandran et al., 2006, p. 212; Sen, 1993, p. 4). Although missionaries had a strong presence in India during the 18th century as well, the British East India Company successfully led efforts to restrict their actions from the territory it controlled. These restrictions were removed by the Charter Act in 1813, which led to a significant increase in missionary work. Consequently, associated charitable and other social activities, such as the building of missionary schools and hospitals, increased (Kapoor & Singh, 1997, p. 16). The Indian elite, particularly those studying in missionary schools in Bengal, were strongly influenced by their actions and began synthesizing their social reform efforts with Hindu charitable activities in the early 1820s (Sen, 1993, p. 4).

Most prominent among these early leaders was Raja Ram Mohan Roy who formed the Atmiya Sabha in 1815. Although the Atmiya Sabha allied with the Christian Unitarians to start the Unitarian Committee in 1821 (Ravichandran et al., 2006, p. 213), the coalition failed to maintain the interest of the Hindu base (Kapoor & Singh, 1997, p. 17) and dissolved. However, Hindu voluntary action did not disappear, and a number of purely Hindu councils (*sabhas*) sprung up in its wake. The *sabhas* undertook a number of health, education, and other social service initiatives in addition to proselytization and religious reform efforts.

In the 19th century, the *sabhas* evolved into more formal organizations and institutions (Ravichandran et al., 2006, pp. 213–214), three of the most significant of which were perhaps the Arya Samaj, the Brahmo Samaj, and the Ramakrishna Mission. The late 19th and early 20th centuries also marked the advent of a number of working-class organizations, such as the Bombay Association of Textile Workers (Kapoor & Singh, 1997, p. 18) and missions of volunteers working to uplift the underprivileged. Many of these charitable and volunteer efforts were combined with Hindu religious instruction, such as the Depressed Classes Mission (1906), the Nirashrit Seva Sadan (1907), and the Free Institution for the Depressed Classes (1909) (Singh, 1968, pp. 262–264).

Although most of these organizations were focused on religious and social reform, the Ramakrishna Mission was unique in the emphasis it placed on social service. Named after the Hindu sage Ramakrishna, who helped to bring about a synthesis of the ancient Indian tradition of service and the modern western tradition of charity, the Ramakrishna Mission was dedicated to social services, medical relief work, and the promotion of education through charity and volunteer efforts (Natarajan, 1962, p. 77). The Mission was founded by Ramakrishna's disciple, Swami Vivekananda (1863–1902) who was instrumental in popularizing and encouraging the perception of social service voluntary action as *sadhana* or spiritual preparation, using the powerful imagery of service as worship of the "living God" (Beckerlegge, 2007, p. 2). He emphasized its links with the concepts of liberty, equality, and free thinking. Great emphasis was placed on Ramakrishna's spiritual message of "Serve *Jiva* as *Siva*" (seeing God in each human being served), which made voluntary action a form of worship.

Vivekananda has been credited with bringing Ramakrishna's message to the people by making Vedanta (the teaching of the Vedas or ancient Hindu scriptures) practical, so that it was no longer the exclusive domain of the learned classes and Brahmins but could be practiced "both by the monk and the ordinary householder" (Narottamananda, 1982, p. 38f). Vivekananda also traveled abroad in order to raise money to train wandering monks. These monks would then act as volunteer educators, providing secular as well as religious education to poor rural children who were unable to attend school (Singh, 1968, p. 245). Ramakrishna is credited with inspiring the formation of a number of charitable and voluntary organizations and missions that have continued to operate across the country long after his death (Datta, 1956, p. 206). These organizations and missions have provided venues for voluntary action for countless individuals.

Due to the relative privilege and influence of upper-caste men at this time, it is not surprising that the vast majority of early reformers were of this demographic. They had the added advantage of access to higher education which, combined with their social status, helped them to take on leadership roles in setting social norms in the practice of charity and voluntary action. However, there are also examples of lower-caste individuals and women being involved in initiating social service movements and institutions in the 19th and early 20th centuries. One example was Mahatma Jyotirao Phule, a low-caste son of a vegetable vendor, who in

addition to leading a variety of social reform activities, such as movements for equality of the sexes and castes and promoting widow remarriage, also opened a home for orphans and children born to unmarried parents in the mid-19th century (PRIA, 2001, p. 7). Another example was Bhandaru Acchamamba, a female author in the Telugu language, who set up a number of women's organizations in Andhra Pradesh. These organizations provided shelter and support to needy women and children and relied on charity to meet their goals (PRIA, 2001, p. 9).

Another major upsurge in institutions resembling modern NGOs in India during the colonial period occurred with the Swadeshi Movement of the early 1900s. The movement was a response to the 1905 decision made by the British to divide Bengal into eastern and western sections. It was marked not only by political protests promoting self-sufficiency and independence, but also by the proliferation of voluntary associations that focused on organizing efforts to promote "self-help in economic and social life." This plan for self-help included the establishment of a number of district associations promoting local industry, community assistance programs, and even cooperative banks (PRIA, 2001, p. 12). The objectives of the Swadeshi Movement were later championed by Mahatma Gandhi who ultimately proved to be the most influential figure in the development of voluntary associations in India.

Gandhi and Tagore

During the early 20th century, religious philanthropy continued to operate and religion-based voluntary organizations focused on welfare and empowerment (Sen, 1993, pp. 8–9). A number of Muslim groups with associated charitable institutions and volunteer corps arose as well (Sen, 1997, p. 408). However, the two most significant figures in the evolution of the volunteer movement during this period were Rabindranath Tagore (1861–1941) and Mahatma Gandhi (1869–1948). Both Tagore and Gandhi viewed the village as the basis of Indian society and the key to its regeneration. Both also felt that the British had worked to destroy the self-reliance of the Indian people and their sense of social responsibility. Moreover, Tagore and Gandhi both viewed social responsibility as congruent with religious duty. There was, however, one important difference between the two thinkers. Gandhi believed in direct political action to remove the British from power whereas Tagore was explicitly apolitical and

focused on internal reform. Ultimately, perhaps in part, because political movements required greater voluntary action from citizens, Gandhi's influence on the evolution of voluntary action in India proved stronger than that of Tagore (Gupta, 2005, pp. 38–57). It was a consequence of Gandhi's efforts that voluntary action began to acquire an expressly political context, which departed from the more issue-based volunteerism of the 19th century (Sen, 1993, p. 8). In fact, his influence on the evolution of voluntary action in India has been so significant that, 44 years after his death, India's Association of Voluntary Agencies for Rural Development (AVARD) identified Gandhian ideology as the most prominent guiding philosophy of NGOs in India, alongside that of Christianity (Tripathi, 1992, p. 10).

Gandhi argued that India's development was only possible through voluntary action (Sen, 1993, p. 6). Like earlier leaders of the reform movement, Gandhi identified himself as a Hindu and took much inspiration from Hindu teachings. He was also profoundly influenced by Christian and western secular thought and the teachings of other religious traditions. For example, although Gandhi held the Bhagavad Gita to be the single greatest inspiration in his life, he identified the Sermon on the Mount as his first significant influence (Tinker, 1964, p. 265). In his formative years, he dreamed of synthesizing the teachings of the Gita, Buddha, and Christ (Datta, 1956, p. 211). Gandhi's religious ideals combined with philosophies on economic development that were strongly influenced by Russian and western populist tradition (Hettne, 1976, p. 230). He believed that, in order to serve God, man must be devoted to the service of others (Kantowsky, 1980, p. 11; Rothermund, 1969, p. 318) and that human actions should thus contribute to both social and spiritual progress (Weber, 1994, pp. 201–203).

Gandhi's syncretic religious beliefs and populist economic leanings manifested themselves in his philosophy of *sarvodaya*. *Sarvodaya* is a word that Gandhi coined to reflect his belief in the importance of service to mankind (Harris, 1987, pp. 1036, 1038). With the aim of furthering his agendas of spiritual and social development and political liberation, Gandhi devised a "Constructive Programme" that included 18 items of voluntary action that required the participation and support of the people of India. These items included various educational, health, economic, and political initiatives. Gandhi promised that true self-realization would occur through the voluntary service to the community (Kantowsky, 1980, pp. 8–10), and his Sarvodaya Movement was perceived by many

as providing a "guiding star" (Harris, 1987, p. 1036) for the future welfare of the nation.

Post Independence

After India achieved independence, voluntary agencies were considered an integral part of the nation-building process, and their numbers increased considerably. Although the philosophy of the newly formed Indian government emphasized the importance of a strong state, Nehru and other early leaders took the position that social service activities should be left to the voluntary sector. They offered government-funded economic and technical assistance to voluntary organizations (Rajesekhar & Biradar, 2002, p. 3). In the First Five Year Plan, the Indian government acknowledged its own responsibility for providing social welfare services. It also established the principle that the major responsibility for such services should be shouldered by voluntary organizations (Taylor et al., 1965, p. 464). To this end, ₹40 million were allocated for the support of voluntary organizations in the First Five Year Plan (1951–1956), and this allocation increased in each subsequent plan (Sooryamoorthy & Gangrade, 2001, pp. 48–49).

The central government also founded the Central Social Welfare Board (CSWB) in 1953 to support and promote voluntary organizations and to strengthen and expand the reach of these organizations into unserviced and rural areas. The significant number of Gandhian voluntary organizations that emerged in the early years of Independence may be largely attributed to this strong government support (Sen, 1993, p. 9). Many Christian and non-Christian religion-based voluntary organizations continued to operate as well, although these tended to focus on relief work (Sen, 1993, pp. 1–2).

The Indian government's enthusiasm for such voluntary organizations (now often referred to as NGOs) existed in part because of the latter's ability to provide social services in areas unreachable by or unattractive to the government. The apolitical attitudes of the early NGO leaders also meant that the government did not have to be especially concerned that they would pose a threat to centralized power. According to Siddhartha Sen, despite the prominent role of NGOs in the early years of Indian Independence, opposition to the state development policy was not an option for these groups. This was due to the "strong monolithic nature" of the state as well as the "enormous prestige" of the national elite, which was extended throughout the country by the patronage links of the Congress Party (Sen, 1999, p. 335). Sen argues that the democratic structure within the Congress Party extended to the grassroots level, allowing the party to knit together the state and society, and that the Congress-linked elite enjoyed such enormous prestige in the years immediately following Independence such that it was unlikely that any individuals or organizations would go against their agenda (Sen, 1999) without seeming unpatriotic. This is significant because, at this time, Nehru was at the head of the Congress Party, and there was a stark disparity between the ideas put forward by Nehru and those advocated by Gandhi—the ideological head of the blossoming NGO movement—regarding development. In fact, according to Nehru himself, the newly independent government had never considered adopting Gandhi's societal prescripts of cottage industries as an ideal for the new social order (Kantowsky, 1980, p. 14). Quite the contrary, Gandhi and his followers advocated cottage industries and local governance whereas Nehru and his associates promoted a version of capital-intensive, centrally directed growth. These radically different philosophies were in part held together by the common nationalist roots of both movements.

Despite this ideological contribution, the government did attempt to incorporate a few of Gandhi's ideals into the plans for the country. For example, Gandhi's constructive program of building economies at the village level was institutionalized by the government in the creation of Khadi and Village Industries Commission (PRIA, 2001, p. 16). Within a short period of time, however, disagreement between the two development ideologies began to manifest itself in outward conflict.

Perhaps the earliest major sign of friction between the Gandhian grassroots ideology of the nonprofit sector and Nehru's philosophy of a strong central government occurred when Mahatma Gandhi's protégé, Vinoba Bhave, was invited to meet with the Planning Commission for the government's First Five Year Plan. Vinoba walked out of the meeting early when he realized that the government was not interested in considering a Gandhian bottom-up style of development, adhering instead to a style of growth marked by "big industry, large production, and consumerism" (Harris, 1987, p. 1042).

However, Vinoba was strongly opposed to direct participation in politics, and his opposition to Nehru's style of development never posed a serious threat to the government. The conflict did not peak until after Vinoba retired to an ashram and the movement was taken over by Jai

Prakash (J. P.) Narayan. Having lost faith in the Indian government, Narayan started agitating against it with the support of thousands of workers of the Sarvodaya Movement who were active in the NGO sector (Sen, 1999, p. 339). This movement included a significant majority of the members of the Sarva Seva Sangh, an organization that had been formed by Vinoba out of a number of Gandhian groups with the intention of carrying out the work of the Sarvodaya Movement better (Harris, 1987, pp. 1039–1041).

The opposition of the J. P. Narayan-led movement occurred at a time when the Congress government was feeling especially vulnerable and continued into the Emergency period declared by Indira Gandhi (1975–1977). During this Emergency, a number of leaders associated with the Sarvodaya Movement were arrested. The Foreign Contribution Regulation Act (FCRA), which regulates foreign contributions to NGOs in India, was also enacted during this period to bring the NGO movement under greater government control. The FCRA includes a clause that allows NGOs "of a political nature" to receive foreign funding only after obtaining prior permission from the federal government (John, 2007).

Despite these efforts by the Congress government, the opposition Janata Party, which Narayan supported and had helped form, was victorious in the elections following the Emergency period. Once in power, however, the Janata Party chose to disregard the NGO-supported Sarvodaya Movement's goals for development in India (Harris, 1987). To make matters worse, when Congress returned to the helm in the following election, there was a major backlash against a number of NGOs. A commission was set up to investigate those who had been in opposition to Congress. The Sarva Seva Sangh, the Gandhi Peace Foundation, and AVARD were particularly singled out (Harris, 1987). The FCRA number of the Gandhi Peace Foundation was withdrawn. A number of other NGOs faced harassment, funding and project obstruction, and a government-supported campaign against them in the press.

During the five years of the commission's life, over 900 NGOs were accused of subversion, and by the mid-1980s, most radical NGOs began to disappear from the political scene. Funding restrictions were tightened even further by way of a 1985 amendment to the FCRA legislation, the Finance Act of 1983, which removed tax exemptions for industries donating to the NGOs ended tax exemptions for income-producing activities of the NGOs (Sen, 1999, pp. 341–343). In this way, the J. P. Narayan-led movement, which had initially brought about a radical shift toward political activism in Gandhian and other NGO activities, contributed to an atmosphere of greater mistrust between the government and the NGO sector. This mistrust ultimately led to greater government involvement in and restrictions on voluntary organizations.

Government Involvement in the Voluntary Sector

The government had allowed considerable independence and autonomy among grassroots-oriented NGOs as long as the organizations were politically harmless. From the perspective of many in the government, the proper role for NGOs was the delivery of a wide variety of services to the people while legitimizing the ruling party. But it soon became clear that the power structure of the relationship between the government and the NGOs could not be relied upon to remain static without legislative enforcement. The central government used its superior position to bring the much weaker NGO sector back down to size so that it would no longer pose a threat to the ruling party. It was able to take such decisive action in part because of its power and sovereignty in international aid negotiations, aided by the strong centralized nature of the expansive socialist state. As Sen (1999, p. 344) explains:

> Unlike many countries in Africa and Asia, bilateral and multilateral donors did not reallocate development assistance away from the [Indian] state to NGOs and set conditionalities, thereby reducing the state's role as the primary developmental actor.... In this policy climate, the state could establish a well-defined role for NGOs and even try to make NGOs adhere to it. This role envisioned that NGOs follow the state's development model and implement it.

Accordingly, the state chose not to attempt to cut the NGO sector out of the development process but to coerce it into following the central government's model by cracking down on dissenters while attracting others through increased governmental grants (Rajesekhar & Biradar, 2002; Sen, 1999). It was at this time that the government began to be a "key player" in grassroots development (Sharma, 2006, p. 63), even forming some of its own quasi-governmental NGOs, known as government-operated nongovernmental organizations or GONGOs (Sen, 1999, p. 338; Sharma, 2006).

Since the late 1980s, government programs and financial assistance channeled to NGOs have increased substantially, which has decreased dependence on outside funding sources and increased their dependence on the government (Rajesekhar & Biradar, 2002, p. 2). It has also arguably led to an increasing professionalization of the NGO movement and a corresponding decline in its grassroots, voluntary nature. The government has continued to take steps to reduce the influence of political NGOs. However, at the same time, the government recognizes the importance of decentralizing its development strategy and allotting a more significant role to those NGOs that it does not view as threatening (Sen, 1997).

A number of centrally directed programs initiated by the government in the late 1970s and early 1980s[3] did not have the impact that had been hoped for, leading the government to be more open to a broader form of development and one in which the NGOs play a major role (Kapoor & Singh, 1997). With this in mind, the government formed the Council for the Advancement of People's Action and Rural Technology (CAPART) in December 1986 (Kapoor & Singh, 1997), which handles the distribution of government and other indigenous funds to the NGOs (Tripathi, 1992). Any NGO that has been legally registered for at least one year can apply to CAPART for projects (Kapoor & Singh, 1997). This change in policy was explicitly recognized in the Eighth Five Year Plan (1992), which emphasized the importance of decentralization and human development (Dhesi, 1996).

Voluntary Organizations in India Today

According to AVARD, the NGOs in India today can be loosely grouped into three types: charity, relief, and welfare organizations; groups involved in service delivery, innovation, and development work; and those organizations focused on social transformation (Tripathi, 1992, p. 10). They exist across the country with a relatively greater number operating in the southern regions, perhaps a consequence of the stronger presence of Christian welfare organizations in that area (Riley, 2002, p. 83). They also tend to be greater in number in those regions in which infrastructural facilities and human and material resources are more easily obtainable (Kapoor & Singh, 1997, p. 24).

---

[3] Such as the Integrated Rural Development Programme (IRDP) (1978–1979), Training of Rural Youth for Self-Employment (TRYSEM) (1979), National Rural Employment Programme (NREP) (1980), Rural Landless Employment Guarantee Programme (RLEGP) (1980), and the Development of Women and Children in Rural Areas (DWCRA) (1982–1983).

In the first detailed survey of NGOs in India,[4] Tandon and Srivastava (2003) write that this sector is largely invisible and widespread. According to their count, which is based on surveys conducted throughout the country, India has 1.2 million NGOs with a majority (51 percent) of them registered, mostly under the Society Registration Acts (Tandon & Srivastava, 2003, p. 4). This sector commands nearly ₹18,000 crore[5] with more than half of this money self-generated through fees and charges for services. Nearly 13 percent of this funding comes from domestic and foreign donations.

The authors also find that more than 75 million Indian households (40.7 percent) report giving to charitable causes and 10 million households (5.4 percent) report volunteering. Indian NGOs are largely reliant upon this volunteer labor. The survey revealed that nearly three-quarters of all NGOs are either completely volunteer-run or have only one paid staff member. In total, over 20 million people work in these NGOs either as paid staff or volunteers, with the total number of volunteers estimated to be roughly 16.5 million. Outside of the agricultural sector, one out of every eight people in the workforce is engaged in nonprofit work on some level, although only 1.8 percent has full-time, paid employment with a nonprofit organization. Tandon and Srivastava contrast this with a 1999 cross-national study which showed that, among the 22 countries surveyed, an average of 4.8 percent of the population was employed full time with nonprofits. Given the size of the nonprofit sector in India, the relatively low percentage of full-time paid workers in the sector may indicate that although the sector is becoming increasingly professionalized, it remains more reliant upon volunteer labor than in many other countries.

Conclusions

The evolution of the voluntary sector in India has been shaped by many different individuals, ideals, and turns of historical circumstance. The religious impetus for social service was perhaps the earliest motivation for

---

[4] Tandon and Srivastava (2003) use the abbreviation "NPO" and do not include self-help groups, cooperatives, political parties, and those establishments focused solely on religious worship. We refer to them as NGOs in keeping with our text.

[5] For the time period 1999–2000, a crore is equal to 10 million.

charitable volunteering and is still strong today. Tandon and Srivastava (2003) report that 26.5 percent of the nonprofits in the country that are engaged in social development activities have a primarily religious identification. We will explore these organizations in greater depth in Chapter 6, although on some level, distinguishing between secular and religious NGOs may be somewhat arbitrary. As we have seen, many of the secular organizations that have proliferated in India are based on Gandhian ideals that, although noncommunal, are explicitly spiritual in nature. Moreover, the early reform movements that encouraged Indians to work for the betterment of the less fortunate in their community were also based on a reevaluation of religious ideals rather than on their rejection.

The reform and Gandhian movements were also closely tied to, influenced by, and influential in the movement for Independence. It is no great stretch to extend the ideal of community service to that of serving one's country. Thus, to many of the early nationalist leaders, as with many NGO leaders today, economic self-sufficiency and softening the sharp divisions of power within India are essential elements of social and economic development. It is, perhaps, for this reason that in independent India there has been a tenuous relationship between the state and the voluntary sector. Both see themselves as heirs of the spirit of the nationalist movement and both, at times, regard the other as a potential threat to the social and economic progress of the country.

Not all volunteers or voluntary organizations should be considered a part of this quasi-political NGO movement. As we will explore in later chapters, the reality is more complex. Many NGOs take advantage of government initiatives and, thus, work unambiguously within the government plan for development. They recruit and attract volunteers who do not perceive their work as a political statement but rather as an expression of a personal or spiritual commitment to help others. (Chapter 2, on youth volunteerism, gives a number of examples of volunteering of this type.) Others work within the contexts of their places of employment, which may be local businesses or large, multinational corporations, as we will discuss in Chapter 4. These companies have their own agenda, which is rarely explicitly political or likely to be perceived as a challenge to the state. The corporations often work with more conventional NGOs to initiate their programs and these NGOs tend to be focused on the communities from which their customer and employee bases are derived. The involvement of the companies likely accords them some influence on the NGOs with which they work with regard to the types of programs pursued.

This complexity in the interrelationships of the many development programs, in which Indian volunteers serve, is rapidly increasing. Over the last 30 years, the scope of foreign influence (and, in consequence, foreign interest) in Indian development has been increasing dramatically. This interest manifests itself in the form of investment from bilateral and multilateral donors and in the presence of foreign businesses and Indians returning from long stretches of work and study abroad. The opportunities provided by technological development, and the Internet, in particular—for Indians to go abroad for volunteer work and for foreigners to come to India for the same purpose—are also making a mark on today's volunteer scene, as will be discussed in Chapter 7. In this book, we will seek to disentangle some of these interconnected threads of voluntary action in India. We will do this by examining a wide variety of types of volunteers who work in a wide variety of organizations, and we will find both consistency and variety in the motivations and activities of the vast numbers of Indians drawn to serve in their communities and beyond.

2

Volunteering: Who Is a Volunteer?

Introduction

This chapter asks the question "Who is a volunteer?" and will attempt to answer this question in a manner appropriate to the Indian context. First, we discuss the various classifications and definitions that have been proposed for volunteering and the underlying frameworks they are built upon. We then develop and explain the "net-cost theory" on which we based our research. Next, we present our four hypotheses and describe the methods used for collecting data in collaboration with other scholars (Handy et al., 2000; Meijs et al., 2003). We then examine our findings as they pertain to India before comparing our results to findings in other countries using a rank-order analysis. A cross-cultural examination reveals that there is a general and universal perception of a volunteer that holds true across cultural boundaries, although there are interesting cultural and country-specific differences among regions as well. We conclude with narratives of two volunteers, each with a different style and manner of volunteering, and we examine their volunteering in the context of our study.

Classifying and Defining Who Is a Volunteer

Although we are accustomed to using the term "volunteer," there is little that defines what a volunteer is in a rigorous and precise manner. A volunteer, in daily parlance, is someone who gives freely of his or her time and does not receive any monetary compensation for services rendered. Using this qualification alone to define a volunteer, however, would result in an incomplete and imprecise understanding of the concept, as too many different activities and situations are encompassed within it (McCurley & Vesuvio, 1985). For example, a person who volunteers to help a disabled person by arranging weekly meetings and outings with her or him for a period of a year and a person who organizes a one-time picnic for his or her school class are both considered volunteers by most published definitions (Ellis & Noyes, 1990; United States Department of Labor, 1985; The President's Task Force on Private Sector Initiatives, 1982; Scheier, 1980; Shure, 1991; Van Til, 1988). Both individuals meet the required specifications of volunteers as they perform their tasks with free will, receive no remuneration, and their acts benefit others. However, as these two volunteers perform tasks that are unique, applying the term "volunteer" to both does not convey sufficient information regarding the nature of their activities. Such lack of clarity makes it difficult to generalize from different studies on volunteers, to measure the incidence of volunteering with any accuracy, or to make appropriate policy recommendations (Lyons, Wijkstrom, & Clary, 1998).

In the for-profit sector, nobody would consider paid employment a homogenous activity. An employee can be a CEO, a vice president, manager, sales clerk, or a janitor, and it is rarely useful to simply classify them all as "employees." In studies dealing with various aspects of employment, it is necessary to classify employees into distinct categories in order to comprehend issues related to recruitment, compensation, contracts, management, and so forth. Likewise, volunteering is not a homogeneous activity, and studies of volunteers need to delineate the different types of individuals engaged in volunteer work (Smith, 1994). Unfortunately, most of the literatures on volunteers do not differentiate between the volunteer who sits on the board of a trust, the one who delivers meals to the poor, and the one who organizes a picnic.

In an effort to devise strategies for better managing and/or recruiting volunteers, several scholars have attempted to classify volunteer workers by what they do. One such classification is based on the frequency with which an individual volunteers. Indeed, it has been suggested that volunteers could be classified according to the number of hours donated (Yavas & Riecken, 1985). Others have suggested a classification based on the type of organization in which individuals volunteer. This classification uses six key groups to segment volunteers: human service, arts and culture, religion, youth development, education, and health (Wymer, 1997). Other proposed groupings include charities, sports clubs, business associations, social clubs, health clubs, self-help groups, political groups, religious groups, and support agencies (Wilson & Pimm, 1996). Earlier work by Handy and Day (1988) suggests three categories of mutual support organizations: organizations where people with shared enthusiasms come together, service delivery organizations, and campaigning or cause-specific organizations.

More recently, Wymer (2006) suggests classifying volunteers by the intensity of their commitment. He distinguishes between "ongoing volunteers" (those who come on a regular basis [e.g., weekly or monthly] to perform tasks that the organization relies on for its regular operations) and "episodic volunteers" (those who come on an ad hoc basis, respond to a particular task, or come once or twice a year to do a special event for the organizations and who are not part of the NGO's day-to-day operations). It is important to note that the "episodic" category does not qualify the nature of the work undertaken by the volunteer. It gives no indication how many hours were volunteered, what kind of task was accomplished, or to what extent the volunteer is interested and invested in the cause or the NGO. For example, in 2004, over 3 million people volunteered in the United States on "Make a Difference Day," completing thousands of projects in hundreds of towns across the country (Salvoza, 2004). The individuals who participate exclusively in such one-day events are episodic volunteers, although their contribution has great value.

In a comprehensive literature review, Cnaan, Handy, and Wadsworth (1996) showed that most definitions of volunteers are based on four key dimensions: free will, availability of rewards (i.e., remuneration), formal organization, and proximity to the beneficiaries. Volunteering is an activity that encompasses these dimensions, albeit to varying degrees, and the various systems used to classify volunteers that were discussed earlier, may all be factored into an analysis that situates a volunteer along these dimensions. For each dimension, a spectrum encompasses a variety of types of volunteers, ranging from a broad definition to a more narrow (or "pure") definition of the volunteer.

A volunteer meeting the criteria of the "pure" or ideal case in the "free will" dimension undertakes the activity without intimidation or compulsion, including social pressure. This means that he or she is not volunteering simply to avoid the social or professional awkwardness that may come with rejecting a request or suggestion from a friend or employer. On the "availability of rewards" dimension, a volunteer may not receive payments (indirect or partial) or rewards for the work undertaken. For example, a lawyer donating his or her time to a nonprofit orchestra may receive complimentary tickets to performances as a "thank you" and a student volunteering for a local hospital may do this with the purpose of meeting a school graduation requirement. Neither of these examples meets the requirement of the ideal case.

On the dimension of "formal organization," volunteering can take place formally with an ongoing commitment on the part of the volunteer or in a more casual fashion, in which the volunteer is free to show up if she or he has the time. An ongoing commitment may require a volunteer to sign a contract and participate in training sessions, and the organization may insist on a commitment for a certain minimum number of hours, given on a regular basis, over an extended period.

Finally, the fourth dimension ("proximity of the beneficiaries") is also an important factor in understanding volunteering. In the ideal case, the beneficiaries are unknown or at arm's length to the volunteer. For example, a mother looking after her own children would not be considered a volunteer, though this work is unpaid, has long hours with an extended commitment, and may be considered voluntary.

Another formulation that may be employed in defining a volunteer uses the concept of "net costs." The scholars advancing this strategy (e.g., Cnaan et al., 1996) argue that, because volunteering is a social construct, the public perception of the "volunteer" is important in defining volunteers. Specifically, people's perception of the net costs incurred by the individual volunteering in a given volunteer situation plays a vital part in defining who is a volunteer and who is not. Net costs are defined as the total cost of volunteering minus total benefit to the volunteer. Accordingly, the public can view two people performing the same task in which each individual benefits society equally and designate the individual who accrues greater net costs in completing the task as being more of a volunteer.

This framework does not negate the four key dimensions but incorporates them in a unified way. Again, a spectrum ranging from "broad" to "pure" is identified for each dimension. In this framework, however, as one moves from "broad" to "pure," the perceived cost to the individual is higher. Free will is an important factor in this framework. Consider, e.g., two hypothetical volunteers: first, a student who helps the elderly as part of a school social service program for which he or she receives credits and second, a student helping the elderly out of his or her free will, with no school requirement to do so. The latter, "pure" volunteer is assumed to bear a higher net cost, as he or she does not receive any reward for his or her work. The same is true on the remaining three dimensions: moving from broad to pure implies a perceived higher net cost to the individual, either in lower benefits or higher costs. In this chapter, we look at the public perception of individuals in India to see whether the net-cost theory has meaning for individuals in India. We then report on the results of a study testing a similar instrument in other countries in order to check if the net-cost theory could be universally applicable.

Theory and Hypotheses

Given that the concept of a volunteer is a social construct, we propose that the explanation of who is a volunteer or what constitutes a volunteer activity be based on the public perception of net cost of volunteering. Our conjecture is that the public perception of volunteering will be based primarily on the perception of the net cost incurred by the individual— broadly defined as all costs minus all benefits associated with the volunteering activity that accrues to the individual undertaking the activity. Furthermore, we propose the hypotheses that the individual incurring higher net cost is likely to be perceived as "more" of a volunteer than someone with a lower net cost. We argue that only costs and benefits to the volunteer are relevant in net-cost theory; therefore, we exclude the benefits of the work to the beneficiary or society.

Using a model based on rational behavior (suggested by economic theory), we argue that for an individual to undertake any activity, the benefits must be greater than the costs incurred for that action. Volunteering activities are not exempt from this rule. The benefits to the individual are the private and public benefits of the activity. Private benefits to the individual include monetary remuneration, enhancement of social status (i.e., reputation) and social and business opportunities (i.e., networks), improvement of potential earnings capability (i.e., wealth), social interaction and leisure activity, a sense of satisfaction from working for a cause one supports, and a good feeling about oneself.

The individual's public benefits are his or her valuation of those public benefits associated with increasing the supply of those goods and services for which the individual volunteers. For example, if the individual volunteers for an activity that increases adult literacy in the community, then the increased adult literacy is an output that the volunteer values. As such, the public benefit of this output is valuable to society and the volunteer. The benefit of the activity, however, which is included in the individual's rational decision making, is his or her own valuation of the public benefit. It can generally be assumed that this valuation is positive (or at the least zero) because the individual, by choosing the adult literacy program, indicates a preference for that specific public benefit. The costs of volunteering to the individual include items such as the time spent volunteering, effort or money expended in supporting the activity, and the opportunity cost of income and social pleasures foregone.

By applying a rational-choice approach, we assume that the sum of the benefits (private and public) must outweigh the costs to the volunteer in order for the individual to voluntarily choose the activity. In other words, the volunteer will undertake an activity if the net private cost (i.e., private costs minus private benefits) incurred is less than the individual's valuation of the public benefit associated with volunteering. Consequently, the higher the net cost of volunteering, the higher the volunteer's valuation of the public benefit associated with the volunteering is presumed to be. Furthermore, the higher the volunteer's net cost, the greater the value the volunteer must attach to the public benefits of the activity relative to his or her private benefits and costs. Thus, the volunteer with high net cost is perceived to be more public spirited or altruistic (and more of a volunteer) than a volunteer with lower net cost. Based on this theory, we examine the extent to which the public perception of who is more or less of a volunteer accords with the predictions of the net-cost theory and to what degree these perceptions are culturally mediated or universal.

The net-cost framework enables us to deduce several hypotheses and to test them empirically by varying the costs and benefits. To this end, we provide some examples of variations in net cost and formulate specific hypotheses for empirical testing. Each variation is associated with a particular testable hypothesis.

Four Hypotheses for Testing

Different Opportunity Costs of Volunteering (with Equal Benefits)

> *Hypothesis 1: In volunteer situations where people have different opportunity costs while doing identical volunteer work with relatively equal benefits, a person with a higher perceived opportunity cost will be considered more of a volunteer.*

Let us assess the volunteering situations represented by the doctor, the trainer, and the teenager, each of whom volunteers an hour of his or her time to a soup kitchen. The individual benefits of serving in a soup kitchen are limited, and we may assume that these accrue equally to the doctor, the trainer, and the teenager. Furthermore, the costs of the volunteer activity itself are similar for each volunteer in terms of effort and time. As explained earlier, however, their individual opportunity costs differ. Thus, viewed through the filter of net costs, which includes opportunity costs (such as foregone income), the ranking should reflect that an hour given to volunteering is most expensive (higher costs) to the CEO, followed by the doctor, the trainer and, finally, the student. In other words, the CEO, whose hourly income is greater than the hourly income of the doctor (or the trainer or the student) and who, therefore, foregoes the most income by volunteering for an hour, would be viewed as more of a volunteer than the doctor. The doctor, in turn, would be considered more of a volunteer than the teacher as he or she will forego more income than the teacher, who, in turn, will forego more income than the teenager whose time is least expensive.

Different Implicit Costs of Volunteering (Benefits Relatively Equal)

Hypothesis 2: An individual volunteering at a recognized charity will be considered more of a volunteer than an individual volunteering at an unrecognized charity.

Similar volunteer activities may require more or less effort from volunteers depending on where and how they are performed. Thus, the context of the volunteer activity, we argue, will change the costs incurred by the volunteer. For example, working for a recognized and reputable charitable organization will be perceived as requiring greater effort and commitment on the part of the volunteer compared to volunteering at a less well-known agency. Consider the following scenario: To protect its reputation, a highly regarded agency will be more demanding that a volunteer meet certain codes of work and ethics, require a commitment over a longer period of time, and ask the volunteer to undergo training, thereby increasing the costs to the volunteer. For example, compare the costs to a person who assists a disadvantaged child under the supervision of a reputable social service agency (e.g., Big Brothers Big Sisters) with one who performs a similar activity on his or her own. The former may require that the volunteer undergo training, have a fixed number of weekly contacts, help the child with certain types of services, and perhaps, provide regular reports to the agency. Furthermore, the child, his or her family, or teachers have an attentive "agent" to complain to if service is not provided as needed and desired.

On the other hand, a volunteer who works alone to help a disadvantaged child has a greater opportunity to shirk in providing the service when it is inconvenient or to provide lower quality service and, hence, to lower his or her cost. The same activity performed under the auspices of the Big Brothers Big Sisters versus the activity performed under the auspices of an unknown agency may also require greater levels of effort and commitment from the volunteer because a more reputable agency will often have stricter supervisory procedures and will demand higher accountability and quality of service from its volunteers. Thus, a volunteer at a more reputable and organized agency will be perceived as incurring higher costs because of the (assumed) higher demands placed on them by the agency.

Different Explicit Costs of Volunteering (Relatively Equal Benefits)

Hypothesis 3: An individual who engages in a volunteer activity that is perceived to be more demanding, will be considered more of a volunteer than an individual involved in a less demanding volunteer task.

In the case of differing tasks, the time and effort involved can vary significantly, although the benefits to the volunteer may be relatively equal. In the first case, we examine a scenario in which an individual volunteers to chair a committee or carry out a particular task but then delegates the work to an assistant. Which one of them is more of a volunteer: the individual volunteering or his or her assistant? The former willingly volunteered but did little actual work, whereas the latter did most of the work but, more likely, less willingly, because he or she is under some compulsion to do what his or her boss desires or risks incurring heavy costs (e.g., losing their job). There are private benefits for both individuals, e.g., status for the boss in society, status for the employee in the eyes of the boss as well as the potential for social contacts and other indirect rewards. We assume that these benefits are relatively equal, although the costs to each individual are different. In this scenario, the net cost to the assistant is higher than the net cost to the boss. We expect that the boss will be regarded as less of a volunteer than his or her assistant.

Another example of this hypothesis is an individual who organizes a crime-watch group versus an individual who leads a group of joggers every week. The former task is more difficult as the individual must invest more effort in order to arrange a daily neighborhood watch than the task performed by the individual who leads a group of willing joggers. Doing a neighborhood watch is inconvenient and rarely done for pleasure; it may require more effort to get it going and the volunteer organizing it may face greater resistance than the volunteer organizing and leading the group of joggers, most of whom are jogging for pleasure or health. Moreover, recruiting people to do a task that needs to be done on a daily basis is more difficult than recruiting people for a weekly activity. Because both tasks are neighborhood oriented, the benefits to both volunteers in terms of social status and the like will be relatively equal, but because the costs to the neighborhood watch leader are higher, we predict that he or she will be viewed as more of a volunteer.

Different Explicit Benefits of Volunteering (Relatively Equal Costs)

Hypothesis 4: When an individual undertakes a volunteer activity, presumably for no explicit personal benefit, he or she will be considered more of a volunteer than an individual who volunteers for explicit personal benefit.

Similar volunteering activities can be undertaken for different benefits to the volunteer. Here, we consider cases in which the costs to the volunteer are kept relatively constant and the benefits to the volunteer vary. For example, we consider a teacher who provides an hour of his or her time to help in a soup kitchen with no apparent personal benefit, and contrast her or him with another teacher engaging in the same activity with an explicitly acknowledged motive, e.g., in order to impress his or her date. According to the net-cost framework, the costs are the same for the both cases, but in the latter case, the benefits are higher, which results in a lower net cost. Thus, the teacher who is perceived to work in a soup kitchen as a volunteer in order to impress his or her date will be perceived as less of a volunteer than the teacher who works for no explicit benefit.

Methods

To test the variations in public perception of who is a volunteer, we adapted and extended the 23-item instrument used by Cnaan et al. (1996). The original 23-item survey was expanded with 27 new items, which were specifically developed to test the net-cost theory regarding perceptions of volunteering for the aforementioned hypotheses. Each item was measured on a five-category Likert-type scale ranging from 1 = not a volunteer to 5 = definitely a volunteer. The questionnaires were self-administered and took 12–15 minutes to complete.

We conducted the survey in eight countries. The data consisted of over 5,000 responses from the United States, Canada, India, Italy, the Netherlands, Germany, Israel, and Belgium. The data was collected over a period of two years and was used for testing the net-cost concept of volunteering and to see if this theory was validated across different cultures in the eight countries (Meijs et al., 2003). The questionnaire had to be translated to meet language requirements and social conventions in each region. The survey was pretested to ensure that the scenarios presented made sense in the cultural and social contexts where they were being carried out. For example, in India, the notion of volunteering "to impress a date" did not fit the cultural norms and we substituted "to make personal connections." Our samples in each of the regions were samples of convenience. We attempt to compensate for the lack of randomness in our sample by having a large (i.e., over 500 in each region) heterogeneous sample.

First, we report on our findings in India before we turn to a cross-cultural comparison. In the latter case, in order to determine the relative universality or cultural differentiation of the theory's relevance, we extend our hypothesis testing to include data from all regions studied.

Findings from "Who Is a Volunteer" Study in India

In India, over 500 adults over the age of 18 were surveyed for this study. This sample was one of convenience and was largely aimed at those who could speak English. Thus, the sample is biased in the sense it overrepresents a well-educated, English-speaking population.

Our sample characteristics appear in Table 2.1, and we note the overrepresentation of well-educated individuals, which is unrepresentative of the population in the region where the study was conducted.

The literature on volunteering shows that in many countries where national surveys are conducted (e.g., the United Kingdom, the United States, Canada, and Australia), volunteers tend to be better educated and well-off compared to the general population. Thus, although our sample is biased, it is biased in the same direction as samples that contain individuals participating in volunteer activity and to whom the concept of volunteering was less likely to be foreign.

Table 2.1: Sociodemographic Characteristics of Respondents in India (n = 502)

Variable	Category	(%)
Gender	Male	55.1
	Female	44.9
Age	18–24	18.1
	25–34	18.9
	35–44	20.7
	45–54	23.3
	55–64	12.5
	>65	8.4
Marital status	Single	29.3
	Married	59.3
	Widowed	8.4
	Divorced	2.6
	Separated	0.4
Education	Some high school	0.6
	High school graduate	3.0
	Some college	4.8
	College graduate	55.5
	Postgraduate	36.1
Income	Lower class	29.0
	Middle class	51.5
	Upper class	19.4
Volunteered in lifetime	Yes	64.8
	No	35.2
Volunteered in past 12 months	Yes	61.0
	No	39.0

Source: Authors.

Rank-order Analysis

To test the hypothesis that the public perception of who is a volunteer is related to an individual's net costs when volunteering, we look at those items that appear in the top and bottom five of the 50 volunteer scenarios. Table 2.2 shows the rank ordering obtained on the mean of the Likert

Table 2.2: Rank-order Analysis

Volunteer Activity	Ranking Out of 50 Items*
Top five	
A person who donates blood to a local hospital	1
An adult who offers his or her time to be a Big Brother/Big Sister	2
A teenager who volunteers to serve a meal at the soup kitchen for the homeless	3
A teacher who volunteers to serve a meal at the soup kitchen for the homeless	4
A childless adult who wants to engage with children and offers his or her time to be a Big Brother/Big Sister	5
Bottom five	
The teenager who presents a program on youth leadership to an audience of peers at a religious youth conference in order to make personal connections	46
The medical doctor who agrees to offer his or her services in case of an emergency at the symphony concert in exchange for a free ticket to the concert	47
A teacher who volunteers to serve a meal at the soup kitchen for the homeless in order to make personal connections	48
An IBM executive who volunteers to serve a meal at the soup kitchen for the homeless in order to make personal connections	49
A teacher who agrees to offer his/her services to the symphony orchestra (for three hours) in exchange for a free ticket to the concert	50

Source: Authors.
Note: * The rank is that of the means given to each questionnaire item (on a scale of 1 to 5).

scales for the five top and bottom items. We look at whether there are any general trends inherent in the way respondents over all the regions ranked volunteers. Specifically, we examine whether there are similarities in who is perceived to be at the high end ("definitely a volunteer" [i.e., close to 5]) and the low end ("not a volunteer" [i.e., close to 1]) for all the regions. We argue that net costs are significantly higher for the top five than for the bottom five and that this suggests the validity of the net-cost theory.

What is striking about the results is that in all of the scenarios at the bottom of the ranking, respondents were least likely to consider individuals whose activity was undertaken with an expectation of a reward to be volunteers. And the contrary is true for the ranking at the top end. Those individuals who volunteered with no expectation of rewards, and at considerable cost to themselves in terms of time, effort, or physical discomfort (e.g., donating blood), were most likely to be considered to be volunteers.

In contrast to the bottom five, none of the top five scenarios indicates that the volunteer receives an implicit or explicit remuneration. This finding supports the net-cost concept that the lower the benefits to the volunteer—and, therefore, the greater the net cost—the more likely it is that the person will be considered a volunteer.

Hypotheses Testing

Hypothesis 1: In volunteer situations in which people have different opportunity costs while doing identical volunteer work with relatively equal benefits, the person with the highest perceived opportunity cost will be considered more of a volunteer.

To test the first hypothesis, we used four individuals performing the same activity in three different situations. We compared a student, a teacher, a medical doctor, and an IBM executive, each of whom volunteered to serve a meal at a soup kitchen for the homeless, to serve on the board of a local library or to provide a status-appropriate service to the symphony (from ushering for the teenager to board membership for the IBM executive) in exchange for free tickets. In each of the three situations, we would expect the IBM executive to be considered more of a volunteer, followed by the medical doctor, the teacher, and the student, in descending order (see Table 2.3).

Table 2.3: Comparison of Means of Items Depicting Different Opportunity Costs for Similar Activities by Four Individuals—an IBM Executive, a Medical Doctor, a Teacher, and a Student (Using One-way ANOVA Tests)

Serving on the board of a local library	IBM executive: 3.65 Medical doctor: 3.76 Teacher: 3.64 Student: 3.65 F-value 1.21, Significance N.S.
Serving a meal at the soup kitchen for the homeless	IBM executive: 3.92 Medical doctor: 4.05 Teacher: 4.48 Student: 4.56 F-value 44.59, Significance .000***
Helping the symphony orchestra in exchange for free tickets	IBM executive: 1.88 Medical doctor: 1.79 Teacher: 1.67 Student: 1.80 F-value 2.91, Significance .033*

Source: Authors.
Note: $^*p < .01$, $^{**}p < .05$, $^{***}p < .001$.

Although the differences are significant, in two of the three cases, the hypothesis is not supported in India. No significant differences were found with the library service. Regarding the soup kitchen, however, the teenager and the teacher were each considered significantly more of a volunteer than the medical doctor or the IBM executive. This suggests that the perception of the IBM executive and doctor doing volunteer work at a greater opportunity cost than a teacher or student is not supported. In other words, the "underdog" approach (a reverse status) took precedence and those who are viewed as least socially and economically strong, were considered to have invested more by volunteering, which contradicts the opportunity-cost hypothesis.

There was only minor support to the opportunity-cost theory regarding the symphony. The teacher was considered significantly less of a volunteer than the IBM executive, whereas all other differences were not statistically significant. Thus, we conclude that our first hypothesis was not supported by our findings.

Hypothesis 2: An individual volunteering at a recognized charity will be considered more of a volunteer than an individual volunteering at an unrecognized charity.

To test the second hypothesis, we compared volunteers in three different situations in which the same volunteer engaged in similar volunteer activities at recognized charities versus unrecognized charities. The rationale here, as explained earlier, was to see if the costs associated with volunteering at a formal, well-regarded organization are perceived to be higher than that costs incurred when working informally. To test this hypothesis, we used paired *t*-tests. Our findings appear in Table 2.4, and we find support for our hypothesis in two of the three volunteer scenarios involving a recognized charity.

The trainer who does a workshop for the recognized charity is ranked significantly more as a volunteer than the trainer who does the workshop for an unrecognized organization. This finding was also true for

Table 2.4: Comparison of Means of Items Depicting the Same Volunteer Activity to Unrecognized (UNREC) and Recognized (REC) Charities (Using Paired *t*-Test)

The student who is doing a community service project as part of a high school graduation requirement	Mean UNREC 2.67 Mean REC 2.72 *t*-value 1.54 Significance N.S.
The student who is helping a *recognized charity* as a high school graduation requirement	
The trainer who does a free workshop for an organization as a marketing device	Mean UNREC 2.58 Mean REC 2.77 *t*-value 4.65 Significance .000***
The trainer who does a free workshop for a *recognized charity* as a marketing device	
The paid staff person who serves on the board of a nonprofit in a slot that is reserved for his or her agency	Mean UNREC 2.34 Mean REC 2.97 *t*-value 9.64 Significance .000***
The paid staff person who serves on the board of a *recognized charity* in a slot that is reserved for his or her agency	

Source: Authors.
Note: *p < .01, **p < .05, ***p < .001.

the individual who sat on the board of the recognized charity versus that of an unrecognized nonprofit organization. This suggests that individuals who give their time to recognized charities are more likely to be seen as volunteers, presumably because the demands on their time and effort (i.e., costs) are thought to be greater than the time and effort of volunteering with unrecognized groups.

In the case of the student volunteer, however, this finding, although it points in the right direction, is not statistically significant. It may be possible that a student who volunteers is equally likely to be considered a volunteer regardless of what costs he or she incurs due to the reverse status effect discussed earlier. Overall, these findings give partial support to our hypothesis.

Hypothesis 3: An individual who engages in volunteer activity that is perceived to be more demanding will be considered more of a volunteer than an individual involved in a less demanding volunteer task.

To test the third hypothesis, we compared two pairs of questions. We compared a CEO of a local corporation, who is a volunteer chairperson of the United Way campaign and who delegates all the volunteer work to his assistant, and we compared an individual, who organizes a crime-watch group with a member of a community sport club, who leads a group of joggers every week.

The assistant to the CEO exercised little or no free will in carrying out the task delegated to him by the CEO. As seen in Table 2.5, however, the assistant is perceived to be more of a volunteer than the CEO who willingly accepted the task but did not do the work himself. The findings suggest that the individual who incurs higher net cost and who actually does the work is considered to be more of a volunteer.

Table 2.5: Comparison of Means of Items Depicting Volunteer Activities with Different Costs to the Volunteers (Using Paired *t*-Test)

The CEO of a local corporation, who is volunteer chairperson of the United Way campaign and who delegates all the work to his assistant versus the assistant to this CEO, who does the job for his boss	Mean CEO 2.0258 Mean assistant 2.54 *t*-value 7.90 Significance .000***

Source: Authors.
Note: *p < .01, **p < .05, ***p < .001.

This finding also suggests that the concept of net costs as perceived by the volunteer may be more significant than whether the individual undertook the task freely or not. Along the dimensions used in the definition of a "volunteer," "compulsion," and "positive net costs," our respondents weigh the net costs incurred as more significant in determining who is more of a volunteer.

> *Hypothesis 4: When an individual undertakes a certain volunteer activity for no explicit personal benefit, he or she will be considered more of a volunteer than an individual who volunteers for an explicit personal benefit.*

To test this hypothesis, we compared four individuals (a student, a teacher, a doctor, and an IBM executive), each engaging in the same activity twice, once without an explicit personal benefit and once with a benefit. In the first instance, we presented them as providing time and effort in a soup kitchen, whereas, in the latter, we presented them as doing the same work to make personal connections.

It was our hypothesis that if the benefits of a volunteer service increase (e.g., enhancing social contacts), the net costs are lowered and, hence, the individual who undertakes the volunteer service to impress a date or make personal connections will be perceived as less of a volunteer than the individual who does it for no explicit personal benefit. As seen in Table 2.6, in all comparisons, the hypothesis was strongly supported.

Table 2.6: Comparison of Means of Items Depicting the Same Volunteer Activity Performed with and without Explicit Personal Benefits (Using Paired *t*-Test)

IBM Executive	Medical Doctor	Teacher	Teenager
Mean with personal benefit 1.24	Mean with personal benefit 1.81	Mean with personal benefit 1.77	Mean with personal benefit 1.94
Mean without personal benefit 3.92	Mean without personal benefit 4.05	Mean without personal benefit 4.49	Mean without personal benefit 4.56
t-value 33.93	*t*-value 29.90	*t*-value 39.03	*t*-value 35.57
Significance 0.000***	Significance 0.000***	Significance 0.000***	Significance 0.000***

Source: Authors.
Note: *p < .01, **p < .05, ***p < .001.

A Cross-cultural Analysis

Is the perception of volunteers in India different from that in other parts of the world? Since volunteering is a worldwide phenomenon, we compared data obtained from eight different countries: Canada, Germany, Israel, the United States, India, Italy, Belgium, and the Netherlands. We found that, although the hypotheses of opportunity costs can be rejected, the remaining hypotheses are supported, suggesting that in terms of the public perception of "who is a volunteer," the net-cost theory holds. A comparison between the rank-ordering across countries reveals provocative differences; however, there are interesting variations in how people from various countries rank the different volunteer scenarios. In this section, we discuss these variations with respect to cultural differences.

The demographic characteristics of the samples for the countries are similar. Some notable variations include the following:

- In India and the Netherlands, half the sample is composed of males, whereas in the three North American samples, males constituted only about one-third of the sample.
- The Canadian sample is relatively younger (31.6 percent of the participants were under the age of 24) and, hence, composed of more people who are single (49 percent).
- The Dutch sample has a relatively high percentage of widowed participants (14 percent) and is less educated (only 16.1 percent were postgraduate, whereas 14.3 percent had some high school education).
- The Italian sample was also less educated (16.4 percent had only some high school education). This sample was also younger (56 percent under the age of 34) and mostly single (48.6 percent). The Italian sample reported the lowest rates of volunteering in the past.
- The Indian sample had the lowest rate of respondents who had volunteered at any time or in the past 12 months, a finding that may reflect the magnitude of volunteering in India. The sample comprised of highly educated Indians; 55.5 percent were college graduates and 36.1 percent were postgraduates—not typical of the population at large but may have resulted because the questionnaire was in English, a language used mostly by educated Indians.

Regardless of these variations, chi-square tests of association reveal that the samples are not significantly different in a statistical sense.

The findings from the rank-order analysis (see Table 2.7) suggest that there is broad consensus regarding who is most definitely a volunteer. The findings show that remuneration (monetary or otherwise) to the individual has a strong negative impact on people's perception of who is a volunteer. Private benefits reduce the net cost to the volunteer and, accordingly, play a significant role in the public perception of who is a volunteer. When people observe an individual personally benefiting (monetarily or socially) from volunteering, they rank the individual as less of a volunteer than those who receive no such benefits but incur similar costs.

We examine the rank of the means given to each item within the sample from one region compared to the samples from the other regions. We investigate whether there are any general trends in the way respondents ranked the items. More specifically, we examine whether there are similarities in terms of who is perceived to be at the high end (i.e., "definitely a volunteer" [close to 5]) and at the low end (i.e., "not a volunteer" [close to 1]). We argue that if similarities exist, regardless of cultural differences, it will enable us to better understand who is a volunteer in terms of public perception.

Across the 50 items, we identify the 5 items ranked highest among the scenarios. The common items are:

1. A teenager who volunteers to serve a meal at a soup kitchen for the homeless.
2. A teacher who volunteers to serve a meal at a soup kitchen for the homeless.
3. An adult who offers his or her time to be a Big Brother or a Big Sister (except Italy).
4. An IBM executive who volunteers to serve a meal at the soup kitchen for the homeless (except India, Belgium, and the Netherlands).
5. A medical doctor who volunteers to serve a meal at a soup kitchen for the homeless (except Canada, Israel, India, Belgium, and the Netherlands).

It must be noted that all of the exceptions scored within the rank order of the first 10 statements. Another noteworthy point is that providing food for homeless people is broadly accepted as a volunteer activity. The plight of the homeless seems to be recognized as a problem worthy of service across cultures and regions. There is less of a consensus across the

Table 2.7: Perceptions of "Who Is a Volunteer"* across Eight Countries* in Rank Order by Means of Likert Scale**

	Mean	All	SA	GE	IL	USA	IN	IT	BE	NL
A teenager who volunteers to serve a meal at a soup kitchen for the homeless	4.75	1	1	2	2	3	3	1	3	4
A teacher who volunteers to serve a meal at a soup kitchen for the homeless	4.74	2	2	1	5	2	4	2	5	3
An adult who offers his or her time to be a Big Brother/Big Sister	4.71	3	4	5	1	1	2	7	1	2
An IBM executive who volunteers to serve a meal at a soup kitchen for the homeless	4.64	4	5	3	4	4	10	4	6	6
A medical doctor who volunteers to serve a meal at a soup kitchen for the homeless	4.61	5	6	4	6	5	9	5	7	7
A person who donates blood to a local hospital	4.59	6	8	11	8	9	1	3	4	15
An adult who volunteers to teach English as a second language to new immigrants	4.59	7	3	9	3	6	6	8	8	5
An unemployed person who volunteers to teach English as a second language to new immigrants	4.51	8	7	12	7	7	7	9	9	8
A childless adult who wants to engage with children and offers his or her time to be a Big Brother/Big Sister	4.50	9	9	14	15	8	5	6	2	1

A member of Alcoholics Anonymous (AA) who leads an AA meeting every week	4.07	10	15	6	18	16	12	10	10	16
An IBM executive who serves on the board of a local library	4.07	11	11	16	9	10	18	12	14	11
A teenager who serves on the board of a local library as a student representative	.06	12	10	13	14	11	17	16	12	13
A medical doctor who serves on the board of a local library	4.04	13	12	15	10	12	16	13	18	10
A teacher who serves on the board of a local library	3.96	14	16	17	11	13	19	14	17	9
A teenager who presents a program on youth leadership to an audience of peers at a religious youth conference	3.86	15	14	8	20	17	21	15	16	17
A home owner who helps create a crime-watch group to safeguard his or her own neighborhood	3.85	16	13	18	16	14	32	21	11	14
A person who participates in a pharmaceutical study to determine the effectiveness of a new drug	3.84	17	17	30	13	15	20	11	13	19
A member of a community sport club who leads a group of joggers every week	3.83	18	18	7	12	20	13	18	15	12

(Table 2.7 contd.)

(Table 2.7 contd.)

	Mean	All	CA	GE	IL	USA	IN	IT	BE	NL
A person who is ill with cystic fibrosis and participates in a pharmaceutical study to determine the effectiveness of a new drug in treating the disease	3.41	19	19	31	23	19	14	17	19	28
An office manager who accompanies his wife to visit seniors in a nursing home	3.35	20	20	27	24	18	15	22	22	26
A parent who becomes a scout leader because his or her child wishes to be a scout. No one else will lead the troop so the parent agrees but only as long as his or her child is involved	3.32	21	23	10	21	21	43	20	21	18
A child who assists in setting up booths at the volunteer fair because one of his or her parents is volunteer administrator and asks her or him to help	3.11	22	22	19	22	22	30	19	31	27
A teenager who offers to program the computer at a nonprofit agency without pay in order to establish "résumé experience." After three months, the teenager plans to quit and apply for a paying job	3.02	23	21	20	32	23	37	42	20	25
An hourly wage worker who, by his or her own choice, works overtime without pay	2.86	24	26	37	17	24	8	26	23	37

An office manager who, by his or her own choice, works overtime without pay	2.71	25	29	42	19	25	11	29	26	45
A teenager who volunteers to serve a meal at a soup kitchen for the homeless in order to impress his or her date	2.70	26	24	22	28	30	41	25	29	21
An assistant to the CEO of a local corporation who is volunteer chairperson of the United Way campaign who does the job for his or her boss	2.69	27	27	21	38	26	33	24	27	29
A teenager who presents a program on youth leadership to an audience of peers at a religious youth conference with hope of finding a suitable date	2.61	28	33	23	27	36	<u>46</u>	28	25	24
A student who is helping Special Olympics as part of a high school graduation requirement	2.61	29	31	28	34	27	27	40	24	36
An IBM executive who volunteers to serve a meal at a soup kitchen for the homeless in order to impress his or her date	2.60	30	28	24	29	32	<u>49</u>	33	35	20
A teacher who volunteers to serve a meal at a soup kitchen for the homeless in order to impress his or her date	2.59	31	25	25	33	31	<u>48</u>	35	34	22

(Table 2.7 contd.)

(Table 2.7 contd.)

	Mean	All	CA	GE	IL	USA	IN	IT	BE	NL
A medical doctor who volunteers to serve a meal at a soup kitchen for the homeless in order to impress his or her date	2.56	32	30	26	30	33	44	36	39	23
A student who is doing a community service project as part of a high school graduation requirement	2.55	33	32	29	35	28	28	43	28	35
A lawyer who provides legal services to a nonprofit organization at half his or her regular rate	2.39	34	38	32	25	35	26	27	44	–
A trainer who does a free workshop for the Breast Cancer Foundation as a marketing device	2.34	35	34	41	42	29	25	45	40	42
A college student enrolled in the National and Community Service program who gives his or her time to Big Brothers Big Sisters and receives a stipend and partial forgiveness of tuition	2.33	36	37	40	41	38	34	32	30	38
A college student who is enrolled in the National and Community Service program and for doing community service receives a stipend and partial forgiveness of tuition	2.27	37	40	39	39	39	35	37	36	39
A person who takes care of a spouse's children from a previous marriage (i.e., stepparenting)	2.26	38	43	45	40	<u>46</u>	22	38	32	40

Item	Mean								
A CEO of a local corporation who is volunteer chairperson of the United Way campaign but who delegates all the work to his or her assistant	2.24	39	35	33	36	43	40	31	45	30
A paid staff person who serves on the board of the United Way in a slot that is reserved for his or her agency	2.23	40	41	43	26	40	23	23	46	49
A teenager who agrees to offer his or her services as an usher at a symphony concert in exchange for a free ticket to the concert	2.21	41	42	35	45	41	45	39	38	33
A trainer who does a free workshop for an organization as a marketing device	2.20	42	36	44	44	34	29	47	42	43
An IBM executive who is granted a year of social service leave with pay to become a temporary staff person with a nonprofit organization	2.16	43	39	48	31	37	31	44	47	47
A medical doctor who agrees to offer his or her services in case of an emergency at a symphony concert in exchange for a free ticket to the concert	2.16	44	46	34	47	44	47	41	37	32
A teacher who agrees to offer his or her services to a symphony orchestra (for three hours) in exchange for a free ticket to the concert	2.15	45	47	38	46	42	50	34	33	31

(Table 2.7 contd.)

(Table 2.7 contd.)

	Mean	All	CA	GE	IL	USA	IN	IT	BE	NL
An IBM executive who agrees to offer his or her services on the fund raising committee of a symphony orchestra in exchange for free tickets	2.10	46	45	36	43	47	42	46	41	34
A medical doctor who delivers a research paper at a conference held by the American Medical Association (AMA)	2.05	47	44	46	48	48	24	48	43	41
A paid staff person who serves on the board of a nonprofit group in a slot that is reserved for his or her agency	1.98	48	48	47	37	45	36	30	49	48
A six-month old baby who accompanies his or her parents to visit seniors at a nursing home	1.59	49	49	49	49	49	39	49	50	44
An accountant charged with embezzling who accepts a sentence of 250 hours of community service in lieu of prosecution	1.45	50	50	50	50	50	38	50	48	50

Source: Authors.

Notes: Figures in bold denote the top five rankings. Underlined figures indicate the bottom five rankings.

*CA = Canada, GE = Germany, IL = Israel, US = United States, IN = India, IT = Italy, BE = Belgium, NL = The Netherlands.

**Scale range: 1 = not a volunteer, 5 = definitely a volunteer.

regions for the five items ranked lowest at the end of the scale, as shown by the list of exceptions. Overall, the lowest five are:

46. An IBM executive who agrees to offer services at the symphony concert in exchange for a free ticket to the concert (except Germany, Israel, India, Belgium, and the Netherlands).
47. A doctor who presents a paper at the annual meeting of the AMA (except Canada, India, Belgium, and the Netherlands).
48. A paid staff person who serves on the board of a nonprofit group in a slot that is reserved for his or her agency (except Israel, India, and Italy).
49. A six-month-old baby who accompanies his or her parents to visit seniors at a nursing home (except India and the Netherlands).
50. An accountant charged with embezzling who accepts community service in lieu of prosecution (except India).

The six-month-old baby and the embezzling accountant were consistently ranked lowest in Canada, Germany, Israel, the United States, Italy, and Belgium (49th and 50th, respectively). In addition, in the Netherlands, the embezzling accountant was ranked last but the baby was ranked 44th. In India, the baby was ranked 39th. These findings indicate that respondents felt that "free will" and "free choice" are important components in determining who is or is not a volunteer. The remaining choices indicate that those who receive overt remuneration are ranked lower as volunteers. With some modest exceptions, this pattern is consistent with the rankings found at the bottom third for all of these regions.

In India, the five items ranked lowest include the individual serving at the soup kitchen to make personal connections and those working at the symphony in exchange for tickets.[1] This change may have elicited a lower rating for these individuals in India because making "personal connections" is tantamount to volunteering to further oneself socially and economically. If items involving "personal connections" are excluded, the bottom five ranks include all four individuals who agreed to offer services at the symphony concert in exchange for a free ticket. A parent who becomes a scout leader because of his or her child is also included in the bottom five rankings. It should be noted that, unlike in North America, in India, scout leaders are school teachers for whom this obligation is

[1] As mentioned previously, because the concept of dating in India is not common for adults, "to impress his or her date" was replaced with "to make personal connections."

part of the required extracurricular duties of their job. Furthermore, scout meetings take place on school premises. Thus, teachers may be regarded as fulfilling their professional duties through such activities and, therefore, are not considered volunteers.

These findings from India suggest that the tendency to rank an individual, who receives remuneration as less of a volunteer, which was found in all other regions, is true for India as well. In some areas, however, there appears to be a greater degree of cultural subjectivity. For example in Canada, Israel, India, Italy, and the United States, those scenarios in which a volunteer receives an explicitly stated personal benefit for volunteering (e.g., tickets to a symphony), survey respondents ranked these scenarios the lowest. In Germany, Belgium, and the Netherlands, getting a free ticket in return for volunteering is less problematic. In the Netherlands, in fact, the norm is that if an individual volunteers for any association, the services of that association should be freely available to that volunteer. In many cases, the volunteer is exempt from membership dues. As a result, free symphony tickets are not considered exceptional private benefits to the Dutch volunteer. In the Dutch nonprofit sector, there also seems to be a lower correlation between donating time and giving money than in the North American context.

Comparisons between India and the other regions (Table 2.8) suggest underlying sociocultural differences. For example, in India, working overtime without pay is seen as volunteering, whereas serving meals at a soup kitchen to make personal connections is not! The idea of receiving a benefit dominates—making social connections for personal benefit, even if combined with the act of serving meals, is seen to be too self-serving to be considered an act of volunteering.

Table 2.8 shows the differences between the means of India and those of other regions. A difference of −1.2 in the first case between India and Canada indicates that in India, a teacher is perceived as less of a volunteer in comparison to a teacher in Canada. An office manager and (especially) an hourly wage worker working overtime without pay are perceived to be more genuinely volunteers in India compared to other regions, with the exception of Israel. (Table 2.7 shows that this is not the case in the other regions.) It seems that in other countries, people perceive overtime work as part of a paying job. In the United States, an hourly employee working overtime without pay is considered more of a volunteer than he or she would be in Canada but the opposite is true for the office manager working overtime without pay.

The differences are especially large with respect to the Netherlands. This would suggest that to Dutch people, a person who tries to impress

Table 2.8: Comparing India to the Other Regions* on Eight Situations with the Greatest Differences Means of Likert Scale**

Volunteering Situations	CA	GE	IL	USA	IT	BE	NL
A teacher who volunteers to serve a meal at a soup kitchen for the homeless in order to impress his or her date (or, make personal connections)***	-1.2	-1.55	-1.2	-22	-.3	-17	-2.25
A medical doctor who volunteers to serve a meal at a soup kitchen for the homeless in order to impress his or her date (or, make personal connections)***	-1.05	-1.5	-1.2	-1.05	-.25	-14	-2.05
A teenager who presents a program on youth leadership to an audience of peers at a religious youth conference in order to find a suitable date (or, make personal connections)***	-1.05	-1.55	-1.4	-.9	-.6	-1.1	-1.9
An IBM executive who volunteers to serve a meal at a soup kitchen for the homeless in order to impress his or her date (or, make personal connections)***	-1.2	-32	-1.4	-1.15	-.35	-.85	-2.3
An office manager who, by his or her own choice, works overtime without pay	1.5	2.4	.5	27	2.05	-1.60	2.75
A home owner who helps to create a crime-watch group to safeguard his or her own neighborhood	-1.9	-1.25	-1.7	-1.9	-.55	-2.3	-2.45

(Table 2.8 contd.)

(*Table 2.8 contd.*)

Volunteering Situations	CA	GE	IL	USA	IT	BE	NL
A parent who becomes a scout leader because his or her child desires to be a scout. No one else will lead the troop, so the parent agrees, but only as long as his or her child is involved	-1.9	-2.8	-2.0	-2.05	-1.5	-1.7	-2.8
The hourly wage worker who, by his or her own choice, works overtime without pay	1.8	2.6	.7	1.55	2.25	1.75	2.8

Source: Authors.

Notes: *CA = Canada, GE = Germany, IL = Israel, US = United States, IN = India, IT = Italy, BE = Belgium, NL = The Netherlands.

**Scale range: 1 = not a volunteer, 5 = definitely a volunteer.

***The concept of dating in India is not common for adults, so "to impress his or her date" was replaced by "to make personal connections."

a date by volunteering is considered more of a volunteer than he or she would be elsewhere. Apparently, the Dutch perceive the personal benefit of finding a date not significant enough to consider the person in that situation to be less of a volunteer. This result corresponds to the situation described earlier in which a personal reward (e.g., symphony orchestra tickets) is included as a free benefit to volunteers.

For example, the negative numbers in all the cells in the case of the "home owner" and "parent" suggests that in all other regions, a home owner organizing a crime-watch group and a parent becoming a scout leader are considered significantly more genuinely volunteers than they are in India. One possible explanation is that such activities are more common in those regions than they are in India.

Discussion

The findings from the rank-order analysis suggest that a broad consensus exists regarding who is most definitely a volunteer. The findings show that remuneration (monetary or otherwise) to the individual has a definite negative impact on people's perception of who is a volunteer. Private benefits, either monetary or nonmonetary in nature, reduce the net cost to the volunteer and, accordingly, play a significant role in the public perception of who is a volunteer.

Many of our hypotheses regarding net cost were supported in the studied regions. The results obtained when comparing the individual who performs the same service to society with or without a private benefit demonstrate that people regard an individual receiving a private benefit as less of a volunteer. In addition, when the costs to the individual of volunteering are higher (demanding agency [Hypothesis 2] or demanding work [Hypothesis 3]), he or she is rated as more of a volunteer.

The finding that the opportunity costs of volunteering (Hypothesis 1) do not enter the calculus of net cost, *a priori*, contradicts the net-cost theory. We suggest, however, that in light of the support for the net-cost theory from the other hypotheses, the reason for this may simply be the public's lack of awareness concerning opportunity costs. Economists have shown that the general public does not always take opportunity costs into account (Ferraro & Taylor, 2005). Another possible explanation may be that the time taken for volunteering is perceived to come from an individual's leisure time. In this case, opportunity cost is relatively equal across all volunteers and, hence, opportunity costs do not need to enter the net-cost calculus. Although there have been some studies relating volunteerism to leisure (e.g., Stebbins, 1996), this issue needs further research.

The data support the theory of net cost in explaining public perceptions regarding who is more of a volunteer. What actually constitutes benefits and costs to the volunteer, however, is a complex calculus requiring further investigation. Nevertheless, the data show that the higher the perceived net cost to the volunteer, the higher the individual is ranked as a volunteer. This trend was prevalent for all items, and without exception, it is significant at the polar ends of who is "definitely" a volunteer and who is not.

Our model suggests that the public views the volunteer's private net cost and infers from this the volunteer's valuation of the public benefit of the activity. In other words, if the volunteer is undertaking some activity with high net costs, then the onlooker assumes that the volunteer must value the public benefits of that activity. Hence, the public perception of the volunteer is someone who is more altruistic to accept such costs; hence, he or she is regarded as more of a volunteer than the individual who incurs lower net costs. Hence, we focused our attention on the net cost to the volunteer and ignored the public benefit of the particular activity as we are more concerned with the inputs rather than the outcome of the volunteer efforts in our perception of who is a more or less of a volunteer.

We also note that the public perception of a volunteer is more sensitive to benefits than costs incurred. This is especially true regarding opportunity costs, which do not seem to enter the cost calculus. The data showed that opportunity costs had little impact on the ranking of the volunteers in all scenarios. By contrast, the benefits received did play a crucial role in the degree to which the individual was perceived as a volunteer.

We are not able to say much about motives for volunteering that are not explicit. We assume that most volunteers are not purely altruistic and acknowledge the fact that they benefit from the volunteer experience (or they would likely soon quit). For an individual to be perceived as a volunteer, however, the perceived costs should outweigh the benefits.

In this chapter, we demonstrated that in India and in seven other countries, net cost serves as the common denominator in all four of the dimensions of volunteering identified by Cnaan et al. (1996). The rational perception of costs and benefits in making judgments regarding the degree to which a person is perceived as a volunteer transcends cultural boundaries (at least in the countries studied). In all four dimensions, the higher the perceived net costs, the more altruistic the volunteer is understood to be. It seems to us that this application of net cost to volunteering is helpful in drawing attention to the fact that it is an activity that is undertaken at some cost to the individual and that it is this cost that renders her or him as an altruist in the eyes of his or her peers.

Narratives

The Formal Volunteer: Nafisa S. (Mumbai)

Nafisa was your typical rich little girl. She grew up in Pune in an affluent family. When she completed high school, her parents did not believe that it was socially acceptable for her to work nor did they allow her to continue her education. This was in the 1940s, and girls of a certain social status were expected to conform to societal roles. Unlike some other girls of her social stratum, however, Nafisa quickly grew bored with socializing and wanted to do something more worthwhile. She completed a course in typing and shorthand and thought about what she could do to contribute to society. She learnt of an orphanage and inquired if she could help. Soon, she was teaching English to the young girls there every day between 10 AM and 1 PM. Nafisa experienced a great sense of satisfaction with her work. Her parents supported her work and the orphanage was pleased that they had a helping hand. After a few years, however, Nafisa became engaged to a wealthy young man from Mumbai, and before long, she was married and settled into the upper echelons of Mumbai society.

Her life in Bombay gave her a sense of *déjà vu*; her husband did not want his young bride to work, but Nafisa was restless. She was lonely and bored and wanted to do something constructive. True to the adage that opportunity comes to the one who is looking for it, Nafisa was approached by Fatima Ismail. Ms Ismail had won the Padmashree, a prestigious award given to those who have contributed to the country. She worked with children who had polio, and she asked Nafisa if she would join her in starting a center for the physically handicapped. The government had donated a large area of huts for the project. The greatest challenge, however, was psychological: how do you encourage physically challenged children to come to the center to learn a trade when it was easier for them to raise money by begging? It took a long time to convince the poor and physically handicapped that it would ultimately be better for them to work than to beg.

Nafisa and Fatima Ismail were not alone in this venture. They had formed a committee of seven committed people to tackle the problem. The Tata Group offered to help, providing a van that functioned as a police car. With the help of government officials, they drove around the city and picked up handicapped beggar children. Although spending time in a classroom would have been ideal, Nafisa and Fatima wanted to make sure that the students at least had a safer and more productive way of earning an income. The center enlisted the help of a company, and the children were taught to sort and package small household items into bundles. In addition to the money, the children were paid for the work, and other companies and rich patrons provided free lunches to encourage their regular attendance. Consistent attendance, however, was a problem. The children would show up for work only when they were having a bad spell in begging.

Over time, Nafisa developed an easy acquaintance with the children. Some of them were interested in her paintings, and she suspected that those children had artistic potential. She received permission to start painting classes at the center. She appealed to companies as well as the public to contribute the supplies needed for these lessons and soon paints and brushes arrived along with old tins. Before long, the children had learned to paint flowers and patterns on the tins. The ornamental tins proved to be popular and sold well.

Political leaders were interested in this venture and Dr Rajendra Prasad, who was the president of India at that time, called on the center regularly. Jawaharlal Nehru, the charismatic first prime minister of India, praised the Center for its work and cited it as a model for such endeavors. A Fellowship for the Physically Handicapped was initiated and the most promising candidates received special education and training. It took many years to fully develop the center. Tata, the Indian industrial giant, gave the center a printing machine and offered to provide instructions on its use. A carpentry department was also set up so that vocational training classes could be offered. These courses were intended to teach the children skills that would allow them to earn money on their own. As the center became more popular, the number of students increased and the facilities expanded. The hutment area proved to be too small to accommodate the growing programs and the increased number of students. Wealthy families, such as the Tatas and the Birlas, who were renowned for their philanthropy, offered to finance a new, modern center. So the center moved from its humble origins in the hutment district to Worli, one of the most sophisticated regions of Mumbai. The Center for the Physically Handicapped is now housed in a modern four-storey building. Nafisa remained a part of the committee running the center until she felt she should step down and make way for younger committee members. The center remains a popular success story and is regularly visited by dignitaries. Nafisa, however, the lady who devoted so much of her life to helping others, is not at the center any more. She is now 80 years old and has suffered a heart attack. Following the heart attack, she began to spend her time in more passive ventures, such as painting; when that proved too strenuous, she began focusing on pencil shadings. But she remains the quintessential volunteer—she continues to be known as the "social worker," and whenever she feels strong enough, she teaches art to less-privileged people. When we asked for her by name, we did not locate her immediately. When we described her as "the social worker," however, many could still identify her and led us to her. A volunteer never stops being a volunteer in the eyes of her community!

The Informal Volunteer: Anita (Mumbai)

Anita is the quintessential informal volunteer—she did not belong to any formal organization and simply began volunteering on her own one day. She had been running a small general store, and she and her sibling gradually took over its management from their aging parents. Over time, larger chain stores, benefiting from economies of scale and mass marketing, began to take more and more business from the shop. The family had never been well-off, and their income dwindled even further. As the store was small and did not require all the children to run it, Anita's brothers began looking for work elsewhere. One moved out and went to work in a different country; her other brother continued to live at home, but worked elsewhere. Anita and her sister ran the store, sometimes with their father's assistance. Both the sisters had completed high school and had made the store the center of their lives.

The shop was on a busy main road, Hill Road, in a suburb of Mumbai, which was even busier on weekends when traffic from a perpendicular street feeds on to the main road just across Anita's store. The road, St. Andrew's Road, is particularly popular on weekends because it leads to the rocky beach at "Lands End," which is crowded with people visiting the waterfront. For Anita, the weekends, especially the evenings, repeatedly presented the same scenario: traffic would come to a standstill as cars from St. Andrew's Road attempted to converge on Hill Road. People would honk their horns in frustration and tempers would fray. Occasionally, drivers would get out of their cars and curse one another or engage in a shouting match. There were also occasional fistfights.

One weekend, Anita and her father could no longer take the cacophony of honking horns and shouting people. They walked out of the store and surveyed the scene in front of them. Then Anita walked to the middle of the street and began directing the traffic.

Anita was no stranger to directing traffic. As a high school student, she had been a member of the Road Safety Patrol, which fulfilled the social service requirement of her school. But she had only directed traffic under supervision. It had been many years since high school, and, now, here she was, attempting to direct traffic by herself. Anita was surprised to see that she could actually bring a system into play and tame the chaotic traffic.

Anita was initially worried about the public reaction to her intervention. She had simply come to the rescue without any thought beyond making the traffic flow better. As she stood there, she wondered if anyone would become violent with her. What right did she have to do what she did? She had her father at her side for support but was that enough?

The first time she tried to direct traffic, she stayed just for half an hour and went home worried. She wondered why had she done this and whether anyone would react adversely. Despite these concerns, she soon began directing traffic for a little while every weekend when the traffic became chaotic. Sometimes her father joined her. Other times she ventured out alone. A couple of months later, there was a write-up in the local newspaper with the headline, "We Appreciate Your Work." The senior traffic inspector came to visit her and she asked why the traffic police did not allocate a policeman to the busy intersection. He said they were short-staffed. Nonetheless, he asked Anita if she would like to become a warden. Anita agreed and completed the training, which lasted one week. She never received the promised stipend, however, and when the police failed to provide the uniform as well, Anita sewed her own. Today, Anita's father is no longer with her but Anita is confident, strong, and determined to continue directing traffic for a few hours every weekend.

Anita's volunteering has been recognized by the neighborhood parish and she has been told that she will win an award on "Women's Day." She has been featured twice on local television shows and in many newspapers and journals. *The Activist* called Anita "a role model;" other newspapers have praised her volunteerism and civic concern. Anita is happy that her volunteering is appreciated—she loves the people of the community and is glad that she can help. Moreover, she feels respected. When I asked Anita why she bothered with directing the traffic despite all the shouting and honking, she said: "Most of all I feel good about myself. I am happy that I am being a good citizen—I would like to continue being a good citizen. I feel good about being unselfish—I hope that I can continue like this."

She plans to continue volunteering her time as a traffic coordinator as long as she remains fit and is able to do so. She sees what she does as a form of social service and proudly talks about the many Bollywood stars who stop and greet her and commend her for her work. "Now I know some of them on a first name basis," she boasts.

Anita knows that she has developed a reputation for being strict and taking a no-nonsense approach. She treats everyone the same and will not make way for the "big names." All cars are just cars to her and all she cares about is to try and make some order out of the chaos, regardless of who owns or drives the car. This attitude has made her unpopular with those who are in the habit of receiving special treatment. Some such people would like to see her removed from her position of authority. They are upset when she insists that they cannot park on the wrong side of the road and sometimes make threatening gestures. But that does not matter to Anita. She knows that she is doing the right thing. Moreover, there are others who acknowledge her work and her sense of fairness by sending her flowers. Some of these bouquets of flowers are from people she does not know, who simply wish to thank her for volunteering her time and serving her community.

In addition to her work directing traffic, Anita has participated in service clubs throughout her life. She has been a volunteer with civic bodies that helped keep the city clean as well as with the Federation, which deals with larger issues such as encroachment. She continues to participate because of the positive feeling she gets from helping others and from belonging to social service groups, and her enthusiasm is reflected in her shining eyes and big, ready smile.

Commentary

We assess our two chosen volunteers, Anita and Nafisa, against the aforementioned framework of the dimensions of volunteering (Cnaan et al., 1996). The first dimension, free will, tells us that a volunteer should ideally undertake a volunteer activity without any coercion or pressure, social or otherwise. According to this criterion, both Anita and Nafisa are examples of the ideal case. Anita moved spontaneously toward the traffic jam and, after surveying the scene, walked to the center of the intersection and drew one side of the traffic to a halt whilst allowing the other side to proceed. Her father did not pressure her to go but, at her request, accompanied her to provide moral support. As for Nafisa, her parents did not pressure her to volunteer either. They would have been content to see her lead the life of leisure practiced by her peers. Nafisa, however, encouraged her parents to allow her to spend part of her time volunteering.

In order to be considered an ideal case in the second dimension, a volunteer should receive no rewards. Anita never received any reward for her pains. In fact, she even had to pay for the uniform she was permitted to wear while conducting traffic. She also took one week off from her work to receive training—she lost money rather than receiving it. In due course, Anita received recognition of her service from several quarters, which could be viewed as a form of indirect reward. Likewise, Nafisa did not receive any compensation for her services although, like Anita, she was publicly recognized for her volunteerism.

The third dimension requires that pure volunteers serve a formal organization with a commitment for a certain number of hours given on a regular basis over an extended period of time. Although her work with service clubs conforms to this ideal, Anita did not volunteer to do traffic work through a formal organization. Nevertheless, she committed a certain number of hours to direct traffic at the peak times during weekends. She has continued doing so on a regular basis over an extended period of time, and her commitment continues to this day. Thus, although Anita is not volunteering for or through a formal organization, her self-imposed commitment serves a similar function. As for Nafisa, we know that as a young lady, she worked at an orphanage from 10 AM to 1 PM, which represents a commitment of set hours through a formal organization. After her marriage, she worked regularly for years at the Center for the Physically Handicapped. This kind of volunteerism deserves to be acknowledged as an example of the ideal case of the third dimension.

The fourth dimension required that, in an ideal case, the beneficiaries would be unknown or have no personal or professional connection to the volunteer. Both Anita and Nafisa fit the ideal case in the fourth dimension. Anita did not know the people in the traffic that she was directing and Nafisa did not know the disabled people she was assisting.

We may also use the four hypotheses of the net-cost analysis to analyze the degree to which Anita and Nafisa would be viewed in society as volunteers. Hypothesis 1 suggests that, in volunteer situations, in which people have different opportunity costs while doing the identical work with relatively equal benefits, the person with the highest perceived opportunity cost will be considered to be more of a volunteer. Anita would likely not be viewed as an ideal volunteer according to this criterion because she is not giving up a high wage in order to volunteer. Likewise, Nafisa is also not a professional who passed up high wages to volunteer, although she was willing to forego her leisure time to do so. As we noted previously, this hypothesis does not seem to hold in India anyway, which appears to favor an "underdog" approach in which those who are least socially strong are seen as investing more by volunteering. In this case, Anita would be considered more of a volunteer than Nafisa, who comes from a more privileged background.

According to Hypothesis 2, an individual volunteering with a recognized charity will be considered more of a volunteer than an individual volunteering at an unrecognized charity. As we mentioned previously, Anita's work does not match this criteria well because she volunteers informally, without a commitment to a recognized charity. Anita did not consult anyone when she volunteered to direct traffic. She does participate in other civic bodies, however, and it appears that this commitment to social service has always been part of her belief system. Nafisa, was on the other hand, from the beginning more of a formal volunteer. When she was young, she taught reading at an orphanage in Pune. Later, after she married and grew bored, she began to seek opportunities to do something constructive. She was approached by Fatima Ismail to help her start a center for handicapped children, and this was a formal commitment that continued into her painting classes for the children. Although she has done some informal volunteering, such as tutoring students in art, her overall pattern of social service is one of formal volunteering. It is perhaps because of this distinction that Nafisa is known as "the social worker," whereas Anita, despite the praise and attention she has received, continues to be identified as a shopkeeper.

According to Hypothesis 3, an individual who engages in volunteer activity that is perceived to be more demanding will be considered more of a volunteer than an individual involved in a less demanding volunteer task. Anita's work is demanding in the sense that she is a young girl attempting to direct potentially hostile drivers who compete aggressively with and swear at one another to get ahead. Nevertheless, this may not make her more of a volunteer than Nafisa who gave up a life of leisure to serve the disabled. The degree to which one may be ranked higher than the other according to this criterion is highly subjective and would likely vary considerably depending upon the perspective of the person asked to do the ranking.

Finally, according to Hypothesis 4, when an individual undertakes a certain volunteer activity for no explicit personal benefit, that person will be considered more of a volunteer than the individual who volunteers for personal benefit. Although both volunteers have no doubt derived personal benefit (e.g., personal reputation, fame, and personal pride) from their volunteering, there is no reason to believe that either undertook her work specifically for such a purpose. In this way, Nafisa and Anita can each be considered more of a volunteer than those who volunteer for personal benefit.

Contrasting Our Stories

The stories of Anita and Nafisa contrast with one another in many ways. The women come from nearly opposite ends of the social spectrum. Anita is not well off. She runs a small store for a living. The store does not do much business; therefore, Anita does not have much disposable income. She lives simply. She does not have a car or any people to serve her. In contrast, Nafisa has always been very well off and is surrounded by the symbols of wealth and social standing. She has always been something of a socialite with many friends and relatives. She told me that when she suffered a heart attack, there were so many concerned friends who came to see her that the whole apartment overflowed with well-wishers who spilled into the corridors outside. This stands in contrast to Anita who appears to have a smaller social retinue and who never married.

Despite their perceived differences, Anita and Nafisa share many commonalities. They both were educated to the same level. Social norms dictated that Nafisa did not study beyond high school, whereas lack of financial resources required that Anita start working in the store rather than pursue a college career. More importantly, both felt the need to give to society and shared the same sense of satisfaction from volunteering. It is this commonality that led society to recognize them as volunteers and shower accolades upon them.

3

The Young Ones: Do Youth Volunteer?

Introduction

In this chapter, we investigate why youth in India choose to volunteer. Scholars have sought to identify commonalities in what young people face in terms of opportunities, constraints, life views, and experiences. In addition, they have sought the characteristics that distinguish them from other demographic groups and that color their perspectives on how to spend their free time. These attributes influence the degree to which young people are inclined to participate in volunteering activities, the intensity of their participation, their motivations, and the benefits they seek to obtain from their experiences. To date, most of the research on why people volunteer has been cross-sectional and has searched for background characteristics and attitudes explaining why some people lean toward volunteering and others do not. In this chapter, we use a similar approach in our investigation of youth volunteering, focusing on young adults studying in universities. Our analysis also presents the findings of a study we conducted of 600 college students in Pune, India. This was an exploratory study done in one city in India and is not generalized for the whole country. Nevertheless, it was the first empirical study of young Indian volunteers that we know of, and it raises some interesting points regarding where, what, why, and how much youth volunteer that could be investigated more thoroughly in future research.

Before reporting our findings regarding university students and their volunteering habits, we will first explore the historical context of youth volunteering in India. Then we will provide a brief literature review of past studies, which have yielded insights into youth volunteering patterns. Although much of this earlier research focused on young people in Europe, Australia, and North America, it can still provide valuable insights into youth volunteerism in India and elsewhere. Finally, we will discuss the findings of our research before proceeding to case studies of youth volunteers and youth volunteering organizations.

Historical Antecedents of Youth Volunteering

Although it seems clear that certain characteristics make an individual more or less likely to volunteer, it easy to forget that the society in which he or she lives also plays a major role in determining whether this potential will be realized. Omoto and Snyder (2002) suggest that in order for an individual to become a volunteer, his/her society must place a positive value on volunteer activities and, in the case of formal volunteering, organizations must exist in which such activity can take place. Societal expectations give rise to concepts regarding normative behavior and may, thus, produce social incentives for individuals to engage in volunteer activities. In the Indian context, part of this sociohistorical background was discussed in Chapter 1, which explored the religious and secular roots of volunteerism in Indian history and the cultural antecedents supporting such behavior. In this chapter, we look at the institutional and contextual arenas that have informed and continue to inform volunteerism among Indian youth.

The first organization to recruit volunteers in India amongst students was the National Cadet Corps or NCC (National Cadet Corps, n.d.). The NCC was formed in 1948 with the goal of training young men in peacetime with an eye to their eventual military service. The origin of the NCC lies with the University Corps, which was created under the Indian Defence Act of 1917 to help compensate for perceived weaknesses in the military services (National Cadet Corps, n.d.). In 1920, when the Indian Territorial Act was passed, the training given to young people through the University Corps was replaced by the University Training Corps (UTCs) with the intention of making military service more attractive to youth. Roughly 20 years later, the UTC was renamed the University Officers Training Corps (UOTCs) to signal that recruitment efforts were aimed at youth who wished to achieve the rank of officer in the military.

When the movement for an independent India began to gain ground, it became clear to many emerging national leaders that youth should be trained for future leadership and citizenship in the new and independent country, and not simply for military service. The plan was to recruit and train youth across the country to be conscientious citizens and future leaders. The students would become responsible professionals, fulfilling a wide range of the country's needs, both in the government and the private sector. To this end, in 1948, a nationwide youth organization, the NCC, was created through an act of Parliament on July 15, 1948, with its first unit located in Delhi.

Along with building responsible and productive citizens to be leaders in civilian life, national defense remained an important area of activity for the young volunteers. For example, during the wars between India and Pakistan in 1965 and 1971, NCC youth members (or "cadets") were organized to help with civil defense activities, such as organizing camps focused on assisting the ammunition factories, patrolling sensitive areas, and conducting rescue work and traffic control. Military recruitment remains a central part of the NCC's general mission, even during times of peace (National Cadet Corps, n.d.). During peacetime, however, the NCC refocuses with an emphasis on developing personal qualities, like leadership. Accordingly, NCC cadets receive training in areas, such as social services and rural development, and participate in fewer military and defense exercises. Along with various other social schemes, cadets are encouraged to participate in adult education, tree plantation, blood donation, visiting old age homes, slum clearance, and creating AIDS awareness.

The NCC is open to male and female students at schools and colleges from the ages of 13 to 26 years, and there are, at present, over 1,300,000 youth enrolled in the program (National Cadet Corps, n.d.)

A program aimed at involving students in community service, the National Service Scheme (NSS), was launched in 1969. The NSS is an initiative of the government that focuses on involving undergraduate students on a voluntary basis in various activities that contribute to the socioeconomic progress of local communities. The program is meant not only to provide students with the opportunity to help address the problems facing their communities but also to learn about the struggles of their neighbors. It is hoped that the program will awaken social consciousness in young people and inculcate in them a sense of dignity in labor and a desire to work selflessly for the poor. This program received the support of politicians from all parties in many constituencies, which was necessary to secure the required financial, social, and political support needed to generate resources and motivate students to join. Many opportunities were created for students to engage for a limited period of time in social and national service. This involvement was seen as an extension of their academic training, providing them with practical experiences to complement their education.

Over the years, many students have participated in a wide variety of programs through the NSS. The NSS has drawn upon the idealism common among students to encourage voluntary involvement in development activities. It has allowed students to see themselves as agents of social change, directly involving themselves in building both better communities and positive futures for themselves. Moreover, their involvement in development activities has been an essential element in furthering the post-Independence era government's goals of economic development and social justice. It was hoped that by working for NSS for the betterment of India, young Indians would develop a heightened sense of nationalism and pride in the accomplishments of their country.

The National Service Volunteer Scheme (NSVS), another national youth volunteer program, was introduced in 1977 and focused on encouraging volunteerism among students after college graduation. The NSVS provides opportunities to graduates to involve themselves in voluntary nation-building activities for a specific period on a full-time basis. The scheme hopes to make use of the window between the end of college and the advent of adult responsibilities by offering graduates opportunities to pursue meaningful, creative, and constructive volunteer work. The opportunities are meant to give young people a better understanding of the problems facing the poor and otherwise disadvantaged in their country before embarking on careers, with the hope that their experiences will influence them to continue to work for the betterment of society in their adult lives.

The NSVS volunteers must commit to volunteering for a full year. To make the program practical and appealing to students, NSVS volunteers receive a small stipend and a travel allowance. Many students have used the program as an opportunity to discover their own preferences for future careers as well as to obtain references for jobs or admission to postgraduate studies programs. Future employers also see the benefit in the life experiences that the NSVS volunteers gain, which may give them an edge in hiring over fresh graduates who have little knowledge of the working world. In addition, having volunteer experience through the NSVS may send a signal to employers that a young person is more likely to be a committed and productive worker who takes his or her responsibilities seriously.

Youth Volunteerism: Current Trends

Although the NCC, NSS, and NSVS continue to recruit young men and women, the recent demand for young volunteers has also come in response to the sudden growth in the number of development and disaster relief NGOs that began in the early 1990s. Many NGOs in India receive funding from international sources that facilitate the recruitment and training of domestic and overseas volunteers. Young Indians have responded to calls for assistance to the many natural disasters (e.g., floods, famines, earthquakes, and cyclones) that have affected various regions across the country, as well as to the never-ceasing need for development work, by volunteering through their schools and colleges or directly through NGOs.

Some NGOs, such as Center for Youth Development and Activities (CYDA), iVolunteer, and AIESEC[1] are particularly committed to engaging students in volunteer experiences. We will present profiles of these organizations and the work they do at the end of this chapter. However, before we do so, we turn to the fundamental question of why students in India, particularly college and university students, choose to volunteer.

Why and How Youth Volunteer: Literature Review

The literature on volunteerism is rich but mostly limited to North America, Australia, and Europe. Unfortunately, studies that may explain how societal characteristics and environmental factors affect volunteerism trends in India have not yet been conducted. In particular, the literature on motivations to volunteer (MTV), although extensive, has primarily focused on volunteerism in western countries (Wilson, 2000). Scholars have found many similarities in the interplay of altruistic and self-interested impulses of MTV across the various populations studied. However, they have also found notable differences in the mix and intensity of such

---

[1.] AIESEC, originally an acronym for Association Internationale des Étudiants en Sciences Économiques et Commerciales, is an international, not-for-profit, nonpolitical organization run by students and recent graduates of institutions of higher education. It describes itself as "[t]he international platform for young people to discover and develop their potential so as to have a positive impact on society." The AIESEC network, as of February 2008, includes 30,000 students in 113 countries at over 1,100 universities across the globe and realizes around 5,000 exchanges yearly (AISEC, 2009).

impulses, depending on the sample studied. The first study to demonstrate empirically that the various MTV are interwoven was carried out by Cnaan and Goldberg-Glen (1991). They concluded their study by noting that "[v]olunteers are both altruistic and egoistic... Volunteers act not from a single motive or a category of motives but from a combination of motives" (p. 281).

Whether studying human service volunteers or fire fighters (Gabard, 1995; Handy & Srinivasan, 2004; Thompson & Bono, 1993), seniors or youth (Herzog, Kahn & Morgan, 1989; Serow, 1991; Sundeen & Raskoff, 1994), MTV include both philanthropic and selfish incentives. Likewise, national surveys in the United States (Clary, Snyder, & Stukas, 1996; Independent Sector, Panel on the Nonprofit Sector, 2006), Canada (Hall, McKeown, & Roberts, 2001), the United Kingdom (Davis Smith, 1998), and Australia (Baum et al., 1999) exhibit both sets of motivations. Despite this apparent similarity, cross-national comparisons based on these studies are difficult because questions, contexts, and cohorts differ.

Several studies found that the intensity of MTV differ according to certain demographic factors (Cappellari & Turati, 2004; Independent Sector, Panel on the Nonprofit Sector, 2006; Smith, 1994). For example, the fact that MTV of youth differs from other age groups is well established in the literature (Carlin, 2001; Hall et al., 2006; Jones, 1999, 2000; Reed & Selbee, 2000, 2001). Gillespie and King (1985) found that a greater proportion of volunteers over 35 years of age volunteered for altruistic reasons (such as to "help others" and "contribute to the community") than younger volunteers who were more likely to volunteer in order to obtain job training and skills. In a national survey of Canadians, volunteer rates were highest among the youth who also tended to be motivated to volunteer more for self-interested reasons than other age cohorts. For example, 65 percent of 15- to 19-year-olds versus 13 percent of those 25 years and older volunteered in order to improve their job opportunities (Hall et al., 2006). Among the student population, Winniford, Carpenter, and Grider (1995) found that in the United States, college students volunteer primarily because of altruistic concern for others, although they also volunteer to seek self-fulfillment and to meet their own developmental needs (e.g., affiliation, sense of satisfaction, and development of career skills). In addition, Dickinson (1999) reported that, in the United Kingdom, students who volunteer are engaged in a conscious attempt to enhance their chances of success in finding post-education employment.

In the category of nonaltruistic MTV, many scholars have argued that individuals volunteer as an "investment" strategy (i.e., to build up their résumés), which enables them to gain admission to educational institutions, enhance career prospects, command higher salaries, and secure better jobs (Freeman, 1997; Katz and Rosenberg, 2005; Prouteau & Wolff, 2006). Perhaps, not surprisingly, younger people, who often focus on exploiting labor market opportunities or on gaining admission to professional or graduate programs, are more motivated by career enhancement or "investment" objectives than retired people. Our sample of university students acts as an ideal data set to test the strength of the investment MTV in India.

Spence (1973) first proposed the value of "signals" in the context of the labor and educational markets. Signaling involves one party (i.e., the applicant) sending signals to another party (i.e., the employer or educational institution) about otherwise unobservable characteristics that they possess. Applicants for jobs and admissions have to signal in a convincing manner why they should be the candidate of choice. What does volunteerism signal? In a competitive environment, volunteerism signals that an applicant possesses qualities such as altruism and willingness to cooperate for the collective good, which are valued by many employers (Prouteau & Wolff, 2006). Indeed, studies of students have found that those who volunteer are more likely than nonvolunteers to have leadership ability, social self-confidence, critical thinking skills, and conflict resolution skills (Astin & Sax, 1998; Astin, Sax & Avalos, 1999). In those cases in which employers see value in volunteering, potential applicants with such experience on their résumés may have a better chance at landing a job or even of receiving a higher salary (Katz & Rosenberg, 2005). Indeed, in Canada, labor market data indicate a substantial monetary return to volunteering, estimated at 6–7 percent by Day and Devlin (1998) and 4 percent by Devlin (2001).

Likewise, institutions of higher learning, where admissions are competitive, often receive huge numbers of applications from prospective students with high test scores and grades and face the analogous problem of how to select those students most likely to succeed from among a pool of highly qualified applicants. Personal statements or interviews are often used to help decision-makers select students that best fit the institution (Astin, 1998). Volunteering experiences become another mechanism used to screen applicants and identify appropriate individuals. For example, a medical school applicant who has volunteered in a hospice will likely be perceived as a better candidate for admission than an applicant with similar scores and no volunteer experience. This is because volunteering signals certain valuable characteristics required in the making of a better doctor, such as being caring and compassionate. In such cases, volunteering may be used as a proxy for a desirable personality type and result in individuals being perceived more favorably in hiring and admissions decisions.

A recent study found that this type of "résumé padding" is a significant MTV among young people in the United States (Friedland & Morimoto, 2005). The authors write (pp. 10–11):

> Much of this volunteerism ... has been shaped by the perception that voluntary and civic activity is necessary to get into any college, and the better the college (or, more precisely, the higher the perception of the college in the status system) the more volunteerism students believed was necessary.

This suggests that MTV may be related to the prevalent expectations of universities in each country.

Furthermore, Astin and Sax (1998) found that college students, who choose to volunteer for community service projects, are more likely to pursue an advanced educational degree. One explanation for this finding may be that students who choose to pursue advanced degrees see the benefit of putting their volunteering experiences on their résumés and, hence, are more likely to pursue such activities than those with lower educational aspirations.

Such selection and sorting are highly context specific, in that not all labor markets or educational regimes interpret volunteering experiences in the same way. Putting volunteering experiences on a résumé is *de rigueur* in the United States and in Canada, e.g., where admission into competitive programs, such as medical schools or law school typically encourage or even require the applicant to show his or her commitment to the profession by having volunteered in these areas. Many top schools in the United States also use volunteering and other extracurricular experiences to assess the leadership skills of potential applicants. Not surprisingly, then, national surveys in these countries show that youth are more likely to note career enhancement and résumé building as MTV. This cohort is, therefore, an ideal population in which to test how the value of volunteering in society—especially with respect to its signaling value in the labor market or in higher educational institutions—may influence MTV. In addition to its signaling value for students, volunteering can result in productive networking that may facilitate job search, school-to-work transition, and effective long-run job placement (Dickinson, 1999; Jones, 2000), which may also play an important role in self-interested motivations to volunteer.

High schools and universities in some countries encourage "volunteering," sometimes even making it a formal requirement for graduation. In India, the NSS, NCC, and NSVS not only raise awareness of volunteering but also provide young people with opportunities to volunteer, thereby, encouraging the habit of volunteering and raising the rate of participation in such activities (Sundeen & Raskoff, 1994).

If, in certain environments, volunteering is promoted as a means of achieving national goals, helping the poor and promoting a more egalitarian society (as were the goals of India's national volunteering schemes), then this may be reflected in a greater reporting of altruistic motivations among volunteers. On the other hand, if volunteering is perceived as a means to better the odds of entering the labor market or institutions of higher learning, then students may be more likely to report self-interested motivations.

Research Findings

Method

Our data comes from 600 completed surveys of university students in Pune, India. Students were recruited by means of a convenience sample, which was stratified along academic disciplines (specifically, social science, humanities, business and economics, natural sciences, engineering, and "other"). Questionnaires were distributed in classrooms and took 10 to 15 minutes to complete. Although participation was voluntary, there were no reports of students declining to take part in the study, thus, reducing the risk of respondent self-selection. Given that the surveys were not distributed randomly, we must emphasize that our study is exploratory and that caution should be exercised in generalizing the findings.

The population from which we selected participants represents a relatively homogeneous group in terms of age and educational attainment, and the sample was equally distributed across academic disciplines. Given our research interest in this particular population, these sample characteristics, combined with the high number of respondents, support the validity of the data.

Sample Characteristics

Among the responding student population, 62.5 percent are male and 37.5 percent are female. The mean age in the subsample is 22 years. A majority of students who volunteer indicate that they come from a middle-income family (79.9 percent) and 12.4 percent of the students rate the family income as "high" with only 7.7 percent reporting the family income as "low."

Of this group, 502 respondents (83.7 percent) reported to have participated in volunteer activities in organizations in the 12 months preceding the survey. Only a third of the students were exposed to volunteering in school or university as a requirement, whereas over 60 percent reported having had volunteering as an optional requirement. The majority of students reported volunteering occasionally (68.2 percent), whereas fewer reported volunteering regularly with 4.7 percent volunteering weekly and 10.8 percent monthly.

With regard to the sphere of volunteer activity, 41 percent of respondents reported volunteering in sport activities, 34.5 percent reported health-related activities, 33.5 percent reported religious volunteering, 27 percent volunteered in local community projects, 20.8 percent volunteered online, 20.2 percent at university, and 35.3 percent reported volunteering in neighborhood organizations, with 41 percent volunteering informally. Students were also generous with monetary donations with 63.2 percent reporting that they had made charitable donations in the past 12 months. When asked where their donations went, 76 percent indicated that they had donated to disaster relief activities and 68 percent responded that they had donated to religious causes (they could pick multiple causes as to reflect their multiple donations).

Why Students Volunteer

To understand why students volunteer, we asked students to rank on a scale of 1 to 5 the benefits they saw in volunteering and what their underlying motivations to volunteer were. Members of the subsample of 502 students who reported volunteering in the past 12 months were asked to rate 15 possible reasons for doing volunteer work on a scale of 1 (unimportant) to 5 (very important). The items were based on the inventory of functions of volunteering developed by Clary et al. (1996, 1998), modified to include a number of résumé-building motivations to test the signaling model. To determine the set of dimensions emerging from the combined data for the six countries, we conducted an exploratory factor analysis.[2] Using three motivational scales that express altruistic values, career enhancement, and other self-oriented motivations, we examined how and why students differ in their motivations for volunteering.

The first factor incorporates four items that clearly represent résumé-building and career-related motivations, and we call this scale the RÉSUMÉ factor.

1. To put volunteering on the résumé for admission to higher education.
2. To put it on curriculum vitæ (CV)/résumé when applying for a job.
3. To get "a foot-in-the-door" where one seeks paid employment.
4. To make new contacts that might help a business career.

The second factor incorporates altruistic and value-driven reasons for volunteering and we call this scale the ALT-VAL factor.

1. It is important to help others.
2. To work for a cause that is important.
3. To learn more about the cause for which one is volunteering.
4. Volunteering gives one a new perspective.
5. Volunteering makes one feel better.

Following Clary et al. (1996, 1998), this next set of items can be understood as social and ego-defensive reasons for volunteering. This dimensional measure is a useful counterpoint to the RÉSUMÉ scale because it captures other self-interested motivations for volunteering; it is also distinct from the ALT-VAL scale.

The third motivational dimension comprises the remaining five items and we call this scale the SOCIAL-EGO factor.

1. Because friends volunteer.
2. Was advised to do so.
3. Influenced to volunteer by people close to them.
4. Volunteering relieves guilt over being more fortunate than others.
5. It is a good escape from one's own troubles.

---

[2] The results reported here are based on a maximum-likelihood extraction with oblique rotation and Kaiser normalization, which allows the extracted factors to be correlated. The final solution retained 14 items, two with factor loadings above 0.40. They reflect three motivational dimensions with a simple structure.

We treat all measures as summated scales. The three factors are positively and significantly correlated; the positive correlations show that respondents who find ALT-VAL reasons for volunteering important, also tend to rate RÉSUMÉ and SOCIAL-EGO motivations as important. This finding is consistent with previous studies that show volunteers are motivated simultaneously by a blend of altruistic and self-interested reasons (Knoke, 1986, pp. 5–7; Smith, 1994, pp. 251–252). The findings in Table 3.1 reveal the rankings of the 15 individual reasons for volunteering.

Included among the top six motivations, we find those five motivations that are included in the ALT-VAL scale (see above). Correspondingly, the least important motivations by mean rating are motivations of

Table 3.1: Scores on 15 Individual Reasons for Volunteering

Motivation (n = 344)	Mean Score	Rank
Makes one feel better	3.9809	1
Volunteering gives new perspective	3.9032	2
Important to help others	3.9028	3
Make new friends	3.8756	4
Learn more about the cause	3.8340	5
Work for a cause that is important	3.8008	6
New contacts that help business career	3.4702	7
Foot-in-the-door at paid employment place	3.4598	8
Friends volunteer	3.3272	9
Put on CV/résumé for job application	3.2133	10
Relieves guilt of one's good fortune by helping others	3.1803	11
Put on CV/résumé for admission education	3.0828	12
Influence close environment	3.0252	13
Advised to do so	2.9427	14
Good escape from own troubles	2.8855	15
Altruism/value scale	**3.9939**	**1**
Résumé scale	**3.2987**	**2**
Social/ego scale	**3.0621**	**3**

Source: Authors.

the SOCIAL-EGO scale; these refer to the idea of volunteering as a way of relieving guilt for being more fortunate than others or as being a good escape from one's own troubles. Table 3.1 shows that students generally rank ALT-VAL reasons for volunteering first, followed by RÉSUMÉ-oriented motivations and SOCIAL-EGO reasons last. This provisional ranking is also reflected in the ranking of the summated scales: we found that the ALT-VAL scale comes first (3.9939), followed by the RÉSUMÉ scale (3.2987) and the SOCIAL-EGO scale was ranked third (3.0621).

We next examined the impact of variables representing the unique personal backgrounds of the respondents on the MTV scales and found few significant effects. Table 3.2 shows the results of three regression models with dependent variables being the three motivational scales, and independent variables: gender, age, household income, personal values, program of study, and whether the student was exposed to compulsory volunteer requirements in high school or university, as well as the frequency of their volunteer participation in the preceding 12 months.

Table 3.2: Results for Three Regression Models

	ALT-VAL	RÉSUMÉ	SOCIAL-EGO
Gender (male = 0, female = 1)	1.03*	2.23*	−0.48
Age	−0.13	0.24	−0.95
Household income: High (versus middle or low)	−0.57	−0.08	0.32
Material values	0.01	0.48	−3.64***
Nonmaterial values	0.23*	−0.68	1.58
Program: (Business = 1)	−0.41	0.75	−0.69
Volunteer requirements in high school: (no = 0, yes = 1)	−1.32*	−0.52	0.08
Volunteer requirements in university: (no = 0, yes = 1)	0.49	−0.38	−0.86
Frequency of volunteering (ref = episodic)			
Weekly	−0.51	0.01	1.58
Monthly	0.23	1.59	1.60
R-Square	0.07	0.02	0.06
N	339	335	329

Source: Authors.

Note: *p < .05, **p < .01, ***p < .001.

Furthermore, we found that female students, in comparison to their male colleagues, expressed stronger support for ALT-VAL and for RÉSUMÉ motivation scales. Age, family income, and study program had no effect on MTV scales (see Table 3.2). Students with a stronger orientation to nonmaterial values were more likely to rate ALT-VAL reasons as important. Students with a stronger orientation to material values showed a diminished sensibility to social norms and expectations, as the significant and negative coefficient for the SOCIAL-EGO scale demonstrates.

The presence of service requirements in high school has a significant impact on student-volunteer motivations: the results show that service requirements in high school have a significant negative effect on the ALT-VAL scale. This finding suggests that such initiatives do not turn students into socially minded citizens.

Finally, we tested for correlations between volunteer motivations and the frequency of volunteer activity because earlier research had showed that individuals who volunteer on a regular basis expressed more altruistic motivations than those who volunteered episodically. The findings do not corroborate the common assumption that students who volunteer weekly or monthly have different motivations than those who volunteer episodically.

The students were asked to rank the importance of the benefits they obtained from volunteering on a scale of 1 to 5 with 5 being chosen if the student strongly agreed that the benefit was derived from volunteering and 1, if they strongly disagreed. The mean scores of the benefits as rated by students are given in Table 3.3. The top benefit they

Table 3.3: Benefits of Volunteering

Benefit	Rank
Leadership skills	1
Self-satisfaction	2
Builds trust among people in society	3
Opportunity to learn new things	4
Making social contacts	5
Professional networking	6
Recognition from colleague/friends	7
Job/career experience	8
Fulfilling requisites for government or school	9
Provides references for employment or admission	10

Source: Authors.

perceived in volunteering was that it helped them build and develop their leadership skills.

Understanding the role of signaling is important in analyzing student motivations to volunteer. Out of all age groups, students are most influenced by the demands of employers and admission requirements in educational institutions and will do their best to get jobs or placements into professional or graduate schools. In some countries, employers and admissions officers often rely on the applicants' volunteering experience to discern desirable, yet not easily observable, characteristics. However, our sample indicated that this was not perceived to be the case in India, and most students did not see volunteering as providing much benefit in terms of résumé building. Our conversations with five employers in a variety of fields (specifically, information technology [IT], engineering firms, consulting companies, and academia) revealed interesting and contradictory viewpoints on this matter. Although most of them were open to the idea that students who volunteered were indeed desirable individuals in terms of their ability to lead, their experience, and their social conscience, some admitted that they would be reluctant to hire them as they might be "too busy" with their extracurricular activities and hobbies to be passionate about their work. It was seen that the time individuals spend at their volunteering activities may reduce available energies. Even if the activities were carried on outside of office hours or on weekends, it was sometimes felt that volunteering would intrude on their ability to respond to work-related e-mails and phone calls and would affect energy available for work. Such employers wanted their employees' level of interests to be completely aligned with their work and their families, exclusive to other goals.

Some employers, however, saw volunteers as leaders of the future and stated that they would be glad to hire such individuals. They did not see their employees' time as being a zero-sum game in which energies devoted to volunteering would necessarily lead to a loss in work productivity. Instead, they saw synergies between the social commitment of individuals and their work. They believed that contacts made through their employees' volunteering activities might enlarge their personal networks and that such activities might also help them to "think outside the box," thus, making them more valuable as employees. Some employers noted that volunteers may bring the passion and commitment to social ideals that motivates their volunteer work to the workplace with one employer arguing that value-driven people are, in the long run, better employees.

This lack of homogeneity in employer attitudes toward volunteerism may help explain our students' perception of the low value of volunteering in terms of providing "references for employment or admission." On the other hand, in several of our conversations with student volunteers, individuals indicated that they had received job offers while they were students that were solely based on their volunteer work or on having met their employers during their volunteering activities.

Numerous studies have found that the number one reason for volunteering is the desire to help others—an altruistic motive. We found that altruistic motives were rated the most important reasons by students in India as well. To date, only cross-sectional studies have been carried out, and it would require longitudinal studies to give us an insight into if and how extrinsic motivations may become intrinsic motivations. Such studies may shed light on the matter of how community service requirements at school might influence adult volunteering. Nevertheless, despite its cross-sectional structure and nonrepresentative sample, this study hints that youth in India, at least at the university level, may participate in volunteering at high rates. Although many participants in our sample volunteer regularly, the majority (nearly 70 percent) volunteer occasionally. This trend of occasional volunteering is something we will return to in Chapter 7.

Narratives

Organizational Narrative: CYDA (Pune)

Matthew, the founder of the CYDA, has always been involved in social issues and helping others. He believes that the desire to engage in social service has existed since the beginning of human civilization, and he illustrates his point with a tale of ancient villagers. As the legend goes, these villagers, when on a commonly traveled path, would take turns placing stones horizontally, one on top of the other. Each passing villager would add one more stone onto the emerging structure until enough stones had been placed to form a support that passing villagers with heavy loads could use to rest their arms for a while. Then, after having caught their breath, the villagers would be able to continue on their journey refreshed. Matthew sees these villagers as being some of the earliest examples of volunteers.

Ever since he was a young boy in Kerala, Matthew has played his part in adding the proverbial support stone to many social causes. He remembers being a part of the youth movement and taking part in many demonstrations, such as the Narmada Bachao Andolan (The "Save Narmada Movement," a movement formed to protest against a dam being built over the Narmada River in Gujarat, India. The dam is expected to displace thousands of people, including many farmers who will lose their lands to canals and the irrigation system.), the Chipko Movement (a group of female peasants in the Uttarakhand region of India who acted to prevent the cutting of trees and reclaim their traditional forest rights that were threatened by the forest department), and many antinuclear movements in southern India.

Once Matthew graduated, he joined Youth for Unity and Voluntary Action (YUVA), an NGO in Maharashtra, which supported multiple social causes. His role in the NGO was to work with youth and encourage them to become socially active.

Matthew believed that the youth in Maharashtra were surprisingly apathetic. He despaired that the energy and idealism of modern college students was being dissipated in coffee shops and canteens where young people hang out in the late afternoon after finishing their classes. Only 7 percent of students proceed to graduate studies, and Matthew estimated that many of these college students were from affluent families and did not need to hold jobs. Their parents financed their education and told them what they should and should not do, and the students were not required to take on any great responsibility in their lives. Although their state of inaction was often acceptable to their parents, it was not acceptable to Matthew. He saw these young people as an enormous potential human resource that was being wasted. Moreover, Matthew believed that when the time and energy of the youth are not harnessed, they become habituated to being unproductive, and there is a good possibility that they will end up becoming unproductive adults as well.

In order to create a space for youth, Matthew started the CYDA, a center for the social development of youth. Matthew did not have the funds to start the center and began simply with a belief that such a place was needed. By 1999, Matthew was able to start the center with an initial investment of ₹4,500. Now, about 10 years later, he operates on a budget of ₹60–70 lakh (approximately US$130–152,000).[3] There are 2,000 youth members who elect a president, secretary, treasurer,

---

[3] The word "lakh" is frequently used in India to represent the number 100,000.

four executive members, and six general members. The elected members have a term of three years, which can be extended twice. Seventy percent of members are female, and the CYDA finds that female members have higher retention rates. The CYDA now operates in 11 districts of the state of Maharashtra. They also train youth leaders in other districts and assist them in starting their own youth groups.

Matthew explains that the CYDA raises funds through three means: grants, consultations, and the sale of items created by students, including cards and bags. The CYDA recruits, motivates, and engages youth through its three "Is":

Inspire: through lectures seminars and workshops
Involve: through camps and other social activities
Initiate: through lending support to projects initiated by youth

For example, a group of students recently approached the CYDA management with a scheme to present a "crackerless Diwali" to the village children. Instead of simply lighting fireworks on this auspicious holiday, as was customary, a group of youth proposed that they would provide an entertaining theater production to the children. The CYDA agreed to fund and support the idea, which was enacted on the last Diwali holiday. A glimpse of the play showed it to be funny. However, other than eliciting laughs, the play also poked gentle fun at damaging superstitions and exposed them as obstacles that prevented people from achieving personal growth.

A documentary film on the CYDA's activities in the remote village of Givshi gives a good picture of the spirit of youth volunteerism in the organization. This village was far from any other settlement and lacked a proper road to connect it to the mainland. No transportation was available, which meant that the people were forced to remain isolated. The propensity for tall grasses to grow wildly in the area also made the villagers vulnerable to snake bites. In such a remote area when someone does experience the dreaded snakebite, the victim has to be carried in a makeshift basket on a long trek to the nearest town. Despite the fact that the government had never acted to address these concerns, the villagers had always considered the making of roads and the clearing of grass to fall under government jurisdiction. Entrenched in their traditional division of labor, the villages concentrated on their one-crop fields and their cattle and simply waited for the government to take up its responsibilities. All of this changed when the CYDA decided to involve the NSS in their NGO work.

When the CYDA discovered the plight of the village of Givshi, they asked the NSS if they could partner with them, sending some of the NSS members along with their own volunteers to work in the village for a week. Over the course of the week, the volunteers labored to remove the grass that was harboring the snakes and to clear a path that would connect the village to the outside world. When the villagers saw the youth working happily and constructively, the spirit of volunteerism was so contagious that many among them decided to join in as well. The NGO collaboration with youth workers was a great success and went well beyond achieving its immediate goals: not only were the students productive in their efforts, but their work gave the villagers an awareness of the power of collective action that resulted in their setting aside a day each month to work together on a project for the betterment of their village.

The CYDA has come a long way from the time when it simply wished to provide a space for youth involvement. The NGO provides internships to rural students in order to develop leadership qualities that they can then use to mobilize youth and initiate their own social development activities. Having successfully recruited and trained its own volunteers, the CYDA has now turned its attention to managing this important resource. In this capacity, it works with other NGOs, training them in how to recruit, manage, and retain their volunteers. It also runs "Volunteer Management" programs that discourage NGOs from viewing their volunteers as merely a source of cheap labor. Finally, the CYDA involves young people as peer educators so that they can spread the word about HIV/AIDS prevention, encourage gender equality, and run youth camps. The CYDA's work is spreading quickly and has now reached other parts of India, such as Chhattisgarh. A number of former volunteers who have grown beyond the age of qualification for participation in the CYDA (13–25 years) have now started "Friends of CYDA" in order to stay involved in the organization. Others have branched off into working for political parties. Parents of the CYDA volunteers sometimes join their children in voluntary schemes. One prominent example of this is when parents and children worked side by side providing relief work for those affected by the 2004 Indian Ocean tsunami.

Both parents and youth have become aware of some of the indirect benefits of youth volunteerism. One volunteer's parents assured the CYDA that because of their daughter's involvement in the CYDA's volunteer activities, she has grown more mature and focused. She became aware of the academic program she really wanted and prepared herself so well that she was accepted into a prestigious university. In gratitude, the parents donated a large amount to money to the CYDA. Another young girl confessed that after getting involved with the CYDA, she went from "worse" to "better." Such reports of the benefits of volunteering with the CYDA have no doubt been a major factor in the rapid increase in the number of young volunteers working with the organization.

Individual Narrative: Bala (CYDA, Pune)

"When you work for the good of others you accrue the greatest good for yourself in the process," proclaimed Bala, at the very outset of his interview. Balasheb Gore, or Bala, as he is known to friends, admits that he had characteristics that made it unlikely that he would ever become a volunteer. He was not interested in societal troubles because he perceived such things as the problems of "others" that had nothing to do with him. Moreover, he thought "that NGOs were money-making machines." As a young man who had just completed his BA in Ahmednagar and arrived in Pune to begin his program in mass communications, his first experience with the CYDA came about through no choice of his own: he was assigned to work with the NGO as a requirement of his curriculum. Bala knew nothing about the CYDA other than that it was an NGO that worked with youth volunteers in areas of social development. He was disappointed about his placement and apprehensive about working with an NGO, but nonetheless, took on the work at the CYDA with as much zeal as he could muster.

Initially, Bala said little and simply did what was asked of him. His first assignment involved writing and preparing brochures for the CYDA, which outlined the various programs of the organization such as Youth for Change. Gradually, through his experience of working with the CYDA, he became aware that his initial assumptions regarding the organization were wrong. He realized that the NGO really did work for the underprivileged in an attempt to bring about constructive change. As he became exposed to the good that was being done by the CYDA, he also became aware of a subtle transformation within himself. He found that he was experiencing the same joy that others in the office exuded when they helped out. He began reevaluating his priorities and realized that he could no longer focus on his own economic self-interest. Like it or not, he had begun to enjoy his work and to appreciate the input of his fellow staff members. In this, he was helped by the direct and indirect guidance given to him by his seniors. The organization's CEO, Matthew, gave Bala some insights into the reality of the work that was being done and the transformations that the activities of the NGO were bringing into the lives of others. He exulted in this new image of himself as part of a large family, and instead of resisting the work, he felt drawn to return to the CYDA even in his free time.

Bala had previously prided himself on his mastery of his work activities: his knowledge of design and marketing and his unique ability to understand the customer. Now, he realized that by focusing his skills on making a financial profit, he had in fact been limiting himself to a narrow vision. Bala became aware of the way the CYDA worked in times of crisis, collecting clothes and raising money to provide relief to people in dire need. He saw how the volunteers and their families pitched in and worked to help the victims of the tsunami. Bala became aware of the real needs of the poor and disadvantaged and of the manner in which volunteer work lightened the burdens the poor faced. He realized that he, Bala, could make a difference in the lives of others and he wanted to come up with new ways to make this difference.

The "homeless project" assigned to him by the CYDA was a special experience for Bala and the others in his cohort: it exposed them to the unique problems of homeless people. He realized that those without an established residence had few rights and were extremely vulnerable. They were always at risk of eviction and of being robbed and beaten, and they were ignored by government officials who denied them the respect and privileges of other citizens. The police were always prodding them and moving them from one place to the next. And although they were among the poorest of the poor, they were not entitled to ration cards and subsidized foods because they did not have a proper address. This vicious cycle kept them mired in poverty and made their plight seem hopeless. Interviews with the homeless made volunteers realize that the poor are ordinary people with the same dreams and hopes for their families as others in the society around them. Often, the homeless are people who have left their ancestral homes in order to pursue their dreams and look for work in the cities. Instead of improving their situation, however, many of the poor run into even more problems in the new, alien lands and lose the ability to return to their villages. Bala and his volunteer friends managed to obtain some ration cards for homeless individuals and also enrolled them on the voters list. In addition to improving their immediate situation by allowing them access to government food schemes, this mitigated their isolation and allowed the people to feel that they were a part of society.

Eventually, Bala was selected by the CYDA and the National Foundation of India for an internship program outside the state of Maharashtra. As part of this program, he went to Chhattisgarh and worked with another NGO, Ekta Parishad, which focused on campaigning for the return of confiscated lands or fair financial remuneration to those affected by land confiscation. When the government and private companies take over the lands belonging to the poor, the newly displaced people often have difficulty making ends meet. By talking to the poor tribal people of Chhattisgarh, Bala became aware that he was gaining a special understanding of not only their problems but also their unique culture, perspectives, and ways of life. The experience helped Bala to understand the power of empathy and the importance of understanding the way others feel in order to become motivated to help them. The self-interested Bala of yesterday had indeed come a long way!

That same summer, Bala joined a rally that journeyed 350 kilometers from Chhattisgarh to Raipur over a period of 15 days in order to protest the policy of agricultural land being taken over by the government and to oppose the violence that was involved in such confiscation. The people of Chhattisgarh were not aware of their rights and had to be informed about the various types of recourse available to them. To this end, petitions had to be filed, and Bala helped with documentation, photography, and press releases as their cause was publicized. The publicizing of the injustices that often accompany land confiscation efforts has won over many others who have joined in support of the ongoing battle to secure the land rights of the poor.

Bala's enthusiasm for uplifting the less privileged has been infectious. His family members are happy with his transformation and are also doing their best to bring about substantive development in their area. For example, his father has been involved in development schemes that have improved watershed management in his village. The success of these efforts has meant that villagers no longer have to travel long distances to get water and has also led to the development of sugarcane plantations, which have created about 30 new jobs.

Bala has received the Best Volunteer Award for his contribution to the work being done by the CYDA and is now completely converted to volunteerism. He is also appreciative of the many associations he has gained through his work and plans to continue working with the CYDA or a similar organization. He is aware that a volunteer can only feel truly involved if an NGO provides interesting opportunities and values the fact that the volunteer is giving up his or her free time in order to be involved. He insists that he will always be available to the CYDA ("even at midnight") and credits his experience with the CYDA for instilling the right values in him and bringing about the transformation of his character: "I am a changed person," he asserts.

Individual Narrative: Mahadeo (CYDA, Pune)

The CYDA offers internships to rural students in order to encourage them to become involved in their own development. For a period of 10 months, an intern receives a stipend and is trained in leadership qualities so that he or she can initiate development programs. We met Mahadeo, one such intern in the CYDA office. Mahadeo was from Latur, a rural district some distance from Pune. He had just graduated from college and was considering doing postgraduate studies when he received an offer to intern with the CYDA. Mahadeo returned to his village and started a youth group, initially with monetary support from the CYDA.

Mahadeo believes that he has profited immensely from his training with the CYDA. "As a young village boy I lacked confidence; I simply listened and learned," he said. Now, Mahadeo believes that he is capable of mobilizing people and running a program on HIV/AIDS awareness or gender equality. Mahedeo would like to continue to work with the CYDA and continues to volunteer his time on Sundays to work on projects from other NGOs as well. He is also pursuing his dreams of postgraduate studies. At present, he is applying for a Master's in social work at the prestigious Tata Institute in Mumbai with the help of the CYDA, and he is even considering doing a PhD someday.

Mahadeo has chosen his future with great care. Although social work is still an unpopular career in India, Mahedeo believes that if he simply takes up a job, he will never be able to devote much time to volunteering. By becoming a social worker, he will be able to earn money and continue to work in programs that influence others. He believes that he has been so fortunate that he must give back to society. "A man must dream and decide to achieve his dream—if he does this he can achieve anything," Mahadeo muses. "You simply make yourself so strong in the direction you wish to go, that you actually make it happen."

Organizational Narrative: AIESEC (Pune)

Originally limited to Europe, AIESEC took form in the 1930s when representatives from various schools with a focus on economics and politics began to meet to discuss cross-national student and information exchange, traineeships, internships, and study tours. AIESEC now has a presence in 1,100 universities in 100 countries, making it a truly global organization. There is no paid staff and the organization is run by youth volunteers. AIESEC caters to its own membership and serves as an international platform for young people to discover and develop their potential. The Indian branch of AIESEC was founded in 1981, and now there are chapters in 15 cities, providing a forum for over 2,500 student members to attend conferences, receive leadership training, and participate in an exchange program that allows them to work and live abroad.

Our focus is on the Pune local chapter, which was founded in 1987. The chapter has roughly 40–50 staff members who help find assignments for volunteers. In Pune, as in other chapters, the recruitment of volunteers is done twice yearly when 60 volunteers are selected from a large group of young applicants. The volunteers range between 16 and 22 years of age, with about 50 percent between the ages of 13 and 18 and another 50 percent between the ages of 19 and 35. AIESEC's internship programs are popular, and AIESEC members, who join specifically for the internship programs, are usually young professionals between the ages of 21 and 30.

Most members are from the middle and upper classes and are students studying at the post-high-school level (generally in India, and usually in undergraduate programs in local colleges). The majority of the members of the national or international committees and of those going on internships have completed college. The religious orientation of the volunteers seems to mirror the distribution of religions in India broadly, and there is an equal distribution of males and females. The organization hosts a number of events on an annual basis, including an annual general meeting, an annual business dinner, a recruitment session, a session focusing on empowerment, and a two-day leadership development workshop for school children between the 9th and 12th grades. Companies that act as partners in these events provide the necessary financial support. Companies also buy brochure space to advertise for these events. The other major source of revenue for the organization is the exchange program. Every company or organization that requires a trainee pays an administration fee to AIESEC for their services. Correspondingly, every student who wishes to enroll in the traineeship program toward an internship also provides an administrative fee. Partly because of this fee structure and its all-volunteer staff, AIESEC is financially sound (indeed, they have a budget surplus) and does not need to apply for grants.

AIESEC International, which is made up of the president and his or her team, heads the global governing structure of the organization. Likewise, at the national level, the National Committee is made up of a president and his or her team. The local chapters within each country are led by a local committee president, supported by a team of six vice presidents who are in charge of in-coming exchanges in the corporate sector, incoming exchange in the development sector, outgoing exchanges, external relations, people development, and finance. Each team member serves for one year.

At the middle management level are leaders who head separate projects for a period of six months. These projects are: Organizing Committee President (OCP) "Let's Unite" (HIV/AIDS); OCP "School of Entrepreneurship"; OCP "Recruitment"; OCP "National Development Seminar"; OCP "Genesis" (HIV/AIDS); OCP "Footprints"—Children's Development; OCP "Eureka" (dealing with entrepreneurship incoming exchange); OCP "Tronix"—Technology; and OCP "Eureka" (dealing with entrepreneurship and outgoing exchange).

Once recruited, volunteers are committed to one of these projects as part of an exchange. One set of interns comes to India to work with NGOs or Indian companies (known as the "incoming exchange"), and another set of interns leaves India to participate in their chosen projects in other parts of the world where AIESEC has a presence (known as the "outgoing exchange"). AIESEC's Web site solicits interns from overseas and spells out the benefits of interning in India: "An Internship in India will challenge your perspective on the world, help you develop personal and professional skills, and will allow you to have a positive impact on the community you are working in" (AIESEC, 2009). The AIESEC internship exchange programs provide valuable opportunities for students to broaden their horizons and gain diverse experiences that enhance their teamwork and leadership abilities. Because they are drawn away from their comfort zones and exposed to new environments, interns are allowed to explore and develop their potential in often life-changing ways.

Volunteers are recruited through the sale of application forms at universities twice a year. A talent analysis is first done at a local chapter. This provides an understanding of the needs of the chapter in terms of the numbers of members as well as a determination regarding the skills or competencies that their members should possess. Promotion campaigns are then run within local colleges to spread awareness. Application forms are available at minimal rates and all applicants are screened through a group discussion and then through personal interviews. Once chosen, the processes that follow ensure the mutual development of both the organization and the membership, which leads to the retention of most volunteers.

Members first start with an induction procedure that gives them a good understanding of the vision, goals, and values of the organization. Once volunteers are recruited, there is a process of "personal goal setting," which requires each member to chart out short- and long-term goals within the organization to ensure their personal and professional development within the framework of the organization's objectives. This process helps determine the training and workshops required for each new recruit. In this manner, AIESEC matches the volunteer to the program most appropriate for his or her development objectives. Volunteer preferences and competencies are assessed before the goals are set. Each member is then given specific roles and responsibilities within the organization for which he or she is held accountable.

Workshops on various topics (e.g., leadership, communication, teamwork, and entrepreneurship) are held regularly, and international opportunities are offered at intervals, along with a system of rewards and recognition in order to manage the membership effectively and ensure its growth.

There are challenges and opportunities in recruiting volunteers. Often, students prefer working for financial remuneration and do not realize that volunteering can contribute to their long-term growth. Moreover, despite the rigorous screening process, it is hard to retain all the members that have been recruited. However, there are many opportunities for recruitment in Pune. The city has a large student base, making it easy to find competent members. At the same time, AIESEC provides unparalleled international opportunities, which makes it an attractive option to young people. As the emphasis is on gaining leadership skills through internship, the members have the opportunity to take up leadership positions through the organizations in which they are interning, which contributes to the growth of both the members and the organizations. As previously discussed, goal setting is an integral part of the volunteer-orientation process and appraisals are offered every six months to assess the performance of members in meeting their goals.

The feedback the members provide regarding their MTV suggests that most youth believe that volunteer work allows for a constructive use of time that might otherwise be frittered away idly. As noted, the opportunities for leadership and international exposure as well as for taking on the responsibility of managing an organization provides a work experience that is prized. Having the chance to work in a professional environment with heads of companies,

NGOs, and educational institutions also contributes to the value of the experience for volunteers. Moreover, the opportunity for interactions with trainees and interns visiting from different countries and from international conferences allows members to build a strong global network.

Individual Narrative: Jenaan (AISEC, Pune)

Jenaan remembers the day as if it was yesterday. She was 16 years old and had just entered junior college. She was excited and apprehensive at the same time at the prospect of the new experiences ahead. She had barely had a chance to get used to college life and here she was, ready to embark on yet another new experience. She had just learned of AIESEC and knew that the group was involved in cultural exchanges, although she was not sure what these cultural exchanges were all about. She simply knew that opportunities were spread across over 90 countries of the world, which had her interested enough to compel her to spend the required ₹30 to buy the application form. Before too long she was invited to the group discussion, followed by the personal interview and, finally, the acceptance call! She had enjoyed the process thus far; now she went to the first local training seminar where she was introduced to the students in her batch as well as to the general body of Pune local chapter. Here, Jenaan felt that she was being pulled out of her comfort zone and forced into an environment of highly charged energy and participation where diverse opinions seemed to be tossed about aggressively and lively discussions and debates were the norm. There was much that she did not understand initially, and her perceptions about the organization were constantly changing. However, in this rapidly moving flux, she was sure about two things: she loved the vision of the organization and she knew that she was excited to be a part of AIESEC.

In the months that followed, Jenaan became involved in the development sector of the organization and, a year and a half later, she became the department head. Her tenure at AIESEC allowed her to evolve from a seemingly average, confused 16-year-old into a motivated dreamer with grand plans. The international conference was the catalyst that transformed her into a determined youth with a clear goal and the drive to achieve it. She was passionate about the development sector, and her experience at the conference helped crystallize her dreams of working in this area.

All of the next year, Jenaan knew that she wanted to be the next person to head the portfolio. She knew that her age was a factor working against her, but she also knew that she was capable of handling the position and she had become astute at recognizing her own strengths and weaknesses. The year was a tumultuous one. She learned the importance of healthy competition, ethical behavior, and being a team player. She accepted her shortcomings and learned to overcome them. She remained focused and worked her way through what seemed to be an obstacle course, surmounting each challenge, picking herself up after a fall, and working hard throughout the year until, at the age of 17, Jenaan attained a position in the leadership body as the vice president of the development sector. She loved her new team, which consisted of a president and five other vice presidents. Many of these young people had been recruited with her, and she had much in common with them. But it was their determination to provide the best possible leadership through learning and innovation that united them. Jenaan began to "eat, sleep and breathe AIESEC." It was not always smooth sailing: there were moments of dissatisfaction and a number of breaking points—but the team had an indomitable spirit that kept them fighting till they achieved most of their goals.

Jenaan has now been with AIESEC for three years and is currently handling a project called "Talent Management." The sum of her experiences has made her creative, confident, and ready to handle new experiences, obstacles and all. She looks back to the days when she was young and unsure of herself, which now seem so long ago. Yet, in a span of a few years of volunteering, the gamut of opportunities and experiences provided by AIESEC and the wide range of people from diverse regions have all chiseled away much of the uncertainty and insecurity of her youth, leaving a confident and radiant young woman. She credits AIESEC for changing her life. She claims that she enjoys devoting time to AIESEC because "the more you give, the more you get back." Unlike other graduates, Jenaan does not have to worry about getting a job that allows for self-actualization. Her internship experiences with the development sector have put her in a comfortable position. She has already been offered a job in which she will create and head the corporate social responsibility (CSR) department for a Pune-based company working in her favored area of development. The shy 16-year-old has come a long way and it looks as if she is gearing up to go far!

Commentary

When one encounters a person like Matthew who insists that as far back as he can remember, he has always wanted to help people, it may seem as if the tendency to volunteer is something intrinsic to a person's nature. However, even Matthew's experience makes it clear that social and institutional factors are necessary to encourage volunteerism. For example, it is likely that without Matthew's efforts, many of these students, who he recognized as representing an "enormous human resource potential," would never have become volunteers. At the same time, his organization contributed to the development of societal norms regarding virtuous behavior and encouraged others even beyond Pune to participate in voluntary social action, such as the villagers affected by the NGO's projects who saw and were inspired by the young volunteers.

The case of Bala even better demonstrates the importance of social factors and leading by example in encouraging volunteerism. If Matthew was the inveterate volunteer, Bala was the antithesis: he was self-interested and not concerned with social problems. Moreover, he had a poor opinion of NGOs as money-making machines. He was required to volunteer as an intern at an NGO (CYDA) as part of his mass communications program. Although he was a grudging volunteer, he could not help but realize that the NGO really worked to help bring about change in the lives of underprivileged people. He also became aware of a certain sense of joy the volunteers felt not only for having helped to bring about a change in others' lives, but also from being a part of a family that enjoyed such work. He began to realize that he could actually make a difference in the world with the help and support of the people he could trust and who were similarly motivated.

The fact that Bala had to volunteer as part of his internship and that this led to his realization of the good that volunteerism brings to volunteer and beneficiary alike, signals that compulsory volunteering for students would allow some of them who might not otherwise have considered voluntary work to experience the rewards of volunteering and encourage them to pursue it on a noncompulsory basis later in life. Bala's experience, thus, lends support to the case for making student volunteering mandatory. However, there is also evidence to suggest that such requirements may be counterproductive. For example, some studies argue that mandatory student volunteer programs bring about resentment and resistance to volunteering and even our own survey on "Youth Volunteering in Pune" suggests that the presence of service requirements in high school has a significant negative impact on the ALT-VAL scale. Thus, mandatory volunteer programs seem to encourage volunteerism in some students while creating a resistance to volunteerism or a focus on its personal benefits in other students, and further investigations explaining this variation are necessary before one can make any confident statements regarding the advisability of such policies.

Mahadeo received an internship from the CYDA to train in leadership and start his own development program. Because he has been helped so much, Mahadeo would like to devote his life to helping others. Although he is completely happy simply acting as a volunteer with various NGOs, he is also aware that he has to earn a living. Thus, his volunteering experience motivated him to work for social change professionally, and he plans to do a degree in social work and perhaps a related Master's or a PhD someday. Prior to his experience with the CYDA, this young man from the village never had such dreams. It was only when he received the opportunity to intern with the CYDA that he became aware that he might be able to make a career out of helping others. We can assess Mahadeo as a mix of the ALT-VAL factor and the RÉSUMÉ factor—with the latter as a necessary building block to establishing a career involving the former.

Finally, Jenaan is part of the youth cohort that believes that volunteering provides opportunities for leadership and international exposure, while encouraging volunteers to make constructive use of their time. She had a preexisting interest in and commitment to development, but also volunteered with an awareness of the way in which an internship experience with AIESEC would make her a viable candidate for a good career. Thus, Jenaan's volunteer experience exhibits the typical tension between altruistic motivations and self-interested motivations, and she would likely score on all three summated scales (ALT-VAL, RÉSUMÉ, and SOCIAL-EGO). This finding is consistent with previous studies that suggest that the three factors are positively and significantly correlated and that volunteers are motivated simultaneously by a blend of altruistic and self-interested reasons (Knoke, 1986, pp. 5–7; Smith, 1994, pp. 251–252).

In sum, the student volunteers we have showcased seem to represent a wide range of student volunteers. Matthew is an ALT-VAL high scorer who provides the venue for other student volunteers. Bala is the archetypal cynic turned into a high ALT-VAL scorer. Mahadeo, a beneficiary of a volunteer internship program, climbed out of his rural poverty and is now working with a focus on RÉSUMÉ factors in order to turn volunteering into a career in social work. Finally, Jenaan combines all three types of motivations. All of our student volunteers have benefited immensely from their experiences and plan to continue volunteering. It is likely that this may encourage other students who witness their progress and satisfaction, as well as their confidence in their futures, to consider volunteering themselves.

4

Corporate Social Responsibility: Promoting Employee Volunteering?

Introduction

In this chapter, we look at volunteering in the corporate sector. Such volunteering arises as part of corporate initiatives aimed at meeting their social responsibilities to the communities in which they exist and that support their businesses. We first trace the origins of CSR and its roots in India, especially in the early years following Independence when corporations became stronger and more nationalistic. We then examine how CSR is practiced in India today and follow this with a brief literature survey of CSR in India and elsewhere. One of the ways many CSR initiatives are carried out is through employer-supported volunteering (ESV) programs. This is what interests us in this chapter, insofar as it involves individuals volunteering, albeit at the behest of—or with the support of—their employer.

Sometimes companies and other organizations encourage employees to participate in sponsored projects by offering incentives. Sometimes they simply provide approval and support, tangible or otherwise, for employee-initiated community projects. In this chapter, we will explore these types of ESV initiatives in India and discuss the linkages that NGOs often establish with corporate entities in support of such programs. We conclude with a brief look at what the future may hold for ESV programs before presenting several organizational and individual narratives to showcase the range of ESV programs in India.

The History of CSR in India

The origins of the concept of CSR may be traced back to the Industrial Revolution, when exceptionally large amounts of wealth were amassed by independent businessmen. Some of these early millionaires, such as Andrew Carnegie, were concerned with the glaring inequities of wealth and sought ways to lift business out of the sordid atmosphere of the "struggle for dollars" and transform it into a noble career (Carnegie & Titchi, 1902, pp. 140–141). The quest for public approval led many businessmen to introduce an ethical perspective to their business strategies and to recast themselves as "social benefactors" of their communities.

In India, the notion of wealth bringing with it social responsibility has also long occupied an important place in the national discourse. The concept of CSR was a key element in the societal precepts of Mahatma Gandhi who described large business as "trusts" of the "wealth of the people" and emphasized the larger social purpose that industrial wealth was supposed to serve (Sudip & Kumar, 2005). Gandhi never laid out clear guidelines as to how this doctrine was to be defined and enforced. At the heart of the doctrine, however, was the idea that the wealthy have the privilege of managing and controlling property and wealth, and rather than viewing themselves as private owners of this wealth with the right to use it primarily for their personal benefit, they should see themselves as trustees with an obligation to use their means primarily for the good of the society as a whole.

Gandhi's trusteeship doctrine helped gain the support of the wealthy for the nationalist movement by offering an alternative to socialism and other class-based strands of thought, which more aggressively challenged the power structures of Indian society. Gandhi masterfully used the doctrine to gain the support of both wealthy Indian industrialists and landlords as well as poor tenants and workers for the Nationalist Movement, insisting to the businessmen that he stood firmly against the forceful redistribution of wealth and property between classes while assuring the poor that the nation's wealth was to be used for their benefit. Gandhi knew that this strategy was essential to the success of the Independence movement, which could be irreparably harmed should the industrialists join forces with the British against Congress or should the "ignorant and famishing millions" initiate a large-scale violent uprising against the landlord and industrial class (Frankel, 2005, p. 44).

A number of Gandhi's contemporaries, however, especially those to his left, including his ally, Jawaharlal Nehru, had radically different ideas about what was required to build a prosperous and just society in independent India. Viewing Gandhi's strategy of appealing to the wealthy to voluntarily work for the good of society as hopelessly naïve, Nehru suggested that it was unreasonable to "give unchecked power and wealth" to "frail human beings" and expect that they would be able to discern between their own personal interest and the public good (Rolnick, 1962, pp. 439–460).

Although many of Gandhi's foes ultimately accepted the trusteeship doctrine (at least in principle), there was some dispute following Independence as to how Gandhi's ideas should be interpreted and incorporated into the evolving policies of the fledgling state. Although, as India's first prime minister, Nehru continued to find it unrealistic to believe that the moneyed classes could be convinced to share their wealth and behave ethically simply by appealing to their values, he recognized the threat to India's fragile stability that any direct attack on their wealth could bring, be it in the form of government policy or popular uprising. Thus, although legislation was introduced by the young government that was meant to bring the capitalist class under greater central control, the Congress stopped short of directly challenging private property rights (Frankel, 2005, pp. 107–109). The state did serve to encourage CSR to some degree, however, through the development of large public sector companies (Arora & Puranik, 2004, p. 96). This "statist" model of CSR, which used the law and nationalization policies to enforce certain elements of corporate responsibility, still survives to some extent today, especially in those companies that have not been fully privatized (Kumar, Murphy, & Balsari, 2001).

Beyond their role in influencing government policies Gandhi's ideas regarding trusteeship also had a direct impact on many of the leading industrialists of his day. A number of these early capitalist leaders, such as members of the Birla and the Tata families, were vocal supporters of Gandhi's ideas and incorporated the concept of trusteeship into their operations long before CSR became popular internationally (Parashurama, Jafadish, & Siddegowda, 2008; Rolnick, 1962, p. 448). In fact, many of these early industrialists were Gandhi's friends and major financial contributors to his and the Congress Party's social and political programs prior to Independence. For example, even in the early years of Gandhi's political career, when he was focused on securing rights for Indians in South Africa, he received funds from the Tata family. In addition, and later on, after Gandhi had shifted his focus to securing independence for India, industrialists and other businessmen took part in a number of Congress activities such as funding no-tax campaigns in rural areas, expanding social welfare programs in village industries, and developing basic education programs (Frankel, 2005, p. 34).

Although in the years following Independence and Gandhi's death, his philosophy of trusteeship may not have materialized in the exact manner he had hoped, Gandhi's ideas regarding the social responsibility of the wealthy continued to inspire many Indian corporations to voluntarily adopt philanthropic programs. Such programs initiated by corporations were framed in terms of charity and signaled the virtues of a company benevolent enough to share their profits with the public at large. This view of CSR as being equivalent to philanthropy remained current until the 1990s. The early emphasis on the generous corporate benefactor and the grateful societal supplicants, however, has evolved into a stakeholder-participation-based model. In this model, ethical environmental, economic, and social policies are expected to factor into all business decisions, ideally complemented by a high degree of transparency, accountability, and dialogue with workers and community members. Since the advent of this model, CSR initiatives have been increasingly seen less as charity and more as an obligation of the company, which has the responsibility to give back to the community that provided it with its wealth. In this way, CSR in India may be seen as progressively returning to the original ideals of Gandhi's trusteeship doctrine.

CSR

Outside of India as well, large corporations face growing pressure to act in a socially responsible manner (Mullerat, 2005). "Corporate social responsibility" has been the buzzword of the last two decades, with a greater number of companies taking on this mantle. More and more governments and the public expect corporations to give back to the communities in which they conduct business and make profits. This change in philosophy has been reflected by a shift in the theories in vogue in management literature. For example, in 1960, Douglas McGregor devised the terms "Theory X" and "Theory Y" to describe two fundamentally contrasting theories about the nature of work and human motivation. Theory X is the view that workers basically do not want to work and will do anything to avoid it; the essential business of management is to use a combination of threats and rewards to keep workers at work. Theory Y is the view that work is, in fact, as natural to human behavior as play or rest; management can function best by harnessing this natural human tendency in order to make the workers' own motivations harmonize with the needs of the organization. One of the ways of encouraging and motivating employees is to make them feel good about the work they do and the organization in which they work (McGregor, 1960).

Traditionally, Theory X was the hypothesis more widely accepted in management literature, but in recent years, the supporters of Theory Y have been growing. A number of other management hypotheses also have been developed that have drawn on the basic ideas of Theory Y. Among these are Maslow's theory of the "hierarchy of needs," which suggests that once a human's basic needs are satisfied, he or she yearns for a sense of belonging and the intrinsic rewards of self-esteem and self-actualization (Maslow, 1943) and Hertzberg's "two-factor theory" (Hertzberg, Mausner, & Snyderman, 1959) which emphasizes that challenges and accomplishments help employees derive satisfaction from their work. A number of sophisticated environmental management systems theories have also been developed that suggest that when employees take on challenges that contribute to social welfare over and above their work commitment, there is a spillover effect that leads to improvement in their work performance (Zutshi & Sohal, 2003). Govindarajulu and Daily (2004) noted that employees who are involved in company-sponsored projects to safeguard the environment, demonstrate a marked improvement in their work performance and sense of satisfaction in their work place.

Management literature has also provided some unique attempts to harmonize the concept of CSR with the Indian culture. For example, Subash Sharma (2005a, 2005b) has put forth a Vedic interpretation of CSR that he describes as a new-age corporate model that is embedded in the social discourse and the holistic vision of development. Sharma sees the holistic concept of CSR as representing a fusion of socialist, capitalist, and spiritualist thoughts that can be translated through the philosophies and terminology of the Vedas to create a new and better social order. Sharma builds upon this ideas to develop six specific Indian management models reflecting the underlying ideals of CSR that are based explicitly on Hindu philosophical traditions. He suggests that his ideas may help to bring about a new type of "Vedic management" that would give due deliberation to holistic and transcendental notions in management and leadership and would make certain that businesses and other social institutions add to the progress of the people and society.

Employer-supported Volunteering

Although CSR encompasses a wide variety of company activities and policies, the strategy most relevant for the purposes of this book is the practice of employee volunteering. Employee volunteering has been referred to by a number of names including "corporate volunteering," and, now, most popularly, ESV. According to Graff (2004, p. 6), "ESV can range from simple acknowledgement that employees perform volunteer work in the community, through to ongoing staff time-off and in-kind support of community efforts and charitable causes." Corporations often devote their financial resources as well as their expertise and manpower to ensure the successful implementation of employee volunteer schemes.

We are particularly interested in the ways in which employers support their employees in their volunteer activities as part of their CSR efforts. For example, in the late 1970s, Excel, a Mumbai-based agrochemical company, created an NGO, Shree Vivekananda Research and Training Institute (VRTI), to do community development projects. Over time, VRTI has grown to be one of the largest development agencies in Kutch (Shrivastava & Venkateswaran, 2000).

Employees from Excel are encouraged by their employer to participate in VRTI's development efforts and to use their skills to make a difference in their local communities (Shrivastava & Venkateswaran, 2000). Among its many projects are watershed development programs, promoting drip irrigation, providing families with smokeless stoves, building public toilets, planting fruit trees and vegetables, and providing training for youth employment. VRTI has, with the help of volunteers from Excel, started a leadership program that supplements local children's education. In addition, Excel employees have volunteered with VRTI to help set up camps for polio and cancer detection.

Another example of employee volunteering is that of the employees of the Taj Mahal Hotel in Delhi. Employees (mainly chefs) joined hands with an NGO, Katha Khazana, to teach women from a neighboring bakery how to improve their cooking and baking skills. Katha Khazana had set up an income-generation program for women in a neighboring slum. Although a bakery was up and running, it lacked the capacity to be successful. Employees at the Taj Mahal Hotel volunteered to redesign the bakery to improve its efficiency and to teach the women the importance of keeping their workplace and products clean. The chefs then conducted an eight-week course and spent two hours after their work each day teaching the women a variety of skills. Over time, the women learned to bake standardized high-quality breads and rolls; cookies; fruit cakes; muffins; pastries; patties; sandwiches; sponge cakes; and vanilla, chocolate, pineapple, and black forest cakes. The employees of the Taj Mahal Hotel helped the bakery become a successful income-generating project (Shrivastava & Venkateswaran, 2000, pp. 166–168).

Titan Industries, a joint venture of the House of Tata and the Tamil Nadu government, offers another interesting example of employee voluntering. Titan Industries partners with local NGOs to help local communities. The company's employees are encouraged to volunteer at these NGOs and devote time and effort to community development activities. The company initiated a "community development forum" run by its employees that meets every month to decide on the activities the company should promote. To recruit volunteers, these activities are listed on the staff notice board with details of what is required of the volunteers. On average, there are about 200 employees who sign up each month to volunteer for these activities. The company also helps recruit volunteers for other programs by matching employee skills with the needs of NGOs. Volunteers are allowed to use office equipment for their projects. Employee volunteering programs generate goodwill in the communities and build team spirit among employees involved in volunteer activities, which encourages further participation by Titan in such programs (Shrivastava & Venkateswaran, 2000, pp. 168–172).

Some corporations claim that their involvement in community projects is motivated primarily by their "philanthropic commitment to communities" (Hall, Easwaramoorthy, & Sandler, 2007, p. 9). Of course, this self-reporting may be subject to skepticism as respondents tend to overestimate their altruism. Partners in Change, which conducted three large-scale surveys of CSR in India,[1] found that a significant majority of Indian companies claim philanthropic motives. However, Partners in Change's own impressions were that many of the respondents give this answer out of concern that other responses may not be acceptable and which, when prompted, admissions of other more business-focused motivations increased. The researchers also found that most CEOs, as opposed to other business representatives, openly emphasized the more business-focused motivations, such as building public goodwill or motivating employees (Arora & Puranik, 2004, p. 97; Partners in Change, 1997, pp. 46–47).

---

[1] The surveys were conducted in 1996–1997, 1999–2000, and 2003–2004.

An additional interesting finding of the these studies is that many of the CEOs viewed their social responsibilities as extending no further than their own employees, their families, and their immediate communities (Partners in Change, 1997, p. 18). Only a small minority of companies were interested in activities outside of the communities in which their factories were located, and the few that were willing to consider programs in other areas were largely service-sector companies lacking factories or companies with high visibility across the country (Partners in Change, 1997, p. 45). This suggests that profit motives may be more prominent than many companies are willing to admit.

Further, a number of companies in India involve their employees in social projects that have obvious and direct benefit to their businesses, taking the view that "social responsibility is good so long as it pays." This approach, which we call the "self-interested CSR" approach, is focused on deriving maximum benefit for the organization and its stakeholders. For example, ITC has been reforesting degraded lands that could provide raw materials for its paper factory in the future, and Hindustan Lever has been helping to improve the quality of water in communities, which also serves to ensure its own supply of good quality water for the manufacture of its food products. Cadbury India is helping farmers to grow better crops, which will augment their raw materials (Kadrolkar, 2008); Voltas, an air-conditioning and engineering services provider, had its employees develop a syllabus "based on the needs of the air conditioning industry" and use it to provide technical training to students from underprivileged backgrounds (New Academy of Business, 2004, p. 38).

Even in those cases in which companies truly are largely or exclusively motivated by philanthropic sympathies, there are still likely to be significant benefits from a business standpoint. For example, those employees, who are proud of working for a socially responsible company, may improve their work performance when they are involved in socially beneficial schemes (Easwaramoorthy et al., 2006; Graff, 2004; Peloza & Hassay, 2006; Rog, Pancer, & Baetz, 2004). The ESV literature also suggests that companies with good community involvement records are able to attract and recruit the most talented people (Hall et al., 2007; Rochlin & Christoffer, 2000). Once hired, employees develop increased goodwill toward employers who provide opportunities for community involvement (Points of Light Foundation, 2005). A survey conducted by Market Explorers in 2000 found that 71 percent of employees want to work for a company that commits to social and community concerns (Kadrolkar, 2008). The CSR literature also asserts that ESV improves employee satisfaction, loyalty, team spirit, and morale and provides opportunities for enhancing existing skills and/or acquiring new ones (Easwaramoorthy et al., 2006; Graff, 2004; Hall et al., 2007; Peloza & Hassay, 2006; Points of Light Foundation, 2005; Rog et al., 2004).

Benefits to a company's reputation, which secures customers and business partners in addition to employees, may also be significant. For example, a survey of 1,003 members of the Indian public, 107 Indian workers, and 102 Indian company executives concerning perceptions and expectations regarding CSR found that more than 60 percent of the general public believed that companies should be held responsible for "bridging the gap between the rich and the poor, reducing human rights abuses, solving social problems, and increasing economic stability;" 32 percent found environmental, labor, and social issues to be the most important factors in determining their opinion of a company (Kumar et al., 2001, pp. 10–11).

The potential for certain tax benefits exists as well. Tax incentives may significantly influence CSR patterns in any country. For example, whether a company decides to consider the expenses of its philanthropic programs to be charitable or business related may have significant repercussions regarding the amount of tax money it owes the government. In the case of India, the tax law may, to a certain extent, work against purely philanthropic CSR activities, while encouraging other types of CSR activities, such as employee volunteerism, as alternatives to donations or other forms of assistance. This is because if expenses can be written off as business costs, they are 100 percent tax deductible, whereas if they are written off as charitable expenses, they are in general, only 50 percent deductible. This may make Indian businesses more inclined to emphasize the "corporate image building" aspects of their CSR work as well as to choose projects with more explicit business benefits (Agarwal & Dadrawala, 2004, p. 155).

Partnerships with NGOs

Many corporations choose to implement their projects in partnership with an NGO. We found many examples of this among the companies we interviewed including General Electric (GE), Mumbai, which worked with the NGO Aseema to arrange education outings that the NGO could not have afforded on its own for underprivileged students.

Rather than working with an NGO to implement a program, companies sometimes do not become directly involved in the implementation of programs and instead provide services to NGOs involved in charitable initiatives. Examples of this include Citibank India whose employee volunteers have developed a computerized microfinance package for its NGO partners and AT Kearney whose management consultants do *pro bono* work for Deepalaya, an NGO working in the slums of Delhi (New Academy of Business, 2004, pp. 17, 20).

It is not clear exactly what fraction of companies involve NGOs in their CSR initiatives. For example, although about 54 percent of the 50 companies questioned in the survey "Enhancing Business-Community Relations: India National Research Report" mentioned that they had worked with or were working with the NGOs (New Academy of Business, 2004, p. 6), among the 46 percent of the 647 companies surveyed in a Partners in Change survey that had been involved in an activity supporting social development, only 16 percent had worked in partnership with an NGO (Partners in Change, 1997, p. 51). The companies surveyed provided various reasons for engaging—or not engaging—in such partnerships. Although roughly one-third of the CEOs interviewed in the Partners in Change survey felt that some sort of alliance with an NGO would be beneficial, another third were indifferent to the idea, and the final third expressed a belief that their companies should avoid such arrangements. Those who opposed the NGO partnerships generally expressed concerns regarding NGOs' handling of funds, a lack of faith in the NGO work or, in some cases, simply indicated that the company had already established the necessary infrastructure for operating on its own (Partners in Change, 1997, pp. 54–55).

The distrust of the NGOs seen among some CEOs does not seem to be shared by the general public, however, and respondents to a 2001 Altered Images survey indicated a much greater trust of the NGOs than of businesses and a belief that verification activities should be done by NGOs or other independent agencies (Kumar et al., 2001, pp. 16, 21–22). This suggests an area in which India's extensive NGO sector could play a major supporting role in CSR activities. Businesses have not done a good job of making their work known, which significantly decreases the benefits to them and cuts down on the "bandwagon factor" that may encourage increased efforts at community involvement. The Altered Images survey demonstrates that although the public prizes CSR activities, there is actually little awareness of which companies were and were not engaged in such activities (Kumar et al., 2001, p. 14). A more consistent use of organizations with a "charitable" reputation (such as NGOs) to verify, monitor, support, and publicize CSR activities could have a significant impact on the scope of CSR activities and on the rewards reaped by businesses by helping to publicize corporate efforts and building public trust.

Corporate Employee Volunteering Programs in India

There have been a number of studies in recent years that explore the extent of, motivation of, and patterns present in CSR efforts in India. A few examples among these are the three aforementioned Partners in Change surveys; the "Enhancing Business-Community Relations: India National Research Report" of 2004 completed by TERI, UN Volunteers, and New Academy of Business (New Academy of Business, 2004); and the 2001 Center for Social Markets report, "Corporate Social Responsibility: Perceptions of Indian Businesses." Some of these surveys yield interesting information about employee volunteering initiatives.

For example, the Partners in Change survey found that 13 percent of the 647 respondent companies had "seconded" or "deputized" staff for projects and that 33 percent of these companies said that such activity was their company's primary mode of supporting social development. Where such a strategy was used, the CEOs claimed to have chosen it because it was viewed as "the deepest form of involvement" that would "give the company personnel a greater sense of satisfaction rather than making donations of items or money." The employee volunteers were involved in a wide variety of activities, including running health camps (18 percent), education and training (11 percent) as well as providing more general assistance (13 percent) (Partners in Change, 1997, pp. 61–62).

A much higher percentage (77 percent) of the respondents in the study "Enhancing Business-Community Relations: India National Research Report"[2] claimed to engage in corporate or employee volunteering. The companies reported that most employees volunteered on their own initiative, although some businesses had rewards in place for volunteers: "awards, cash incentives, weightage in performance appraisals, certificates and praise in in-house magazines" (New Academy of Business, 2004, p. 4).

A recent report in the *Times of India* (Menon, 2006) on corporate volunteering notes the rise of companies interested in CSR programs

---

[2.] This study used a small sample of 50 companies and 30 NGOs.

that incorporate employee volunteer initiatives. Menon (2006) notes that businesses often have significant financial resources that have allowed them to be effective and important contributors to public welfare projects. However, with the newer trend of employee involvement, a new army of volunteers is "emerging from the offices, cabins, and boardrooms and spilling out into the streets," working on projects previously thought to be the exclusive domain of the NGO workers. He points out that businesses often provide organized platforms to employees and give them opportunities to contribute to society, sometimes even offering paid time off from work.

In an attempt to give a broad picture of the degree to which this trend has affected major corporations in India, Karmayog (a unique NGO that will be discussed at greater length in Chapter 7) recently published its CSR rankings for India's largest 500 companies. The criteria used was strict, and no company was given the highest possible CSR ranking of 5, which required that the company's CSR activities "enable sustainable and replicable solutions to problems faced by society" and that the company develop "innovative [CSR] ideas and practices," whereas only 3 percent of the companies received the next highest ranking of 4, which required that CSR activities "form a part of the daily business activities of the company" and be "embedded in the business operations."[3] The majority of the companies received a rank below 2 (Rank 0 [26 percent], Rank 1 [29 percent], and Rank 2 [29 percent]) (see http://www.karmayog.org).

An analysis of the data presented indicates that, in general, those companies with higher before-tax profits tended to receive better CSR scores, suggesting that CSR is, to some degree, a luxury for companies enjoying financial success (ITC Ltd, 2009). Furthermore, the Karmayog study indicates that the size and scope of volunteer operations vary considerably between organizations, ranging from the employee-mentoring programs of five dedicated students to Tata's force of roughly 20,000 volunteers engaged in activities across 28 companies (New Academy of Business, 2004, pp. 22, 35). Tata, which received one of the highest Karmayog rankings, represents, by far, the most prominent example of a company with an emphasis on CSR and employee volunteerism in India.

Founded in 1907, the Tata Group is a giant family of businesses that dominates Indian markets. Operations are spread across the country

---

[3.] See, Karmayog's ranking criteria at http://www.karmayog.org/csr2009/csr2009_29264.htm.

with headquarters in Mumbai. There is a long history of corporate responsibility within the group, which employed 48,800 people as of April 2002. Considering the need for a holistic vision in business, founder J. N. Tata reflected in 1895:

> We do not claim to be more unselfish, more generous, or more philanthropic than others, but we think we started on sound and straightforward business principles considering the interests of the shareholders, our own and the health and welfare of our employees. . .the sure foundation of prosperity. (see http://www.tata.com/)

As early as 1958, the company established its Community Development and Social Welfare Program. As part of this initiative, the Tata companies conduct IT and vocational training for members of the community. The program continues to this day as management staff volunteer their time to training workshops within their community. A "Directory of Employee Volunteers" was also established by the Tata Group as an efficient way of matching jobs in the community with available employee skills and interests (see http://www.tata.com/). Tata's CSR programs are vast and include initiatives such as literacy and skills training, community development, and health, environmental, and employment programs. Tata has also made efforts to unify and formalize charitable activities as part of its general business practices. For example, in August 2000, its "Guidelines on Community Development" was released, which was meant to enable the formation of a unified CSR strategy across Tata's companies and integrate it into the business process in a manner that recognized CSR-related duties "on par with all other duties of employees" and ensure "explicit" management support of all employee activities in the community (New Academy of Business, 2004, pp. 34–35).

Another example of a company with a relatively large-scale employee volunteering program is IBM, India, which encourages its employees to volunteer in their local communities through its "on-demand community programmes." Fifteen percent of IBM employees volunteer with various NGOs with employees providing skill-building activities, mentoring, administrative support, and technology training. Likewise, American Express encourages its employees to volunteer their time to community projects through its Global Action Volunteer Fund. This fund provides monetary donations to the NGOs based on the degree of volunteer efforts of American Express employees to the NGO. In India, American Express employees have volunteered with several NGOs and have put together events for hundreds of underprivileged children (Menon, 2006).

Like the scope of the ESV programs, the manner in which companies support volunteer activities varies considerably, from subtle encouragement that employees volunteer in their time off to "seconding" their workers to do charitable work instead of their regular duties for a period of time. Allied Dunbar is one example of a company with a "secondment plan" of this type. The company sends its managers to work with Indian NGOs for periods of up to three or four months. A more small-scale example is the Sundaram Finance Company, which nominated one of its vice presidents to be the chief executive of a hospital (to which it contributes financial support) for a minimum period of a year after its former CEO died (New Academy of Business, 2004, pp. 18, 33).

Ballarpur Industries Ltd is one of the few Indian companies that allow its employees to do volunteer work during working hours. The paper processing company employs 10,000 people and has an office at Worli, Mumbai. The company says it needs to foster better relationships in the remote tribal communities where many of its sites are located. "The onus is on us to offer employment, but we can't give everyone jobs. So if we want to sustain our sites in these areas, we need a kind of social license and acceptance," explained Yashashree Gurjar, chief general manager of CSR. The employees work for two days a month on AIDS awareness, promoting polio vaccinations or sharing their professional skills with the community. "Employees take part because it gives them job satisfaction and helps them do something other than mechanical engineering all day. Moreover, they feel they are making a difference," she said.

Microsoft in India also has a similar, albeit more limited, policy allowing its employees to take three working days a year off to engage in volunteer projects. Excel Industries, the Mumbai-based agrochemical company discussed earlier, "informally encourages" its employees to engage in "time offs" if they want to work for the community, as long as they are not required in the office (New Academy of Business, 2004, p. 23). More commonly, however, charitable work completed by company employees is purely voluntary and must be completed outside of business hours.

The celebration of success often breeds more success. Cognizant of this, Hong Kong and Shanghai Banking Corporation (HSBC), India, offers employees an opportunity to celebrate the successful execution of any of their community-development initiatives. After the HSBC marketing team of 60 members visited three villages on the outskirts of Mumbai and engaged in building trenches, teaching children, and interacting with the self-help groups and villagers, they were invited to share their stories at a business-community partnership event called "Breaking Barriers."

HSBC hopes that events such as these will act as catalysts for further volunteering and has started a program called "Catalyst," which is touring all the HSBC branches in India in an attempt to recruit more employees in participation schemes. The bank's 1,000 employees from across India celebrated World Volunteer Day by engaging in over 8,000 volunteer-hours in the community. Such attempts at encouraging and recruiting employees to take a more active role in volunteering are not confined to one company. "Volunteering Action Fortnight," which initially took place between November 14 and November 28, 2006, engaged employees from different companies to work with NGOs in their communities. Employees contributed more than 40,000 hours of volunteer time and large numbers of people were recruited into volunteer projects. This has now become an annual event (HSBC, n.d.).

Wipro, another major company that encourages its employees to volunteer, started its ESV programs in the aftermath of the 2001 earthquake in Gujarat. Involvement in the disaster relief activities increased awareness in a number of Wipro volunteers of the dire needs of the community and instilled in them a desire to continue their service even after the immediate crisis was over. The management of Wipro supported the employee volunteers; Vijay Gupta, a senior executive, asserted that the Wipro companies cannot function as "islands of excellence" in a community that is dismally lacking in the basic necessities of life (DevelopedNation, n.d.). They are astute enough to know that such inequality breeds resentment and that the community is the source from which they will find their future employees. It made good sense to engage employee volunteers to find ways to help their community. Moreover, the employees were anxious to help and offered their time and money freely to programs of poverty alleviation. The popularity of these initiatives led to the creation of Wipro Cares. The company provides half of the funding for Wipro Cares, with the other half of the funding coming from the volunteers themselves.

In order to determine the key issues that needed to be addressed through volunteer initiatives, the employee volunteers did a quick survey of the slums around Bangalore and Hyderabad. They identified three critical areas of need: education, health, and sanitation. Wipro established programs to "train the trainer" in which school principals and teachers are trained to teach in a manner that "opens the minds" of the students as well as educational programs for students that seek to improve on the traditional ways of learning by introducing modes of critical thinking. They are presently in the process of developing two further initiatives meant to address health and sanitation concerns (DevelopedNation, n.d.). Wipro will undoubtedly benefit from development work in the communities around their workplaces: they will allay any local resentment toward their company as well as create a pool of potential employees. But more importantly, they are also helping to build a community of healthy, critical thinkers who can contribute to the development of their communities and nation.

Future Concerns

In a recent report in the *Hindustan Times*, Shalabh Sahai, cofounder and director of MITRA, was quoted as saying that he was struggling to promote an employee volunteering scheme through the volunteer agency iVolunteer (Canton, 2007, p. 2). Sahai said that many Indian employers were not happy to give employees time off to volunteer during company time because they were afraid that this would be tantamount to giving them a holiday. Moreover, the corporate employee programs were floundering despite the rhetoric of CSR. Further, anecdotal evidence suggests that global competition, as well as the downturn in the economy, may require employees to put in long working hours. It may also make it difficult for many businesses, which may be struggling to continue their operations at all and are facing the prospect of employee layoffs to continue to invest time, money, and manpower in charitable work. It seems likely that the ESV programs of organizations such as Tata, which have made efforts to incorporate the CSR and employee volunteer ethic into their general business operations, will be best able to weather the economic storm. However, there is significant risk that many other businesses, for whom employee volunteering has been a supplementary and perhaps not so highly prioritized activity, will be more hesitant in the coming months or years to encourage their employees to volunteer.

Narratives

Narrative: Patni (Computer Company, Pune)

Ramesh and Chandan (the names have been changed) are employees of Patni. Ramesh grew up in Kenya and first encountered volunteering through scouting programs in school. He came to India to go to college and, during his undergraduate years in Bangalore, volunteered with local NGOs that promoted children's rights. Later, he moved to Pune, and while doing an MBA at Symbiosis, started a volunteer program called Sharing Care. The program developed a knowledge base of NGOs working with children's welfare and was eventually funded by his university, which promoted IT.

For many NGOs that lack technical knowledge, capacity building is essential. As students involved in IT, the volunteers wanted to help NGOs develop a knowledge base that would support their activities. An initially difficult but important step was to get support from the NGOs themselves as collecting all of the necessary data on their own took time from their already busy schedules. However, the NGOs soon grew to appreciate the value of the project and became more comfortable sharing information and allowing students to visit and observe their programs. The knowledge base program initiated by Ramesh is now running and has strong support from the university that funds it. Moreover, the university encourages students to volunteer through the program.

When Ramesh graduated and joined Patni, he took with him his passion for children's rights. Patni, an IT company based in Pune, was already involved in many different charitable endeavors, including supporting an old-age home and conducting drives for reusables such as clothing, small appliances, books, and toys for the poor. Among the company's 700 employees, 20 to 30 participated in these programs. When Patni donated computers to NGOs so that they could train students to use them, there was a dearth of teachers available to make use of them. So, in August 2007, a group of employees under the leadership of another employee, Chandan, decided to invite the children to come to the company. Here, the employees themselves volunteered to help train the students in computer skills.

The goals were modest: to impart IT training, to give the students simple presentation skills, and to build their confidence by heightening their ability to use computers (something normally out of reach for young people attending public schools and living in dire poverty). In order to be successful, Ramesh and Chandan realized early on that it was necessary to get the support of all the stakeholders that were to be involved directly and indirectly in this project. This included the parents of the students, the students themselves, the company, and all of its employees. One of the founders of this initiative was a senior executive who decided to pilot this project at a location he managed, using resources he controlled. If it proved successful, he would take it to his superiors and garner support for expanding the project to the entire company.

As the project was being planned, Ramesh, Chandan, and their loyal cohort of volunteers organized an event to sensitize the employees to the problems of children living in the slums not far from their corporate offices. The first pitch was made regarding child labor at an evening event attended by over 3,000 employees and their spouses. The presentation educated the attendees about the current and past plight of child labor through a multimedia production. Interesting and informative songs, short plays, and visual displays made the event successful and, at the end of the evening, an oath regarding child labor was circulated. Chandan recalls a moving moment when all the participants read aloud in unison an oath against the use and promotion of child labor. They were presented with roses to remind them that "although the fruits of child labor are sweet [like the rose]—an increased productivity at lower costs—the price was high [like its thorns], a generation of uneducated children who would never reach their true potential."

The training program started with computers, which were made available by the company for two short periods during the week: 5 PM to 7 PM on Saturdays and 9 AM to 1 PM on Sundays. Students participating in the program were required to come for each of these sessions weekly. They were asked to meet at a local public school from where they were picked up by transportation vans owned by the company and brought to the training facilities. The company also provided meals for the students during the training programs. Initially, 20 students, aged between 9 and 14, enrolled in the program. Because all of the students spoke the local language of Marathi, using English language commands and Microsoft Office with English fonts proved challenging. Furthermore, although the volunteers attempted to account for varying learning speeds and abilities by grouping the students by age, a number of the students, many of whom were children of migrant workers, had not had the benefit of continuous schooling and, consequently, there was great diversity in educational backgrounds among the students in the classes. However, the volunteers found that by exercising patience, using visual aids, and teaching the students some basic English words, they were soon able to make progress. Paintbrush, a type of painting software, proved especially successful, and the children quickly learned to draw pictures on the computer. The volunteers were unanimous in their praise of the students' talents in learning about computers despite their lack of basic reading, writing, and other skills.

To get volunteers for this computer training program, an e-mail was sent out to the 1,900 employees of Patni. Volunteers were required to come for one session on the weekends. Some 45 employees volunteered and were organized into four groups with each group of six to eight people taking the responsibility for training one weekend a month. Ironically, volunteers were relatively easier to secure than were students. This was because initially the parents did not want their children, especially the female children, to go to the venue set up for the training. There were suspicions about the kind of training the children might get and of the use of the word "club" in the name of the location. Only after one of Patni's young employees who also lived in the slum met with the parents to convince them that there were no ulterior motives to the project, did the parents relent and let the children go. To further reassure the parents, when young girls came for training, the group of volunteers always included a female volunteer who was assigned to look after them. A female student was also picked to cut the ribbon that ceremonially inaugurated the program and the parents were invited to participate.

When the students had mastered some basic computer skills, they made presentations to other employees in Patni, which doubled the rate of employees signing up to volunteer. Resources from the headquarters were committed to the program in terms of computer space, volunteers were encouraged to make lesson plans and coordinate their efforts via interoffice e-mails, and time and resources were made available to employees to plan events that showcased their efforts.

The success of this pilot project, which had come from the grassroots efforts of a few employees, allowed it to become an important and ongoing effort receiving official company support. This does not imply, however, that all managers or senior executives are wholly behind the undertaking. Some of the employees actually feel that their commitment to the project and events linked to it are frowned upon by certain managers who see their participation as representing a loss of billable hours. At a rate of US$18 per hour, the labor of the volunteers represents a significant sum in a country in which millions live below the US$1-a-day poverty line.

In 2009–2010, the management of Patni decided to formalize its CSR focus and establish a public charitable trust: the Patni Foundation. A global poll among all Patni employees was initiated in 2009 to help determine the focus of Patni's CSR activities. The results showed that the employees favored education for the underprivileged children as a cause for support to create awareness of the need for such education and critical issues as well as to provide opportunities for employee participation in tackling this and other community needs. Patni accomplishes this through their partnerships with NGOs. With the help of their partner NGOs, Patni aims to expose its employees to local social inequities in order to inspire them to make a voluntary choice to participate, and make a difference in their local communities. Patni's overall CSR goal is to create programs that make employees' lives meaningful and inculcate a culture rooted in active employee volunteer participation. Such programs will include support for employee participation in projects that strengthen the quality of education for underprivileged children. A long-term goal involves projects for employee participation in providing vocational training programs for the physically and intellectually disabled.

Narrative: GE (Mumbai)

GE, Mumbai, has been in the business of working with communities since 1902. According to GE management, the company believes that the essence of corporate citizenship is "the inextricable link between integrity and performance to the point that they become one and the same" (GE, 2010). One of the areas in which GE promotes its corporate citizenship philosophy is through "GE Volunteerism," which is considered a core activity of GE and which focuses on community service projects and educational programs in GE communities. Globally, GE employees volunteer more than one million hours of community service each year, backed by more than 145 GE volunteer (GEV) councils in over 40 countries. Employees discover compatible opportunities by visiting the online "GE Volunteers Portal" or by looking within their own neighborhoods. During Global

Community Days, GE coordinates company-wide efforts to support urgent projects around the world. GE's charitable organization, the GE Volunteers Foundation (GEVF), works to strengthen the communities where employees work and live by partnering with local nonprofit charitable organizations to address key needs. GEVF is funded by direct donations from GE employees and retirees and through the proceeds from the GE Volunteers VISA/MasterCard credit card.

The Mumbai Council of GEVs, created in September 2002, was followed by the creation of other India chapters in Delhi, Chennai, Hyderabad, and Bangalore (Dandiwalla, 2008). Council meetings are held quarterly at local GE business offices. All volunteer programs are sponsored by local GE businesses or through the GEVF. Today, GE in Mumbai has over 250 members. Twenty to twenty-five volunteers form the core of personnel from GE Capital, GE Commercial Aviation Services, and GE Energy. Each Council meeting is attended by about six to eight employee volunteers. The number of volunteers at GE has risen since the Council's inception, and volunteerism continues to increase in popularity. Most employee volunteers are between 25 and 40 years of age and have graduate degrees, with many holding MBA's from prestigious Indian business schools.

Global funds are distributed each year to the various GE regional businesses. The corporate office in the United States or Asia or local GE businesses contribute the required funding for each project with local councils sometimes absorbing any expenses that come in over budget. The NGOs send in their proposals for grants and their plans of action to the Council, which then evaluates each proposal and decides which ones to fund. At times, NGOs are given projected budgets so that they can frame their proposal around available funds. There is a stringent proviso that GEV members must be present when administering the funds for a project and their role must be specified in the proposal. For example, if books are to be given to a school or organization, it is mandatory that GEV be involved in some way in the project, such as by taking on the role of teachers or tutors.

The GEV headquarter acts as a corporate structure with a global reach. India has five GEV councils. The Mumbai chapter has a six-member leadership council that consists of a leader, coleader, secretary, treasurer, communications lead and Web master. Fifteen to twenty GEVs participate in several projects on a regular basis.

The projects with which the GEVs are involved are usually episodic and sometimes involve partners/sponsors, such as M/s. Jet Airways (India) Ltd, Hindustan Petroleum Aviation Services, and TajSats In-Flight Catering. GEVs have been involved in initiatives with varied associations, such as Magic Bus and its partner NGOs, Aseema Charitable Trust, Vision in Social Arena, Primary Healthcare Center, and the Indian Red Cross at the Society of the Home for the Aged. Sometimes, the GEVs find imaginative ways to combine their partners/sponsors and the associations to deliver services.

A case in point is the "Flight of Fantasy" project held annually on November 14 over the past seven years. GEVs, Mumbai, in association with primary sponsor M/s. Jet Airways (India) Ltd, commemorated Children's Day, India, in a novel fashion. On Children's Day, the nation pays tribute to India's first prime minister, Pandit Jawaharlal Nehru, who was well-known for his love of children. GEVs, along with staff/ancillaries from NGOs and nonprofit organizations, host 75–80 children between the ages of 8 and 14 for a trip on board a chartered Jet Airways' Boeing 737-800. The plane flies over the city and the shimmering Arabian Sea for 50 minutes, hovering over various panoramic sites before returning to the Mumbai Airport. The pilot explains his role in commanding the flight and the process of education required to obtain his job and the jobs of others on his avionics team. The GEVs participate in and support the event in the hope that it will entertain the children, inspire them to study, and make them aware of career opportunities in the aviation industry.

In addition, annually on August 15, the eve of India's Independence Day, GEVs, Mumbai, visit or invite children from schools adopted and managed by the NGO Aseema. During the Independence Day event, the volunteers distribute sweets, join the teachers and children in singing patriotic hymns, and hold a "paint fest," which brings out the artistic skills of the children. The volunteers also enact a skit that highlights the importance of Independence, education, hygiene, and helping the needy. The money that is spent on this occasion is derived from a corporate budget allocated to GE Commercial Finance, Mumbai, for office festivities.

In the past, the Mumbai chapter celebrated "ECOmmunity Week" by sending its volunteers to accompany 42 children from VISA (Vision in a Social Arena) on a trip to the Nehru Planetarium and the

National History Museum. The trip started with a virtual expedition into outer space where the children were able to witness man's first step on the moon. Later, they had a guided tour of India's culture and history museum. After the trip, a quiz was administered to test the success of the expedition and the children's answers showed how much they had learned. Similar ECOmmunity weeks were celebrated by GEVs in Vadodra, Ahmedabad, and Pune involving tree plantation and rain water harvesting projects as well as the screening of a movie highlighting social problems. In addition, on a recent Christmas Eve, GEVF and GE Money, Mumbai employees individually sponsored 54 Christmas Goody Bags. They then visited 13 NGOs in a bus packed with goodies and distributed them to senior citizens, orphans, and other challenged children with whom the NGOs worked.

GEVs have been involved in many worthwhile projects around India in their short history. They have upgraded facilities at a primary health-care center in Gujarat; conferred a generous grant to Pratham (Pune), an educational foundation with the long-term goal of achieving universal education; visited with seniors in a missionary run by the Sisters of the Poor; and worked with the Cancer Patients Aid Association to celebrate National Cancer "Rose" Day. GEVs also participate in blood donation camps, educational and historical excursions, factory site visits, and tree plantation and make provisions to donate water purifiers and desktop computers and sponsor distribution of hygiene products to less fortunate children.

Industrial Narrative: Ashish B. (GE, Mumbai)

Ashish is a GE employee who volunteers regularly for GE-sponsored events. When I asked Ashish whether his decision to begin volunteering was brought about by the suggestion of another volunteer, he laughed and replied: "We initiated the volunteer program in our office!" Ashish does not volunteer outside of the office and believes that it is easier to volunteer as part of the company because the structure is already in place. One has simply to join the "club" and look for a role to play. There is something for everyone to do depending on what they choose; the process is simple and hassle-free and, of course, it is not mandatory.

Ashish tells us how he initiated two successful GEV projects. For the first project, Ashish took advantage of the goodwill between GE and the aviation industry. The aforementioned project, in which underprivileged children were taken on a flight through the skies of Mumbai, was a direct consequence of his efforts to get the airlines interested in voluntary work. Some of the underprivileged children who participated in the flight were also associated with the "Magic Bus," which was discussed earlier.

Aseema was another NGO that had been invited to encourage the participation of poor street children with whom they worked. Ashish was excited about the prospect of involving these children in the event because he was aware that many of them would never otherwise have access to the places he wished to take them to. He worked hard to incorporate entertaining activities into the day's events and to make the experience unforgettable for them. He even approached the famous Bollywood star, Hritik Roshan, who not only agreed to appear but also danced, sang, and entertained the children. When the captain of the airline who flew the children over Mumbai demonstrated the mechanics of how the aircraft takes off and lands and spoke to them about the education he received that enabled him to do his work, many of the children decided that they would like to grow up and become pilots some day.

Ashish believes that such events are not only fun, but help to plant the seeds of future ambitions. A trip to the Godrej soap factory, organized by one of the factory's employees, was another event that fascinated and inspired the children. This event also involved an inspirational talk regarding the various occupations that the children could aspire to if they continued their education diligently. The success of the two events made a great impact on Ashish, who strongly believes that such actions help inspire poor children to have ambitions and dreams.

Ashish believes that anyone can organize such an event with the existence of an ESV program. Such programs facilate and encourage people to pitch in and help. One simply has to come up with an idea and then things quickly fall into place. Like other GEVs, Ashish volunteers whenever he is interested in a proposed project. He derives enormous satisfaction from volunteering and is happy that he is able to contribute in any way he can, given that so many children are in need of help in the busy metropolis of Mumbai.

Organizational Narrative: Standard Chartered Bank (SCB) of India (Mumbai)

SCB is a multinational bank that embraces employee volunteering in order to forge stronger relationships between SCB and the communities in which they operate. SCB employers are mandated to give employees the

> ... opportunity to use their skills to make a unique contribution to the organisations and causes they support. It also allows them to develop and learn new skills. Under the Bank's Employee Volunteering programme employees are given extra two extra days paid leave a year to volunteer on projects aligned with the Banks' community and environmental programmes. The number of employees volunteering continues to climb, totalling more than 23,000 days in 2008, an increase from 11,000 in 2007. (SCB, 2009)

SCB of India began its employee volunteer program in Mumbai in 2003. Although SCB policy allows employees to volunteer during working hours, this is generally not feasible in a place like Mumbai where the time required for commuting from one place to another makes it difficult to put in a few hours of volunteering in one place and then return to the office to work. Hence, volunteer activities usually take place on weekends. Initially, employees interested in joining the volunteer program met once a month, holding their meetings at individual offices. Now, they meet biweekly and through video conferencing; they also engage with their colleagues globally.

Among the key programs offered to the local communities recently is the Pallasdhare Water Project. As part of this project, SCB employees partnered with a local NGO to provide water to a nearby village. The targeted village was 90 kilometers from Mumbai and had a low-level water body. The volunteers worked on a project in which the water from this body was piped in to the 150 houses of the village. SCB employees also conducted environmental programs for the villagers and donated needed blankets; an effort which was funded by the employees.

AIDS prevention and helping people with HIV/AIDS to live healthy lives continues to be a priority for the SCB volunteer programs, and SCB consults and works with the National Aids Control

Organization, a governmental agency, on its many AIDS-related projects. SCB volunteers operate 99 programs on "Living with HIV" in India. Volunteer members are educated so they will understand what it means to live with HIV/ AIDS and the possible medical interventions that exist to help infected persons live normal lives. They then work with people living with HIV/AIDS, providing them with necessary information, supplying medications, and generally educating them on how to live a relatively healthy lifestyle.

SCB has also made a three-year commitment to the NGO Pratham to contribute funds for running 50 *balwadi*s (kindergartens) per year in the slums of Mumbai. Pratham encourages young executives from SCB to volunteer their time to work in the *balwadi*s as well as in their "Bridge" programs. The *balwadi* program provides preschool education for every child in the 3–5 age group with the objective of preparing children for entry into schools. Alongside this program is the "Bridge Course" Program, which prepares school dropouts in the 6–11 age group to return to their studies. Pratham has developed programs for SCB volunteers to assist in these educational projects (*CSR Digest*, 2009; Harita, 2009).

Organizational Narrative: Honeywell India

Honeywell India encompasses several businesses across India, and in each business their employees are engaged in volunteering for many of the company's CSR initiatives. The management realizes that the company's success needs to be shared within the community they work in, hence, many CSR initiatives are based in or near the towns where Honeywell conducts its business. More importantly, they acknowledge that, although corporate citizenship generally focuses on financial donations, it also extends beyond the checkbook.

Deeply embedded in the Honeywell culture is the idea "that successful companies can make a vital impact in the community" (Honeywell Hometown Solutions, n.d.). It is mostly seen "through the tireless efforts of our employees, who spend their time in volunteer service to help create stronger, healthier, more vibrant communities" (Honeywell Hometown Solutions, n.d.). Understandably, Honeywell sees employees who take time out to volunteer as the "the driving force" (Honeywell Technology Solutions Lab, n.d.) behind their social responsibility efforts. Their employees contribute many hours to NGOs each year, "serving on boards, acting as mentors and rolling up their sleeves to take part in community service activities" (Honeywell Technology Solutions Lab, n.d.).

Many of their community services are intended to benefit children and the aged and focus on education and improving the environment. All of these require the physical presence and effort of Honeywell's volunteers. For example, Honeywell's education projects involve identifying needy children, who are then awarded scholarships in order to enable them to continue their education. The program also provides children with mentors: Honeywell employees, who help them with their studies, conduct computer classes and teach computer skills to physically handicapped children. Children completing computer classes are given certificates that help them in finding work.

Another of their outreach programs to children was dedicated to help the "Slow Learners School" at Lonikand. Employee volunteers visited the school and played with the children. They discovered that the children were in dire need of bedding as well as play equipment. This led them to organize a fundraiser to raise money for mats and bedding for the children. They also enlisted a local maker of the playground equipment to donate the equipment for the playground at the school

The company also runs medical assistance programs, which involve establishing health services in remote villages that would otherwise have little or no access to modern medical treatment. After identifying needy villages, Honeywell works to develop a steady stream of doctors' services, medical supplies, and education in hygiene and preventive methods to ensure healthy lifestyles among the villages' residents. The employee volunteers participate actively in facilitating the medical camps run by the NGO Ramakrishna Ashram in its adopted village, Shivanahalli.

The company's Native Village Adoption programs involve adopting some of the villages their employees come from and enhancing the lives of their residents by building infrastructure and teaching work skills to help make the villagers more financially self-reliant. The idea is to initiate schemes that help teach the villagers to develop their own capacities and help themselves, so that the communities are uplifted and are able to thrive without outside assistance.

For villagers near Pune (the location of one of the Honeywell businesses), there is a program to encourage healthy lifestyles through the promotion of drinking water safety, nutrition as well as awareness of issues such as family violence, addiction, and reproductive health. Volunteers train local women from the villages who take on the work of being "health communicators" to promote healthy lifestyles. Other women and men are trained to conduct health-related activities in local schools. Local youth leaders are selected and trained to communicate to their peers information related to reproductive health awareness.

The process for all of Honeywell's volunteer programs starts with the company stating its principles and key areas of focus for community-development initiatives. Employees then propose initiatives intended to accomplish these objectives and a group of employee volunteers (a board) formulates a work plan with specific goals. The board then identifies the tasks and resources required to implement the plan and draws up a schedule that is presented to employees, who are encouraged to volunteer for the various tasks. After securing volunteers, the board coordinates activities to ensure that the project is completed and will be beneficial to the target population. Sometimes, the board will partner with an NGO to work on a project. Whenever possible, Honeywell leverages its leadership and business experience to combat problems and facilitate the chosen project. For example, the company's in-house software expertise helped to develop a Child Tracker that assisted in tracing missing children. This software was then provided to the local police in Bangalore (Honeywell Hometown Solutions, n.d.).

Commentary: CSR—Promoting Employee Volunteering

Our narratives on CSR paint a picture of the many employers in India today that support and encourage volunteering programs for their employees. We found that the impetus for employee volunteer programs varied considerably between companies. Sometimes, programs are initiated at the upper echelons of the company; other times they are employee driven; there are even cases in which both employees and management are involved in formulating the programs. For example, in the case of GE, the corporate management initiated a number of programs that were sponsored by the head office. Sometimes, however, the employees proposed projects that were then approved and funded by the head office. In the case of Honeywell Technology Solutions Lab, the company determines the key areas of community development that the volunteer programs should address and then employees propose initiatives that fit into these goals. The most appropriate of these schemes are then chosen and a work plan is devised that identifies the tasks that need to be done and the resources available. Employees are then invited to volunteer to fulfill these tasks. The breaking up of projects into discrete tasks is a method also employed by SCB. The bank found that offering task-specific projects to employees was a good way to encourage their involvement because it allowed them to better match their interests, capabilities, and availability of time to the needs of the program.

Overall, we notice a tendency for corporations to work on targeted projects in partnership with NGOs. Working with an NGO often simplifies companies' volunteering efforts by allowing them to take advantage of existing projects sponsored by their NGO partners and to choose specific projects that meet with employee approval. For example, GE partners with Aseema, Magic Bus, and other NGOs; SCB works with Pratham; Honeywell Technology Solutions Lab works with Ramakrishna Ashram, among others. Some of the NGO-linked projects that are supported by the ESV programs are focused on helping to build capacity in the NGOs, such as the "Sharing Care" project by Patni, which involved setting up a database for NGOs to facilitate their work. Other projects involve working alongside NGOs to achieve shared goals.

Some employers (e.g., GE and SCB) demonstrate a tendency to engage in episodic volunteer projects. This often happens when projects are related to specific holidays and events or are employee driven and, thus, continue as long as employees show interest. However, long-term projects are also employed where appropriate, such as in the case of child-mentoring initiatives. From our interviews, it may be fair to conclude that both GE and SCB engage in episodic volunteering, whereas the volunteering schemes undertaken by Patni and Honeywell Technology Solutions Lab tend to involve project-based, long-term volunteering.

As is the case with many other small- and medium-sized companies, the ESV projects are relatively modest and are started by small groups of like-minded individuals. These employees initially come together independently to undertake a project dear to their hearts, only later seeking support from their bosses. A top-down, employer-drive approach is rare, and leadership generally comes from among mid- or low-level employees. However, although many employers are sympathetic to the needs of the poor in India, much of their corporate philanthropy remains at the discretion of boards of trustees or owners. Most requests for charitable involvement are made to the CEOs or boards and decisions are made there. It is only when employers see the successful outcomes of their employees' commitment to projects and are assured that these projects align with the company's interests or philanthropic goals that such projects receive support.

The scope of volunteering by employees in ESV programs is limited. It is often found to be fewer than 10 percent of the overall staff, although one sees instances where a greater number of volunteers will get involved in a specific project. Most corporations usually have a small group of core volunteers, consistently leading and initiating projects. The rest of the employees join in when there are programs already in place that they find attractive on the basis of perceived need. The ESV programs at Patni, e.g., have had successful pilot projects that came about through the efforts of a few employees who felt drawn to a particular project. After coming up with a project plan, the employees e-mailed the plan to their coworkers and encouraged them to get involved. A similar process occurs at GE in which a core group of volunteers (i.e., council members) draw up projects and then publicize them to attract other employees. The importance of such groups of core volunteers who consistently give their leadership and time to projects is confirmed by other studies of volunteer behavior (Reed & Selbee, 2001).

We also found that companies adopting the ESV programs have to deal with many of the same challenges that NGOs and other organizations involved in charitable projects face. In addition to the challenges of understanding the unique needs of the communities served and of coming up with appropriate ways of catering to them, volunteers often face resistance and distrust among the very people they are trying to help. For example, despite the training given to SCB employees on how to run effective education programs intended to improve the lives of a HIV/AIDS population, many volunteers were not welcomed in the community and the project was regarded with suspicion. A program initiated by Patni employees faced similar challenges when the volunteers found that parents were not eager to send their daughters to their schools. In both cases, the employees had to work hard to find ways to understand and allay suspicions in order to continue with their projects.

Certain patterns relating to corporation size also appear when we examine the ESV programs discussed in this chapter. Smaller corporations seem to have more flexibility in their initiatives, and their schemes are often long term and more holistic. However, because they rarely have the flexibility to give employees time to volunteer during work days, the ESV programs for smaller companies are more often scheduled on weekends. Larger corporations, on the other hand, appear to favor more structured programs that offer diverse volunteer opportunities for their employees who generally engage in short-term, episodic volunteering. With deeper pockets, larger corporations are able to come up with monetary donations to help develop their ESV programs with greater consistency.

One important group of questions relates to the distribution of the costs and benefits of such initiatives. Is employee volunteering simply a way for the employers to build morale among their employees and generate business in the community? Is volunteering done on company time really a donation from the company, given that the employees still receive their wages? Most employees, even those volunteering during their work hours, and especially at the managerial levels, need to finish their tasks regardless of whether they do it during regular office hours or not. This might suggest that the employer is the one who benefits from the ESV programs at a cost to the employee who has given up his or her time. For example, the Tata Group of Industries; GE, Mumbai; and SCB give employees short periods of absence from work to be involved in volunteering projects, but there is an unspoken understanding that they will not shortchange the regular work by participating in the volunteering projects.

Companies certainly benefit from the public relations that such employee volunteer efforts generate. Those efforts have the potential to increase business as well as to build goodwill in the communities from which potential employees and customers are drawn. Furthermore, the ESV programs that involve groups of employees working together build morale and team work skills, which helps them to become happier and more productive workers. However, many employees also benefit from these schemes. There is considerable literature showing the mental and physical benefits to individuals who volunteer. Beyond potential social benefits and the feel-good factor of making a difference in the community, volunteering gives employees time away from their work and their own problems, which often helps them to put their own challenges in perspective and to become appreciative of the blessings in their lives. Finally, and perhaps most obviously, partner NGOs and the communities served also benefit from the volunteers' efforts. Our research indicates that the ESV programs promoting volunteering among adults, who may not have volunteered otherwise, is an important way of involving civil society in India's development agenda; hence, as we see, it is a winning solution that meets the CSR agenda of corporations as well as the interests of partnering NGOs, the volunteers themselves, and society at large.

5

Volunteering by Mature Adults in India: Never Too Late?

Introduction

Having investigated youth volunteering, what can we say about volunteering done by the more mature adults in our society? There has been a significant increase in interest in the senior population all around the world. In most countries, the population is aging rapidly, and on average, today's mature adults are living longer, more prosperous lives and enjoying better health and greater mobility than previous generations. They often have the same desire for societal involvement as younger adults do and, as volunteers, have certain advantages over younger individuals, such as a greater amount of free time and the professional, technical, and social skills gained from a lifetime of experience. Given that this sector of the population is often active, intellectually involved, and willing to find fulfillment in volunteering, we consider this group a "demographic dividend." By this we mean that there is an increasing supply of volunteers due to a rising share of active mature adults in the population.

In this chapter, we examine how the condition of mature adults is changing in the Indian context as well as the potential, both realized and unrealized, for them to become involved in volunteer work. As part of this analysis, we consider what factors might influence their participation in volunteering activities as well as the benefits they may derive from such participation. We conclude the chapter with organizational and individual narratives that give an interesting and unique picture on volunteering by mature adults in India.

The trend toward increasing longevity in India and throughout much of the world has had a number of major social and economic consequences. It is not uncommon for the rising percentage of elderly people in society to be looked upon as a collective burden, adding to the financial obligations of younger individuals of working age. However, standards of health and well-being are improving along with life spans, ensuring that for many aged people, being retired from paid work does not mean being retired from making a positive contribution to society. Many individuals with the health, time, and resources to remain active in retirement look for an outlet for their energies and abilities, and a number of studies have found that increasing life expectancies are correlated with an increase in interest in volunteering among older adults (Bass & Caro, 1995).

Several studies, mostly conducted in the United States, tell us about the characteristics of older volunteers. These studies find that older adults who volunteer have better physical and mental health than their counterparts who do not volunteer. They have at least some college education, have higher than average incomes, and assign high importance to religion (Kutner & Love, 2003; Lum & Lightfoot, 2005). No major studies have been conducted of mature volunteers in India, but it is likely that many of these indicators are relevant in the Indian context. Here, especially among those with limited family obligations and those in the middle- and upper-income groups, who are less likely to be compelled to seek employment for financial reasons, volunteer activities may be an attractive alternative to idleness during the retirement years.

Such people might be encouraged to help with many of the social problems besetting India, and outreach efforts by the NGOs help in tapping their productive energies to benefit society. As volunteer labor became an important resource for nonprofits, nonprofits responded by restructuring to provide opportunities to use volunteer labor. Growing organizational similarities among nonprofits around the world led them to structures that would make full use of this resource, thereby, increasing reliance among the NGOs not only on charitable donations of money but also of time by volunteers. Moreover, the weakness or absence of government responses to many pressing social problems in both India and the United States has increased the role of the NGOs and other volunteer-based charitable organizations, which has resulted in a greater demand for volunteers and, in turn, increased volunteerism among the general public.

Initiatives and interventions easing the match between the potential volunteer labor supply and the demand for volunteer goes a long way in facilitating the active engagement of older persons in social work and in encouraging them to contribute their time, efforts, and knowledge to their communities. To do this successfully, it is important to have public policies or community-level interventions with the aim of expanding older Indians' engagement in projects benefiting vulnerable groups and individuals in society. At the end of this chapter, we will discuss a number of these community-based interventions and examine case studies of older volunteers in India.

The Changing Condition of the Aged in India

One of India's major developmental achievements in the last century has been to increase the longevity of its population. The number of Indians aged 60 and above increased from 12 million in 1901 to 19 million in 1951 and 77 million in 2001 and, as seen in Table 5.1, the number of mature Indians as a percentage of the population has also been slowly increasing and is expected to reach nearly 9 percent by 2016 (Registrar General of India, 1996).

Table 5.1: Mature Indians as a Percentage of the Population

Year	Below 5 years	Between 0–15	Between >15–59 years	+60 years
1991	12.80	37.76	55.58	6.67
2001	10.70	34.33	58.70	6.97
2011	10.10	28.48	63.38	8.14
2016	9.7	27.73	63.33	8.94

Source: Registrar General of India, 1996.

Although these numbers show a smaller fraction of older individuals in the general population than in many other countries, the number of mature adults in India is significant in terms of sheer numbers given the size of India's population, which is the second largest in the world.

This continuous increase in the relative number of older people adds to the socioeconomic challenges faced by families, communities, and the government, especially in rural areas. In addition, a number of economic and cultural changes in recent years have unsettled the traditional social safety net of the elderly. Although India is an extremely diverse country, the joint family system has long been a common feature of society across linguistic, religious, and regional divides. Under this system, sons and daughters-in-law are expected to care for their parents in their old age and remain with them in their homes. This system helps to guarantee that, as long as parents have a surviving son, they can expect to be looked after when they become old and feeble. In terms of financial dependence, this relationship does not seem to be weakening and, in fact, there is some indication that Indian mature adults are becoming even more financially dependent on their children (NSSO, 2006). However, in recent years, the trend toward nuclear family homes, the growing migration of youth from villages to towns and cities in search of employment, and the increase in the number of women seeking employment outside of the home has meant that many among the elderly have been forced to maintain a higher degree of independence than they have had to in the past.

The magnitude of this shift is demonstrated by a comparison of the living arrangements of mature adults in India in 1986–1987, 1995–1986, and 2005–2006. There has also been an increasing drop in the percentage of mature adults who are living with their children and no spouse over the last two decades. Furthermore, data also show that the number of older Indians living alone with their spouses has increased across gender and environment, and the percentage of those living with their spouses and "others" has also decreased (NSSO, 2006, pp. 62–65). These changing patterns of living have implications for what mature adults choose to do with their growing leisure as they retire.

Implications for Volunteerism

We may expect this trend toward older Indians living separately from their children to influence patterns of volunteering among Indian seniors in a number of ways. On the one hand, the increasing number of mature adults living alone may encourage more of them to seek social activities outside of the home, such as charitable work. The relative freedom from the types of child-care responsibilities, which many older individuals in joint families are compelled to take on, may also give many elderly Indians, who are living alone, more time to engage in such activities. However, the insecurity inherent in the single family arrangement may also mean that many among them may be forced to seek paid work in order to maintain themselves, cutting down on the leisure time available for volunteering. According to a 1993–1994 study, almost 70 percent of aged males and 24 percent of aged females in rural areas of India were working. These numbers were considerably lower among city dwellers, with 44 percent of urban men and 11 percent of urban women working in old age.

Moreover, in part because almost 9 out of 10 people in the workforce in India are employed in the informal sector, only about 5 percent of rural Indians and 17 percent of urban Indians aged 60 and above have access to some form of retirement pension funds (Visaria, 2001). Although there exists a meager government scheme for destitute persons above the age of 65 (of ₹150), it is insufficient for covering even the bare necessities of life. Only one in five of those eligible actually collect this money because many are illiterate and are unable to meet the bureaucratic requirements of producing certificates or filling out the myriad of forms (*Developments*, 2008). In consequence, many elderly Indians are forced to seek paid work. However, there is no guarantee that all those who desire to work will be able to do so. Physical frailty, which comes naturally with age, affects the ability of many in the lower income brackets to continue doing manual labor. In the middle and higher income areas, there may even be legal obstacles to gaining paid employment, such as the mandatory retirement of civil servants from government service at the age of 60. Moreover, in India, as elsewhere, there is often reluctance on the part of private companies to the idea of hiring older individuals. This means that those who do not have children may have difficulty making ends meet, even if they are physically able to work.

As in other periods of life, women are particularly vulnerable in old age. One reason for this is that they are considerably less likely to have access to pension schemes. Amongst other factors, they may face social taboos that often discourage marriage after the death of a husband, which, combined with greater longevity, makes them more likely than men to be alone in their later years (Visaria, 2001). The relatively greater likelihood that a woman will be by herself in the latter part of her life appears to be worsening: the 1995–1996 and 2005–2006 NSSO surveys show that the number of aged women living completely alone had increased from 6.1 percent to 7.6 percent among rural women and from 6 percent to 6.5 percent among urban women, while the percentage of aged men living alone rose much less in rural areas and even dropped in urban areas from 3 percent to 2.1 percent (NSSO, 2006). Further, in the 2005 NSSO survey, 32 percent of aged males and 72 percent of aged females reported themselves to be fully economically dependent upon others. This number has increased for rural men and women and for urban men in the 10 years following the 1995–1996 survey, with economic dependence decreasing only among urban women (NSSO, 2006).

Overall, a comparison between the 1995–1996 and 2005–2006 NSSO surveys indicates that the economic condition of the elderly has improved disproportionately in urban areas (NSSO, 2006). Thus, it is likely that the generally poor economic conditions faced by the majority of India's aged means that most of those among them with the leisure time and the resources to volunteer are likely to be urban middle class and upper-middle class individuals.

Other Factors Influencing Volunteering Patterns

Beyond income, leisure time, and other quality of life considerations, there are many additional factors that may influence a person's likelihood to volunteer. As discussed previously in this book, volunteers may have a wide variety of motivations, many of which are present across cultures and national borders. For example, individuals may decide to do charitable work because they have friends who are volunteers, because they have a desire to remedy certain societal ills, because they hope to achieve a spiritual reward for their work or simply to pass time in a social manner. Often, the desire to help other less fortunate people is a major motivation to volunteer. Older volunteers, when surveyed in the United States, state most often that the ability to help individuals meet their needs is a strong motivator to volunteer, and it is likely that this is a significant factor among Indian volunteers as well. For example, Mitra and Van Delinder (2007) use selections from interviews of highly educated upper-middle and upper-class female volunteers in Kolkata, India, a number of whom are mature citizens, to argue that such volunteers often view their work as a responsibility of their socioeconomic privilege. These individuals may use volunteering to reify their class status and to maintain social contacts and to gain prestige without abrogating social, religious, and community norms. Furthermore, the moral dimension "that those that have more should help those with less" is an important driver in encouraging older persons to volunteer in their community, particularly among those who are financially comfortable.

For an older person, the decision to volunteer may involve different parameters than for a younger volunteer. For example, for the older person, the decision may be based on the additional surplus time they have when they retire and whether or not they have any family obligations, such as babysitting their grandchildren and, more importantly, on whether they have the mental and physical health and energy to do the volunteer work. Butrica, Johnson, and Zedlewski (2007) found that the key factors in explaining volunteering among older Americans are past volunteer experience and having a spouse who volunteers. For example, individuals who have participated more intensely (in terms of hours) in volunteer activities in the previous years are less likely to quit in the current year than those who have volunteered fewer hours. Furthermore, volunteers who marry another volunteer or those who remain married to a spouse who volunteers, are less likely to quit than those who are not married or those married to a spouse who does not volunteer.

We also know from many studies that the most frequent reason given by volunteers regarding why they started volunteering, regardless of their age, is because someone asked them to volunteer. In one study, older volunteers were approximately five times more likely to volunteer if they were asked to do so. The authors found that people 75 years of age and older volunteered at a high rate when asked, with about 81 percent of people over 75 years of age volunteering when asked to do so by others compared to only 25 percent who volunteered when they were not asked (Saxon-Harrold, McCormack, & Hume, 2000).

Other factors also explain the likelihood of an older individual continuing to volunteer: those who assign a high importance to religion, have recently ended spousal care, have a college degree, and have persistent excellent health are more likely to continue their volunteer activities. Factors that increase the probability of quitting are depression, moving, and family health-care issues (Butrica et al., 2007).

Trends in Volunteering among Mature Adults Worldwide

Although there have been no major studies of volunteering among mature adults in India, there have been a number of studies that provide insights on patterns of volunteering among the aged in other countries. Mature citizens are progressively making up a larger percentage of the population of many nations. Increasing life spans and declining birth rates throughout most of the world have resulted in a relatively large segment of the population being retired from paid work, healthy, and available to take part in many volunteer activities in their communities. Despite the unique cultural and economic condition of older adults in India, some of the trends seen elsewhere in the world may have implications for the future of volunteering among the aged in India as well.

Most of the research on older volunteers have taken place in the United States. Here, in 2009, 9.1 million older adults (aged 65 and older) dedicated 1.6 billion hours of service to communities across the country. Of the total population aged 65 and older, 23.9 percent of older adults volunteered. They were most likely to volunteer at religious institutions (47 percent), followed by social services (17 percent). Their rates of volunteering have been steady, varying between 22 percent and 24 percent from 2002 to 2009 (Corporation for National and Community Service, 2010).

In response to the interest of older individuals in doing charitable work, the 2005 White House Conference on Aging suggested that new volunteer opportunities be created for older Americans (Morrow-Howell, 2006). The Peace Corps, a federal government program that provides long-term volunteer opportunities for United States citizens in foreign countries, has long had mature volunteers, including former President Jimmy Carter's mother Lillian who joined the Peace Corps in 1966 at the age of 68. However, the program has recently begun a scheme to entice a greater number of older people over the age of 50 to join the Corps as they move from paid work to early retirements. The organization also recruits retirees by contacting a number of organizations that work with older adults. The decision to target older individuals results both from the increasing availability of volunteers of this demographic and because such individuals value the maturity and experience older volunteers bring. The Corps's goal is that, by 2009, 15 percent of its volunteers will be over the age of 50. Currently, the record for the oldest Peace Corps volunteer is held by Arthur Goodfriend of Hawaii; who was 86 when he finished a two-year tour in Hungary in 1994.

Many of today's older volunteers are welcomed with assignments created especially for them. Interestingly, it is not unusual for older volunteers to be returning volunteers, who first joined the Peace Corps in the 1960s. Examples of this include Don Hesse, who returned to teach English to the Bedouins in Jordan having served in Sierra Leone in the late 1960s and Charles Ludlam, a former aide to Senator Joseph Lieberman, who at the age of 61, with his wife Paula Hirschoff, returned to the Peace Corps for their second tour of duty in Senegal (Abruzzese, 2007; Schlesinger, 2006). Although there has been no major initiative by the Indian government along these lines, some Indian political leaders have discussed the benefits of involving mature adults in volunteer work. For example, Rajwant Sandhu, India's joint secretary in the Ministry of Social Justice and Empowerment, has argued that rather than seeking paid employment, older adults in India should "work as volunteers and pay back to society" (Sengupta, 2004).

Studies done outside of the United States have shown a variety of trends among mature volunteers, some of which closely reflect the pattern of increasing volunteering among older individuals seen in the United States. In Australia, over half a million volunteers are over 65 years of age. However, this older-age group generally volunteers less than those in the middle-age groups. Furthermore, older volunteers are more inclined to volunteer for community, welfare, and religious organizations. Despite the relatively low numbers of older volunteers, evidence from both Australia and the United Kingdom shows that they are more likely to be highly committed and to participate intensely and that they do so over a longer period of time. This means that mature volunteers are often more cost effective for organizations, which is one reason why they are viewed by many nonprofit groups as a rich resource.

In a comparative study of mature volunteers in Australia, the United States, and the Netherlands, Baldock (1999) found that although there were significant differences in policies regarding older volunteers, there were interesting commonalities as well. For example, since the 1990s, governments have stepped back from the provision of social services. This has led to on increased demand for volunteer, and governments have responded to this demand by designing programs meant to promote volunteering among older adults. The recent trend toward early retirement in Australia and the Netherlands has also boosted the number of mature adults available for volunteer work, and in all these three nations, the overwhelming majority of individuals over the age of 60 who are employed are working on a volunteer basis (Baldock, 1999).

The number of older adults volunteering in Germany is also rising; a report commissioned by the German government's Family Ministry in 2006 found that one in three people aged between 55 and 64, and one in five of those aged between 65 and 74 said they did volunteer work (Kreutzbruck, 2007). Because it is expected that by 2030, one in three people in Germany will be over 60 years old, it is likely that the number of mature volunteers will continue to increase in the coming years (Lehr, 2003). Currently, many older Germans volunteer at local schools, helping to curb school violence by doing crisis mediation when students come into conflict with each other. Schools are just one of many sectors in Germany in which mature adults are volunteering. Web sites, private and publicly sponsored, provide database that list more than 1,200 organizations that rely on such volunteers, and more and more pensioners are visiting these Web sites in search of volunteer activities. As in many other countries of the world, researchers have found that mature citizens in Germany today are more likely to have greater resources in terms of money and time, be better educated, enjoy better health, and live longer lives than their predecessors—all factors that are associated with the tendency to volunteer (Kreutzbruck, 2007).

Although research on volunteering among older adults in Asian countries is scarcer than in western countries, there have been a few studies that have provided insight on this phenomenon. For example, for the years 1999 and 2003, it was found that approximately 6 percent of Koreans aged 65 years and older participated in volunteer programs. The study also found that older Koreans who are either Buddhist or Catholic are more likely to volunteer than those who have no religion. The older volunteers tend to be better educated than their nonvolunteer counterparts and are less likely to have children living at home (Kim et al., 2007).

We also found interest in older volunteers in Singapore and China. One study examined older volunteers in Singaporean and Chinese NGOs and found that both sets of volunteers perceived their work as benefiting not only others but also themselves. The volunteers explained their reasons for participation as resulting from a mix of intrinsic and extrinsic motivation, personal beliefs, and a desire for new experiences. It was important for them to receive the support of family and friends in sustaining their volunteering. Many relied on these networks to find the right opportunities and to facilitate their participation: e.g., lending moral support and providing them with the means to volunteer, such as transportation (Mehta & Yunong, 2004).

Cultural Factors Affecting Volunteering among Mature Adults in India

Although it is likely that such factors influencing decisions about volunteering in the United States and elsewhere may be relevant in the case of India, it is likely that culturally specific factors also play a major role, both in the types of volunteering undertaken and in determining the likelihood of volunteering among older individuals. For example, in the United States, it is common for religious institutions to take an active role in social service activities, including providing services to needy individuals of other faiths, and studies have found that older American volunteers often find out about volunteering through their religious congregations. However, in many other countries, churches, mosques, temples, and synagogues mainly exist to provide worship services and do not act as a community club where members mingle socially and work on community projects together (Cnaan et al., 2002).

In the case of India, as will be discussed in the chapter on religious volunteerism, there appears to be a greater tendency for religious institutions to focus only on their own community or to prioritize religious propagation over charity. Thus, it is likely that secular institutions such as service clubs (e.g., the Lions Club, Rotary Club, Kiwanis, and other membership organizations), places of employment, and NGOs act as the dominant avenues for encouraging and pursuing volunteer activities in India. Indeed, there are certain NGOs in India whose main function is to match volunteers to opportunities (to be discussed in Chapter 7).

Distinctly cultural factors may also be important in affecting how individuals in a given context view volunteering as well as how they view their appropriate role in society, which affects their likelihood of undertaking charitable work. This is perhaps nowhere more true than among elderly individuals, who are more likely to value and yield to the pressures of the traditions and expectations of their societies and to hold views of morality, spirituality, individualism, and fulfillment that are relatively indigenous to their environment.

Savishinsky (2004) explores how such traditional ideals have affected the expectations of the elderly in India and the United States. His analysis, based on interviews with white retirees living in rural New York; textual research on the Brahminical and Buddhist traditions; and interviews with Indian students, teachers, and parents may not be generalizable. It does, however, hint at how the social roles ascribed to ideal types, varying individual experiences, cultural expectations, and underlying beliefs and values give rise to different images of the self for older persons in the two countries, which likely affects decisions regarding the activities they will pursue.

Savishinsky reports that many older Americans view retirement as an entitlement, with an underlying obligation to use their free time to reimburse society for the benefits they have enjoyed preretirement. This moral dimension may lead them to volunteer to help others not as fortunate as themselves and to spend the healthy years of their retirement engaged in volunteer work. On the other hand, the traditional Hindu ideal of old age involves retirement from and renunciation of all worldly things. An elderly man following this path is known as a *sannyasin* (renouncer) and often retires from both public life and family to focus on achieving union with the divine. Although this is a distinctly Hindu tradition and one that has traditionally applied only to men, there is little doubt that it has contributed to a different concept of virtue in old age than that found in the United States. These models of aging reflect cultural values and beliefs and portray different emphases on inner versus outer directedness, self-development versus self-effacement, and personal freedom versus social responsibility.

Benefits of Volunteering for Older Persons

Over the past two decades, there have been many studies that have investigated the effects of volunteering on the well-being of older adults. Their findings indicate that volunteering provides individual health benefits in addition to social benefits. The research shows a strong relationship between volunteering and health: those who volunteer have better physical and mental health, greater life satisfaction, greater functional ability, and lower rates of depression later in life than those who do not volunteer. In addition to cross-sectional studies, some longitudinal studies are able to demonstrate that those individuals who volunteered during the earlier years of the study, had lower mortality rates the later years of the study during, even when health, age, gender, and socioeconomic factors were taken into account. Other studies also report that when older adults who have compromised health status (e.g., chronic or serious illness) volunteer, they too receive benefits beyond those that can be provided by medical treatments (Morrow-Howell et al., 2003; Piliavin & Siegl, 2007; Wilson & Musick, 1999).

Interestingly, research has shown that such benefits are more likely to accrue to older adult volunteers (i.e., those aged 60 or older) than to younger volunteers. Some have argued that this is because as mature adults, they face a higher incidence of illness or because volunteering provides them with physical and social activity and a sense of purpose at a time when their social roles are changing. Although depression may serve as a barrier to volunteer participation in mid-life adults, it is a catalyst for volunteering among older adults who may seek to compensate for the role changes and attenuated social relationships that occur with aging (Li & Ferraro, 2006; Van Willigen, 2000).

Van Willigen's (2000) study addresses if and how volunteer work improves the psychological and physical well-being of elderly persons. Her findings confirm the long-term impact of volunteer work on the physical and emotional health of elderly persons. Because older people are likely to have access to fewer avenues for social engagement, volunteer roles can fill this gap and may allow them to experience greater mental health benefits than younger volunteers. Van Willigen argues that volunteering in old age may be on appealing alternative to having to fill endless hours at home, while volunteering in middle age is often undertaken to fulfill any one of multiple roles, such as being a good parent or a diligent worker. Older volunteers also tended to offer their services to more than one type of organization. The study found that those who benefited the most were more likely to be engaged in church-based voluntarism. Moreover, Van Willigen (2000) and other researchers (Herzog, House, & Morgan, 1991) found that in the United States, the vast majority of adults over 60 years of age believe that older people should contribute to society through community service after they have stopped working.

Researchers working in Canada also found that community volunteering provides opportunities for older adults to maintain their self-esteem and sense of well-being while promoting transformative learning. Volunteering provides meaningful roles for them while promoting participation in the social economy (Narushima, 2005).

These analyses suggest that efforts to encourage mature citizens to volunteer and to make volunteering more possible for elderly persons should continue. However, to determine the types of volunteering most suitable and beneficial for such individuals in India, there must be some effort at collecting nationally representative data to explore how volunteers commit their time, what volunteering means to them, what kinds of activities they engage in when they volunteer, and what explains the differing effects on well-being. Furthermore, researchers should be cautious when choosing a measure of volunteering. Previous research in other regions had erroneously concluded that volunteer commitment does not significantly affect the impact of the volunteer role because including commitment in the same models as volunteer role leads to multicollinearity. Extant studies indicate that the choice of measurement can greatly affect the results of analyses and conclusions drawn.

Volunteering among Mature Adults and Retirees in India Today: Some Examples

Given the established benefits to older individuals of volunteering, it is not surprising that there are a few organizations in India today that aim to promote volunteer activities among older Indians. These organizations work to match older volunteers with needy the NGOs. For example, the Harmony for Silvers Foundation in Maharashtra was founded in 2004 with the mission to enhance the quality of life of the elderly in India by creating an environment in which older Indians, of all religious and cultural beliefs, can find ways of being productive. The foundation helps aged Indians—who are referred to as "silvers"—find paid and volunteer opportunities. They list volunteer opportunities in *Harmony Magazine*, their online magazine, providing their members with links to available opportunities all over India. They frequently publish profiles of their members who volunteer with the NGOs and note with pride that in recent years, many retired professionals have ventured into volunteering or working for the NGOs (Baruah, 2004).

Community Aid and Sponsorship Programme (CASP), a Pune-based NGO, also has a volunteer bureau that helps to organize mature adults working for a wide variety of causes. CASP established The Longevity Centre (TLC), an aging research center in Pune, in collaboration with the University of Pune, the Athashri Foundation, and Bharati Vidyapeeth Deemed University. The center's volunteer bureau is designed to forge relationships between older retired people and NGOs with the goal of using the experiences of retired citizens productively for the benefit of the NGOs. At the same time, the center hopes to promote active and fruitful aging and to help retirees retain strong connections to the society around them.

The volunteer bureau gathers information on available retired people, records their knowledge, experiences, and areas of interest, and then helps to link them with the NGOs who are looking for volunteers, such as hospitals, schools, and institutions for children with physical or mental challenges. The bureau gets around 150 applications a year from older adults looking for volunteer opportunities (Baruah, 2004). "Most of the volunteers are highly qualified, and quite a lot of them are women," observes the agency's director. Many of the volunteers working through the bureau report the same types of motivations seen among mature volunteers elsewhere in the world. For example, one 66-year-old retired professor states, "I see this as an opportunity to interact with more people and make a contribution to society" and another volunteer reports that "[t]here are many senior citizens who want to contribute to society, but don't know how to go about it. Ever since I retired two years ago, I've had a lot of time on my hands. I would like to help others as long as my health permits me to" (data from surveys and personal interviews, 2008).

A good example of a corporation engaging retired professionals in its CSR efforts is Infosys, India. Infosys, India, has various teams of employee volunteers who are actively involved in providing additional support to government schools on weekends. They exploit the skills and experience of retired school teachers in Bangalore to assist them in their efforts to provide free education for children in government-sponsored childcare centers and orphanages (Ezine, 2008).

Some NGOs that have recruited older volunteers, deal with community needs, e.g., building hospitals or schools or aiding the destitute or the mentally challenged. The manager of one participating hospital reports that the institution's experiences working with mature citizen volunteers has been "very good," noting that older adults come without any expectations and bring a positive attitude that helps their patients a lot. The volunteer bureau has matched four elderly citizens to the hospital. These volunteers spend time with lonely patients, attend to people in queues, and take part in counseling and other therapeutic activities. The bureau recognizes that in order to continue to place older volunteers in NGOs, the NGOs need to respect senior citizens and appreciate their work, while also noting that the elderly gain satisfaction from volunteering and are committed to the services they offer. Nearly 200 volunteers were registered with the bureau and were placed in NGOs as of 2004, and the bureau has periodic meetings to review volunteers' experiences and hear their suggestions (Polanki, 2004).

Other NGOs, such as the Agewell Foundation in New Delhi and the Dignity Foundation in Mumbai, also cater to older Indians and put them to work either as volunteers or as employees in NGOs. According to the Agewell Foundation, there are roughly 9,000 mature adults in Delhi alone working in NGOs (Baruah, 2004).

There are anecdotal examples of other local initiatives that use older volunteers as well. Many members of service clubs, e.g., the Rotary Club and the Lions Club, especially those who are retired members, volunteer with a range of organizations such as local women's clubs and groups catering to the needs of the elderly. Another example is the Multi Service Centre for Senior Citizens, which offers aid to mature adults and has developed a volunteer base of individuals who get involved in projects for the benefit of the community. The center's major objective is to help older citizens cope with problems of loneliness while doing useful and productive work for the community. Another example is that of Pune's Mentor Programme, the result of a collaboration between CASP and the police commissionerate, which was envisioned as establishing a relationship connecting mature citizens and students who come to Pune from other parts of the country to study. The program nominates elders as local guardians or mentors to the students, thus, creating a support system for both parties. The center's deputy director, Radha Raj, suggests that it will help the students to have a senior citizen as a mentor, someone to share their achievements and problems with. Furthermore, senior citizens help students by tutoring and following up on their academic efforts and outcomes, and provide students with emotional support (Polanki, 2004).

In order to gain a better understanding of the dynamics of organizations working to involve older Indians in volunteer activities, we now profile two organizations in greater depth: the Non-Resident Indian Parent's Organization (NRIPO) and the Dignity Foundation. We will also explore the experiences and motivations of two long-time Dignity Foundation volunteers.

Narratives

Organizational Narrative: Non-Resident Indian Parents Organization (NRIPO, Pune)

The term NRI needs no explanation in India. Everyone knows that NRI stands for "non-resident Indian" because there are so many who have left India and gone to foreign countries, either for studies or for better employment prospects. Although everyone seems to know about the opportunities of NRIs abroad, there is little discussion about what happens to the families that NRIs leave behind. This is especially the case when the families consist of aged parents who traditionally looked to their children to support them emotionally, physically, and economically as they grew older.

Indian families are generally very closely knit. The "Kodak moment" of old age has always involved the image of a large extended family with grandchildren celebrating birthdays and traditional festivities, with sons and daughters-in-law tending to their aged parents. Instead, as they enter their retirement, many parents are now finding a lonely homestead devoid of children and an extended family. The situation is exacerbated in those instances in which there is only one surviving parent. The parents are often reluctant to go and live with their children in foreign lands. Many have visited their children's homes in the United States, Canada, Australia, or other countries far from the Indian subcontinent and are lonely when their children are away studying or working. Though there is often much more available materially in such places, it cannot make up for the loss of friends and relatives or the social visits that are so much a part of the Indian culture. One often hears the term "golden cage" when parents describe their sojourn in the foreign land of plenty where there is an abundance of material goods and a dearth of emotional support. Thus, many such parents prefer to spend their old age in India even though they know that they will be living alone and perhaps in need of help and support.

It was this recognition that prompted Justice Abhyankar to start a self-help group organization for the parents of NRIs, NRIPO (Non-Resident Indians Parents Organization). The organization was founded in 1994 with 30 parents of NRIs. The key criterion for membership was that the parent must have at least one child abroad. NRIPO has grown to over 1,000 members in just 15 years. Most of the members are from the middle class and are older than 55 years, although the oldest parents are in their 90s. The membership fee is ₹800 per couple and that usually covers most costs. Donations are sometimes received from members and their families.

NRIPO members provide emotional and practical support to NRI parents through a voluntary support committee of 13 executives and 50 committee members. The members have an office and a secretary who is present every day. The president and vice president volunteer approximately four hours a day; other members devote 10 to 12 hours a week. NRIPO has 35 geographical groups, and there are 15–20 members in and around Pune. Regional members meet once a month at the house of a member, and the total membership meets five times a year—three times for entertainment events and twice for educational sessions. Twenty-five to thirty members volunteer their time to organize each event, and the events are often scheduled on festive days that are traditionally spent with families. In this way, the organization's activities work to fill the void left by departing children and allow members to enjoy cultural celebrations together. Although most NRIPO services are focused on the well-being of the organization's members, it does hold events and information sessions related to aging for members of the public as well. Moreover, NRIPO has created a sizable endowment and uses the interest earned on the account to give an annual award to persons or institutions judged to provide the best help to an older person or persons in need.

The organization has set up many practical programs to assist their members. The most noted is the "one-by-two" scheme, which ensures that a single parent is mentored by two groups of supporting parents who help the single parent in times of need. This scheme has saved both ailing parents and helpless children abroad much grief when the latter cannot come to their parents' assistance immediately. Such was the case of Mrs A. who was hospitalized with a grave medical condition. Her son, in the United States, was duly informed, but he could not leave his job right away. The two supporting sets of parents took the ailing Mrs A to the hospital and visited her there every day. When she was released, they looked after her in their homes until she was well enough to return to her own home. Her son expressed his gratitude that his mother had such wonderful support.

The "will-and-after" scheme is another successful support program provided by NRIPO that helps parents draw up their will; NRIPO will even execute them. It also ensures that supporting parents stand in as families to fulfill the last rites in case the NRI children are unable to come to the funeral.

Members are also assisted with travel arrangements, such as tickets, passports, visas, and insurance. Other simple but practical support is also available, such as helping members get quick telephone connections and taxis to take them to the airport. Aside from all the practical support that is, of course, necessary, NRIPO provides the camaraderie and *joie de vivre* that is necessary for the happiness of people of all ages. The support system provides the assurance that members can count on friends to act as surrogate families and to be there when needed. It is this need to connect that keeps the president, the past president, and secretary committed to the organization. The past president reiterates that although he has put in many hours of voluntary work for NRIPO, he believes that he himself has been the chief beneficiary. Visiting the office provides the excuse to leave home and meet with like-minded people. This keeps him fit and active and he is more than happy to pitch in with time and money to help people who are now as close to him as his family. His views are shared by most of the core volunteers, who make up about 10 percent of the group.

The many success stories suggest that the mandate that members provide support for each other is working. When 86-year-old Mrs. J. called to alert members that her husband had been admitted to the hospital after having suffered a heart attack, members rushed to support her. When Mr J. died a little later, members were there to help Mrs J. with the last rites. They called the children in the United States. But the children could not get away at such a short notice. Mrs J. notes that although she is happy that her children have a good future in the United States, she feels that she also has a good future remaining in India with NRIPO and asserts that she would prefer to continue living with her NRIPO family rather than join her children in the United States. She is proud to be part of a group of mature adults who help themselves and does not want to trade this for a living situation that would require her to wait around to be helped by others. She also feels that, through volunteering her time to help other members, she is helping to keep herself in better mental and physical health.

Organizational Narrative: Dignity Foundation (Mumbai)

The Dignity Foundation was established in Mumbai in 1995 by Dr Sheilu Sreenivasan and is dedicated to people approaching the later years of their lives. It has a total of 15 paid staff and at least 20 volunteer staff members at any one time. The Foundation has chapters in Kolkata, Chennai, and Jamshedpur. Every year, it finds volunteer assignments for at least 2,200 mature volunteers, and this number continues to rise.

The Foundation's definition of a senior is anyone aged 60 years and over, and most of the volunteers are of 65 years or older. Many of the volunteers are from the middle class, with a few from the upper and the lower classes. Despite the disproportionate number of middle-class volunteers, the organization stresses that volunteering is not based on class and that the number of volunteers from poorer economic groups is growing. More outreach programs in the future will make more individuals aware of the opportunity to volunteer in their later years. A few of the volunteers have professional, postgraduate degrees (5 percent) and some are college graduates (15 percent), but the majority of volunteers are simply high school graduates (80 percent). The female-to-male ratio is 60 : 40, and most are married.

The Volunteer Retirement Scheme is a workshop offered with the aim of recruiting mature volunteers from corporations. Workshop attendees are told that it is no longer inevitable to face a decline in their health with age; rather, health is their own responsibility, and it is up to them how happily and healthily they age. The workshop creates awareness that one can volunteer at any age and stresses that the later years are in fact the best years for volunteering because it is at this stage that one has the maximum amount of life experience and free time. Most mature volunteers, however, are recruited by word of mouth. They have heard of the Foundation and approach it to see if they can do anything to help. The Foundation's volunteers have said that they are interested in giving back to society and that they would like to stay occupied during the extra time they have in retirement. There is the strong belief among the volunteers that one deteriorates both physically and mentally if one is not occupied as one grows old.

The first step in the volunteer process is a personal interview and, when approved as a prospective volunteer, all applicants must first become members. The volunteer is then trained and asked to ac-company a more experienced volunteer for a while. When both the experienced volunteer and the prospective volunteer are confident that the individual can work independently, the training is complete. About 30–40 members are trained each year, and these volunteers are then matched with programs. Sometimes, a new volunteer may indicate a preference for a program. The interview process allows the coordinator to decide if it is a suitable match. The matching of a volunteer with a program is done with care to ensure that they are doing work that is appropriate for their skills and background and that the client is receiving the best care.

Many of the Foundation's volunteers participate in the helpline, which allows older adults to call in with their problems and have volunteers of a similar age group work to resolve them. Many are also involved in companionship activities. For example, when the Foundation receives a call that an aged person is lonely, some older volunteers go and visit the lonely individual. Other areas of partici-pation for such volunteers are the Dementia Daycare Center and the Counseling Center. The Dementia Daycare Center is a place where aged adults suffering from dementia can be left for the day and provided with activities and care. The Counseling Center allows people to call in with their problems and be put through the appropriate support channels so that they receive the help they seek. Mature volunteers in all programs are encouraged to give feedback on their various volunteering experiences so that changes can be implemented when necessary.

Another form of counseling in the organization that is gaining popularity is peer-counseling for seniors. When older adults receive counseling from volunteers of their own age group, it may be particularly effective because the parties can identify with one another. Some of the volunteers work with the municipal authorities. They have won the respect of both the municipal staff as well as members of the public and have proven to be good, dependable volunteers capable of resolving problems.

The Foundation is also interested in helping mature adults become involved in paid work in retirement and, in pursuit of this goal, it has initiated a program called "Second Careers." The program invites organizations to advertise positions with them so that the Foundation can help them to find a match with an older individual who has the right experience for the job. The Foundation hopes to train older adults to fit those needs so that they can be recruited into second careers during their retirement years.

Individual Narrative: Namjoshi

Namjoshi has always lived in Bombay (now Mumbai). After matriculating from high school, he went on to spend most of his life working, moving up the career ladder to become the assistant branch manager of his bank.

Namjoshi was going to be transferred out of Bombay but chose to retire at 55 rather than be uprooted. His wife continued working and retired some years after him. He has a daughter who is married and a son who is studying. Namjoshi had always planned to do social work, and as he had no major responsibilities after leaving his job and a pension that kept him financially comfortable, when retirement came, he felt it was time for him to begin volunteering. He believed that volunteer work would give him personal satisfaction and, more importantly, that his decision to look after others would lead the Supreme Being to look after him.

Namjoshi had heard about the Dignity Foundation and decided to join the organization as a life member because he was attracted to the idea of serving the needs of older adults. He has now worked at the Dignity Foundation for over 10 years and proudly attributes the fact that he has no ailment thus far to being blessed for his involvement in volunteer work. Aspects that he enjoys most about volunteering are the people he works with, from the lowest ranks to the highest ranks of the staff, whom—he finds to be honest, good, and easy to work with. The time he puts into volunteer activities often depends on the needs of the moment, but on average, he goes to work three to four times a week.

One of the program areas in which Namjoshi has served is the Helpline, launched so that older citizens can call in and receive assistance in resolving their problems. He relates a story of when he received a call from an elderly gentleman who complained that the tenants who lived in the apartment above his had constructed an additional bathroom illegally. This resulted in leakage of water into his apartment, which he believed, was also a fire hazard. He was quite old and lived alone and did not have people to summon to his aid. He felt helpless to tackle the problem until he heard about the Dignity Helpline and called in with his problem. Namjoshi was able to resolve the problem by writing to the erring tenants and appraising them about the illegality of their actions and the penalties involved. He suggested that they resolve the problem before official sanctions were imposed. Fortunately, the tenants did so and that was the end of the case. According to Namjoshi, this informal approach of mediation has helped the Dignity Foundation to resolve at least 75 percent of all the cases of elder abuse.

Cities served by the Foundation are divided into geographical areas or "municipal wards" lettered from A to Z, and Namjoshi is particularly proud of his role as chief dignitarian for D ward, which means that he is in charge of the municipal problems in that ward. All of the wards have senior dignitarians. These dignitarians are usually in charge of wards that are fairly close to their residence. The volunteers physically patrol their wards and check if either the workers or members of the public in the area have any complaints. If there are problems and/or complaints, the dignitarians work to ensure that the issues are resolved. The complaints heard are on a wide variety of topics, such as the garbage not being picked up or the lack of water. The work that the dignitarians do is much appreciated by government bodies such as the Mumbai Municipal Coporation, which lacks qualified staff and are happy to have someone oversee such problems for them. Members of the public also appreciate the fact that they can approach the dignitarians with their problems. A regular schedule is maintained in order to ensure the smooth resolution of problems before they escalate. Every Thursday, dignitarians meet to discuss the problems in their wards and the ward officer is met with once a month to resolve any outstanding problems.

Namjoshi feels that he has made good use in his volunteering of the skills he accumulated while working at the bank. Moreover, he has also acquired new skills from his experiences. More importantly, he is pleased that because of his volunteering, he continues to be a respected member of his community, just as he had been when he was an assistant bank manager. Though he does not gain financially, he believes that he is far richer for being able to give himself to the service of others. This gives him immense satisfaction, as does the fact that he is able to make good use of his faculties and stay fit. He insists that he would like to continue volunteering with the Dignity Foundation as long as he is able to walk.

Namjoshi believes that retirement is a perfect time to turn to volunteering. He enthusiastically sings the praises of volunteer work and of all the benefits that he has received from it. For example, he greatly enjoys using all of his experiences for the good of society and especially other older citizens. It is also important to him that he remains involved in society and that he does not retire simply to grow old in some chair. He also believes that it is only by virtue of the fact that he keeps himself going that he is able to continue to keep going. He is proud of the fact that he has not had any health problems since he has taken up volunteering and emphasizes that his volunteering has kept him fit. He, therefore, believes that if he wishes to remain in good health, he must and will continue to volunteer!

Individual Narrative: Sabar

Sabar seems to have always done things in a proper manner. She completed her schooling at St. Theresa's Convent and then went on to complete her Bachelor of Arts degree. She found work as a secretary in a "good company" where she worked her way up to the position of a senior officer. The company also grew and became one of the largest cement companies in India. She worked there for 30 years, dealing with the insurance for the entire business and their 15–20 factories. This was a huge responsibility and she had a team of eight people to assist her.

When she was 48 years old and married with two grown children, she began to assess her life. As both her daughter, a flight attendant, and her son, who was studying to be a chartered accountant, were now independent, she decided that she would take early retirement and enjoy herself. However, instead of enjoying herself, she began feeling bored. Her husband had continued working and her children, who were accustomed to her being away all day, had developed a routine that did not include her. Sabar felt redundant, as if she was getting in the way; so just a couple of years later, at the age of 50, after a successful interview for a secretarial position, she announced to her husband that she was going back to work. After working for about eight years, she left the position and went to the United States to visit her daughter, who was expecting a baby. However, after returning to Mumbai, Sabar found that she was again left with too much time on her hands. She had always wanted to do some kind of "social work" in order to give back to the society that had given her so much, but she did not know where or how to start. She was a member of a social group of "personal assistants," and after hearing a talk about volunteerism from the president of the Dignity Foundation at one of their meetings, she immediately signed up to volunteer with the organization. This was about nine years ago.

When Sabar first joined Dignity Foundation, she was 60 years old and was assigned to the Companionship Helpline. This was one of the key programs at the center at that time. Over time, the center evolved and began to develop many more programs. One program that interested Sabar was the Counseling Center, and she soon became quite involved with it. The Counseling Center was established to provide assistance to people who needed legal advice. Sabar was responsible for coordinating with a panel of lawyers, who specialized in different areas, such as housing, will making, income tax, or consumer guidance. Whenever there were a number of clients who needed assistance in a particular area of law, she would invite the requisite lawyer to the Counseling Center to provide them with legal advice and coordinate the lawyer–client interaction.

Sabar now spends much of her time with the Senior Leisure Group called *Chai-masti*, which meets for tea and activities between 4 PM and 6 PM each evening. Although she has cut down on her work hours, her volunteerism has not ended, and she continues to visit the Dignity Foundation at least a few times a week to recommend people for legal advice. She remembers helping a woman recently who was frightened that her Internet account had been hacked. Sabar steered the woman toward the right lawyers and her problems were resolved. Her role as coordinator at the Counseling Center is combined with her role as beneficiary of many of the social activities offered to mature adults through the organization, such as bridge, *tai chi* and the Laughter Club. Sabar likes her life the way it is now, and she does not plan to stop volunteering. When asked the reason for her continued interest and loyalty, like Namjoshi, Sabar cannot find enough praise for the people at the Dignity Foundation. She finds them caring and nurturing. Moreover, she thinks that she gets as much as she gives, noting that she has learned a lot about dementia and Alzheimer's disease and that her volunteering has helped her to stay alert and fit.

Individual Narrative: Ebe

> I believe more in giving my time and talents with passion rather than a check book charity; the passion creates a positive energy in the beneficiaries.
>
> —Ebe

Ebe spent most of his adult life in the family business until he became involved in land litigation and began dividing his time between the business and attending to the case. When his young son finished his MBA, he joined the family business and over time, relieved his father of many business-related duties, allowing him time to attend to the litigation. When, at long last, the litigation was over, Ebe found that he was 63 years old and that his son was ably running the family business. At this juncture, Ebe decided that his life was entering its "second innings" and he would devote it to doing what he enjoyed doing most: making a difference in people's lives. Though helping people had always been a part of his life, it had played a secondary role to the more important business of running and expanding his business. However, he had always had a desire to become more involved in social service, and it was this yearning that had spurred him in the past to become an active volunteer at the Rotary Club and to join projects that helped the less fortunate. He recollected a program that he had initiated through the Club. It was an attempt to change the rude and inconsiderate traffic behavior of some drivers. This project had been successful and had won the support of the traffic police as well as the Regional Transport Office (RTO). However, the people heading the traffic police and RTO were transferred after a couple of years and the program ended.

Now, with more time in his hands, Ebe was delighted that he could make helping people the focus of his life. He came into contact with a director of an institute in Pune that offered MBA courses. In 2005, the director started his own institute. As the director believed that managers should devote a part of their lives to catering to the needs of the underprivileged sectors of their society, he decided to make 60 hours of community service mandatory for his students. Ebe became an advisor to these students, guiding them and helping them overcome the roadblocks they encountered in their volunteer experiences. In his first year as an advisor, he helped 160 students complete work on 10 community projects, and in each subsequent year, he repeated this success. Two of the projects with which students were involved included working in the slums and collecting and distributing old clothes. Another project involved replacing plastic bags in shops with bags made of newspapers that could be reused and these paper bags were made by slum dwellers, who earned much needed money from the sale proceeds. Ebe enjoyed coordinating these projects, and their popularity grew until the volunteering requirement was dissolved with the outbreak of the swine flu. Students were no longer permitted to work in unsanitary areas in order to protect them from exposure. However, the project left a great legacy. Some students continued working in rural areas, whereas others have carved out a career funding cooperatives and helping young people to set up businesses. With Ebe's help, many student volunteers have realized the joy that comes from helping others while earning a livelihood.

As Ebe reflects on his life's activities, he realizes that his best moments have been when he helped others, whereas his professional work in finance has taken a back seat. Ebe believes that he has been fortunate to be able to spend the later years of his life doing the things that satisfy him, while his son runs the family business. In fact, he believes that this stage of his life is the most enjoyable as he is able to realize his goals: "All else pales into insignificance compared to what I am doing now." So Ebe continues doing what he does best—remaining happy by helping to make others happy!

Commentary: Volunteerism among Mature Adults and Retirees

Our narratives about mature adults and retirees who volunteer and the organizations that support them suggest that there is nothing "retiring" about these individuals and that their years of experience with life and the working world have provided them with knowledge, wisdom, and grace. They are engaging, lively, and face many challenges in their volunteer work, but accept these challenges as part of life. Mature volunteers often dedicate themselves to serving each other, with the strong shouldering the weak among them. Many, such as Ebe, focus on the joy that comes with voluntary service to the younger generation.

Although the tradition of the older adult as *sannyasin*, the stage of retiring from active social life, is still alive among many sectors of the Indian society, this role is gradually being replaced by a vision of a more active retirement. Many Indians who are active and healthy see their retirement as a time to start a new career, or to take on projects dear to them. Some acknowledge their obligation to their communities and choose to use their free time to pay society back for the benefits they have enjoyed. This path of involvement by volunteering is conducive to staying healthy and occupied, and helps the elderly reconnect with life rather than simply preparing themselves for death. Common to all the narratives we have explored is the volunteers' belief that they need to keep themselves physically and mentally active to retain the functioning of their faculties; we found this to be a common impetus for volunteering among mature adults.

As with other demographic groups, there are many different paths by which older adults may become involved in volunteering. They may take the initiative themselves, searching until they find an organization they feel comfortable with or they may be approached by friends or acquaintances and asked to volunteer. Some mature adults are motivated by spiritual inclinations and work through religious organizations, whereas others prefer groups that cater to the limitations and capabilities of their demographic.

The ability of the aged to donate their time and energy is often contingent on their health, financial independence, family, or other obligations. Despite the fact that the existing literature on senior volunteering is decidedly non-Indian in its focus, most of the older volunteers we encountered in the Indian context resembled volunteers elsewhere. Specifically, most mature adults involved in volunteering were from the educated and middle classes, although the Dignity Foundation suggests that there is a new trend of increasing participation among those from the lower economic strata of society as well.

It is interesting to note that both of our organizational narratives discuss groups that not only seek to encourage older individuals to volunteer but that also focus the volunteers' energies on the needs of their own demographic. It is perhaps not surprising that many older volunteers would be drawn to help others like themselves, given the extremely vulnerable and often neglected status of many among the aged population. The two organizations detailed are unique, however, in terms of organizational form: NIPRO is an example of a membership organization in which members help one another, whereas the Dignity Foundation is more of a client-oriented NGO, serving mature adults in the population at large.

Namjoshi's narrative illustrates how volunteers in the Dignity Foundation are able to facilitate the work of the Mumbai Municipal Corporation by acting as intermediaries with the public. He is an energetic volunteer, completely engrossed in his volunteering work. Sabar, on the other hand, is an example of an individual who is now cutting back on her volunteering time and picking up hobbies. As she gets older, she devotes less time to volunteering and more to availing herself of the leisure activities offered to members. However, she does not want to give up volunteering because that would be equivalent to giving up her "lease on life." Both volunteers are motivated to keep volunteering party because of an awareness of the mental and physical health benefits of doing so (Morrow-Howell et al., 2003; Piliavin & Siegel, 2007). As for Ebe, he has a strong desire to bring about positive change in society, and this desire gets stronger as he ages. When his volunteer efforts, such as the counseling and the driving etiquette programs, ended prematurely, he moved on to find other volunteer opportunities.

Our narratives highlight the fact that mature volunteers also find a sense of belonging through their involvement with others in volunteer projects. This is similar to the psychic benefits that many volunteers of other demographic groups reported in earlier chapters. This sense of belonging is especially valuable to those older volunteers who have lost their spouses and are now living alone or to those who, despite living with other family members, feel that they are no longer recognized as a central part of their families. Companionship with other mature volunteers and with the people they serve creates a new family for those in danger of feeling isolated. Moreover, it gives them a sense of purpose and helps prevent them from feeling useless or burdensome, or from simply "waiting to die." We found this to be true in India, and it is also in accordance with the findings of research focused on volunteering among the aged in many other parts of the world (Van Willigen, 2000). The sense of self-esteem that volunteering provides is especially valuable at a time when the number of social and professional roles diminish for older retirees. This maintenance of a sense of self-esteem has been noted in many studies that show that when mature volunteers take on roles they consider meaningful, they thrive on the resultant feelings of self-respect (Narushima, 2005). Namjoshi is a good example of this: he reports his satisfaction at being able to resolve problems for people through his involvement as a liaison with the municipal authorities and cherishes the respect he receives in return.

All of this suggests that both older adults and the societies in which they live benefit when mature citizens avail themselves of volunteering opportunities. However, as we noted earlier, the richness of their involvement in volunteer work is not well recognized in India, and there are not enough organizations that aggressively provide such individuals with volunteering activities. The Harmony for Silvers Foundation and CASP are two of the newer organizations that are attempting to fill this void by using the experience that mature adults bring when providing mentoring to students or companionship to those individuals. The Dignity Foundation is also doing an admirable job of facilitating the involvement of older Indians in civic activism as well as catering to their needs through the provision of services and leisure activities. The burgeoning membership of older volunteers in such organizations suggests that this is a resource that can go a long way toward benefiting society and its more mature citizens.

6

Religious Volunteering: Serving God?

*Spirituality engenders service. Service without spirituality is like
a body without a soul.*

— Param Pujya Ma, Spiritual Guru, Arpana;
see http://www.arpana.org

*I bow my head before my Creator in humble submission to whatever little
I could do for my suffering people.*

— Maulana Badruddin Ajmal Al-Qasmi,
President, Markazul Ma'arif, "How the Long Journey Began";
see http://www.markazulmaarif.org/home/default.asp

*It is tantamount to a betrayal of the Christ to be overly concerned
with rituals and rites in the face of the challenges offered
by social structures, which deprive men and women and children
of their dignity as children of God.*

— D'Souza, 2000, p. 42

Introduction

In this chapter, we focus on volunteerism through religious organizations, which is one of the most important avenues of volunteering in India today. Approximately, 29 percent of voluntary sector activities in India are social development activities undertaken by religious organizations, and such groups are the largest recipients of charitable donations (Copal Partners Research, 2006, pp. 2–3; see also Tandon & Srivastava, 2003).[1] This may be, in part, due to the fact that religious organizations often have certain social capital advantages over secular groups due to the sense of camaraderie arising from the shared vision and commitment typically found when there is spiritual motivation for group participation (Harper, Rao, & Sahu, 2008, p. 13). Shared religious inspiration also often makes it easier for such groups to secure workers on a voluntary basis and may make them more capable of quickly recruiting large numbers of individuals to confront pressing humanitarian needs as they arise (p. 12).

In this chapter, we will first provide a brief background on the history and forms of religious volunteerism in India, followed by a discussion of religious voluntary organizations associated with the three largest religions of India: Hinduism, Islam, and Christianity. We will look for common themes between and among these three groups by examining the philosophies, motivations, and leadership styles of major examples of Hindu, Muslim, and Christian organizations. Finally, we will provide more detailed information on the backgrounds and motivations of the volunteers for three of the profiled nonprofits through interviews with a number of individuals involved in voluntary service.

The Structure of Religious NGOs in India

Religious organizations have a long history of involvement with charitable activities in India. In the early history of the subcontinent, religious institutions were the most common form of institutionalized social service with Hindu ashrams and *maths*, Muslim *waqf*s and *khanqahs*, and Sikh *gurudwaras* and *deras* often taking on charitable and social welfare duties (Planning Commission, 2002). With the increasing bureaucratization and regulation of organizations that occurred during the British and Independence eras, however, religious charitable activities began to take on new, more secular forms. This has often involved the creation by a purely religious entity of an ostensibly secular organization which, for legal or organizational reasons, may be either partially under the control of the religious institution and partly autonomous or even completely autonomous and connected to a religious institution purely through

---

[1]Tandon and Srivastava (2003) estimate that 26.5 percent of nonprofit organizations engaged in social development are primarily religious in identity.

inspiration (Harper et al., 2008, p. 15). Many religious NGOs have both legal and funding concerns related to their spiritual inspiration, which can encourage them to attempt to distance their charitable activities from their religious mission. It is not uncommon, e.g., for an organization with religious roots to insist that it is completely secular, even when its funding is largely drawn from a single religious community and its programs largely concentrated on areas in which that community is dominant (p. 11).

In India, one reason that religious NGOs often emphasize that they serve all needy individuals without discrimination, is that religious and charitable trusts lose their tax exempt status under Sections 11 and 12 of the Income Tax Act if they work for the benefit of any particular religious community or caste (Agarwal & Dadrawala, 2004, p. 119). Income tax and legal liabilities may also explain why many of these organizations set up multiple trusts with different foci, which are viewed differently for tax and other legal purposes. For example, Arpana, a Vedantic organization to be discussed later in the chapter, operates two separate charitable trusts: the Arpana Trust, which is responsible for research and spiritual activities and is, thus, eligible for a tax exemption as a social science research organization under Section 35.1(iii) of the Income Tax Act and the Arpana Research and Charitable Trust, which runs the organization's health and socioeconomic service programs and is eligible for a tax exemption as a charitable organization, broadly under Section 80G of the Income Tax Act, and on a program-by-program basis through Section 35 AC of the same Act (see http://www.arpana.org; Agarwal & Dadrawala, 2004, pp. 131–132).

This ambiguity in determining which charitable organizations may be properly identified as such makes the discussion of "religious" organizations tricky and makes it impossible to put forth accurate estimates regarding the number of these types of NGOs operating in India today. For this reason, we will not attempt to make generalizations regarding such organizations, but instead will try to find patterns common among them by exploring specific charitable organizations with ties to the three largest religious traditions of India: Hinduism, Islam, and Christianity. Although we have chosen to focus on these three major faith groups, it is important to note that there are voluntary associations associated with the many other religions in India as well, which are also engaged in important charitable work. For the purposes of this chapter, we will consider a religious organization to be any organization that puts forth religious doctrine or a religious figurehead as its main inspirational source or which is funded largely through explicitly religious donations.

Due to a dearth of outside sources providing information on the religious nonprofits of India, much of the specific information about the voluntary organizations we explored is derived from the Web sites and publications of the organizations profiled, and we focus on how these organizations choose to represent themselves. Organizational self-representation is important in understanding the mindset of the groups' volunteers because it is this image that is most likely to attract or repel individuals who are considering offering their services.

Hindu Voluntary Organizations

Relative to Islam and Christianity, Hinduism presents perhaps the greatest challenge in terms of determining which charitable organizations should be considered "religious." Compared to these other two faiths, Hinduism is much less scripturally based and there are significant variations in belief and in the gods and individuals venerated. Many traditions that are viewed as falling within the Hindu fold are also more open to including figures and teachings associated with other faiths within their embrace. That said, there are a number of significant volunteer-supported organizations engaged in charitable activities in India that are explicitly inspired, either directly or through the medium of a guru, by Vedic or other Hindu religious teachings.

Most of the Hindu charitable organizations operating in India appear to derive their inspiration largely from a particular charismatic spiritual figure, who also acts as the group's leader, rather than directly from a textual source. This is in contrast to Muslim and Christian organizations in which the founder, although often highly praised and respected, is generally put forth as simply the originator or guide of the organization and not as its professed inspiration. This focus on the teachings of a leader or guru is so prevalent among Hindu organizations that any Indian movement centered around and inspired by the message of a spiritual guru tends to be categorized by outsiders as Hindu, even if the organization itself eschews connections to any such religious categorization, such as the Sathya Sai Organization.

However, even within this model, there is considerable variance, with some organizations having more of a religious focus than others and some deriving greater inspiration from a single spiritual guru than others. For example, AIM for Seva emphasizes that it is a secular development organization that embraces people of varying "cultural backgrounds" (see http://www.aimforseva.org). Its activities are largely service focused, including running homes for disadvantaged children, schools, health-care centers, hospitals, mobile medical services, and old-age homes; conducting disaster relief and environmental work; and establishing self-help groups for women. In fact, on its Web site, the closest the organization comes to openly promoting religious philosophy in its work is through its statement that it teaches "value-based cultural education" at its homes for poor children so that they may become "proud of their rich cultural heritage," a statement made next to a photo of children appearing to pray (see "Student Homes" at http://www.aimforseva.org). Despite the organization's general emphasis on secular goals, however, its "drive," "energy," and "vision" are derived from the "dynamic leadership" of Hindu guru Swami Dayananda Saraswati (see http://www.aimforseva.org). Saraswati is referred to as "a great visionary, an eminent teacher of Vedanta and a powerful thinker and writer of our times" (see "The Founder" at http://www.aimforseva.org).

Although Saraswati is AIM for Seva's founder and spiritual guide, he is portrayed merely as an inspirational and spiritually attuned teacher. The language the group uses to describe him, thus, contrasts with that used by Arpana in reference to its spiritual guide, Param Pujya Ma. In describing Pujya Ma as "Beloved and Divine Mother, Revered and Eternal Guru, Perfect Embodiment of Truth and Love, Essence of all the Scriptures" (see http://www.arpana.org), Arpana portrays its founder as more than a pious inspiration and teacher, but as a divine figure on earth. The organization believes her speech to be directly divinely inspired and has gone so far as to compile her oral wisdom into what they consider to be new *shastra*s (scriptures).

The primary aim of Arpana is to "carry out research in the Scriptures in the light of Vedanta as elucidated by Param Pujya Ma" ("Arpana's Applied Research," see http://www.arpana.org). However, although Pujya Ma emphasized that the spiritual aspect of the organization must remain key, even opposing the use of the phrase "social service" to describe its work, the group is involved in a wide variety of service activities in India. The programs are centered in the areas around Delhi, Haryana, and Himachal Pradesh and include initiatives such as slum resettlement, health care, women's empowerment activities, vocational training, and microcredit. Such service is viewed as necessary to implement the injunctions of the scriptures and devotee volunteers are called to dedicate their lives to promoting the well-being of society through selfless service.

Not all Hindu charitable organizations follow this model of finding their inspiration solely through the teachings of one particular guru. Although nearly all seem to derive at least part of their inspiration from a spiritual leader, in some organizations, a particular text or thread of Hindu tradition is emphasized more than the figurehead, and many groups are inspired by a string of spiritual figures rather than by a single personality. For example, Bochasanwasi Shri Akshar Purushottam Swaminarayan Sanstha (a.k.a. BAPS), an Indian "socio-spiritual Hindu organization" (see "Introduction" at http://www.swaminarayan.org), which has grown into an international organization, traces its roots back to the Hindu Vedas. The loyalty of the group is to the teachings of the texts as interpreted by a long chain of religious gurus, beginning with Bhagwan Swaminarayan (1781–1830 CE) and continuing on to the present guru, Pramukh Swami Maharaj (b. 1921), who is believed to be the original guru's present manifestation on earth. Perhaps, in part, because the organization has existed under eight different spiritual teachers, it is relatively textually focused, and its Web site devotes considerable space to discussing Hindu scriptures.

BAPS is focused on spiritual and moral education, but it also strongly emphasizes the importance of social action. At the head of its Web site's "Introduction," it states:

Many ask, "How can you mix spirituality and social service?"

We ask, "How can you separate the two?"

Those who wish to sincerely serve society must be spiritually pure and only those who are spiritually pure can sincerely serve society! (See "Introduction" at http://www.swaminarayan.org.)

In line with this objective, the organization's Web site declares that it runs eight hospitals and health-care clinics and 31 educational institutions; awards 5,000 scholarships a year; carries out environmental programs such as recycling, tree planting, and water conservation; has operated 33 disaster relief operation; has established 800 centers for "permanent tribal uplift" and nine mobile medical centers that treat 250,000 villagers a year. In addition, although it is not clear what portion of volunteers are working within India, BAPS boasts of 45,000–55,000 volunteers (The organization's Web site offers these two disparate numbers on different pages. See "Introduction" and "History" at http://www.swaminarayan.org), and claims that each year, these volunteer workers contribute 12,000,000 hours of their time in service of the organization. Although these numbers include its programs overseas and are certainly estimates (and possibly generous estimates), it is clear that BAPS has an extensive presence throughout India.

Like BAPS, the Chinmaya Mission is a Vedantic organization, which originated in and is administered from India, but has developed a considerable international presence as well. Although the group's spiritual leader has a prominent role in inspiring the organization, like BAPS, it is not centered on a single individual, but a chain of gurus with the present leader, Swami Tejomayananda, not deified in any way, but simply portrayed as a highly respectable individual and knowledgeable teacher.

The organization's mission is to "provide to individuals from any background, the wisdom of Vedanta and the practical means for spiritual growth and happiness, enabling them to become positive contributors to society" (see "About Chinmaya Mission" at http://www.chinmayamission.com). This primarily involves running centers of Vedantic teaching and supporting publications; however, the organization also engages in a variety of social development programs. It runs the Chinmaya Organization for Rural Development (CORD), which facilitates victim support groups and discussion forums for rural women and youth, offers informal legal counseling, conducts skills training for girls and women, promotes self-help groups for the government's SHG-Bank linkage program, runs a girl's orphanage, offers rehabilitation services for disabled villagers and a variety of health-care services, and manages a natural resource training program. The Chinmaya Mission recruits volunteers from India and overseas to work on CORD's development projects, accepting both those with professional services to offer as well as unskilled workers. Like Arpana's Research and Charities Trust, the existence of a separate relief and development wing in the form of CORD allows the organization to take advantage of donations that are deductible under Section 80G of the Income Tax Act. The organization also derives funding from the Indian government, the international aid divisions of foreign governments, and philanthropic organizations.

The movement built around the figure Amma (mother), provides another outstanding example of a religious NGO that utilizes volunteers for charitable activities. Amma was born in 1953 in a poor fishing village in the southern state of Kerala. She was given the name Sudhamani and, like many other spiritual figures in the Buddhist, Hindu, and Islamic Sufi traditions in India, she has a unique birth story and childhood. According to the organization's Web site, "[s]he came into this world not in tears as babies usually do, but with a beaming smile on her face, as if prophesying the joy and bliss she was to bring to the world" and "[b]y the age of five, she had already begun composing devotional songs laden with deep mystical insight" (see "Amma: Born with a Smile" at http://www.amma. org). Amma grew to dedicate her life to spiritual and humanitarian work and is viewed by her followers as a living expression of *Karma Yoga* or selfless service. She explains:

> Meditation and studying the scriptures are like two sides of a coin. The engraving on that coin is selfless service, and that is what gives it its real value. Our compassion and acts of selflessness take us to the deeper truths. Through selfless action we can eradicate the ego that conceals the Self. Detached, selfless action leads to liberation. Such action is not just work; it is *karma yoga*. (See "Teachings" at http://www.amma.org)

A number of organizations, centers, and groups have grown up around her and her message. These institutions are meant to embody the Vedic principle of *Tyagenaike Amritatvamanashuhu* (through renunciation alone can immortality be attained). According to Amma, at her ashrams and other centers, her devotees are encouraged to "devote all their time and energy to the remembrance of God, doing selfless service and developing qualities such as love, patience and respect for others" (see "Centers Around the World" at http://www.amma.org).

Volunteers for the movement are recruited from "both the skilled and unskilled alike" (see "Get Involved" at http://www.amma.org), and most of the organization's work is done by these devotee volunteers. Volunteers are engaged in a variety of charitable and development programs in 33 countries, with their greatest presence appearing to be in India and the United States. For example, those participating in the "Circle of Love" program write "loving supportive letters on a regular basis to an elder, someone confined by illness, or someone at a crossroads in life" (see "Get Involved" at http://www.amma.org). A related program, "Circle of Love Inside," commits volunteers to write letters, donate books, and visit people incarcerated, spreading Amma's story and her call for unconditional love. Volunteers are also widely involved in education, health, development, and relief programs and are encouraged to promote environmental sustainability by planting trees and flowers and using oil lamps.

Christian Voluntary Organizations

Along with Gandhian NGOs, Christian NGOs probably make up the most common type of development organizations operating in India today (AVARD, 1992, p. 10). Christian institutions have involved themselves in charitable and development activities in India, such as building schools and orphanages, along with their missionary endeavors since the early 1810s (Sen, 1993, p. 4). Such organizations have affected the growth of voluntary organizations considerably and are largely responsible for the significantly greater presence of the NGOs in the south of India, where Christianity and missionaries have a longer history and a stronger hold (Riley, 2002, p. 83).

From a funding perspective, Christian organizations in India have a significant advantage over organizations associated with other religions because of their disproportionate ability to attract foreign donations. According to the Home Ministry, as of 2001, 60 percent of the total foreign funds received by Indian organizations were donated to Christian institutions and the NGOs; only 15 percent was directed to Muslim and Hindu organizations (Krishnan, 2001). This was true despite the fact that the single largest recipient of foreign aid was a Hindu organization.[2] This funding, which comes from both individuals residing overseas and governments, is directed at a wide variety of organizations, including those with a missionary focus. For example, in 2005, 25 percent of the worldwide partners of United States Agency for International Development (USAID), the economic and humanitarian assistance wing of the United States government, were faith-based organizations, and almost all of these groups offered "personal salvation, biblical infallibility and a commitment to proselytizing" as part of their mission (Berger, 2006, pp. 6–7).

In terms of the types of programs pursued, Christian religious groups in India have traditionally been more concerned with social work than social action and have focused most of their charitable activities on areas such as building hospitals and orphanages. When such organizations have sought to go beyond this, getting involved in more politically charged issues, such as workers rights and indigenous rights, their efforts often meet with disapproval from the church hierarchy (D'Souza, 2000, pp. 32–34, 46). In recent decades, however, calls for social action have been on the rise, and churches and other Christian organizations have been shifting their approach away from charity and short-term poverty alleviation programs and toward initiatives emphasizing social awareness and mobilization and, in line with donor community preferences, self-help (Lobo, 1999, p. 69).

[2]The Hindu organization was Maharishi Ved Vigyan Vishwa Vidyapeetham, a Hindu Vedic group that does not appear to be involved in charitable activities (see Krishnan, 2001 and http://www.maharishi-india.org).

However, the religious message has not faded into the background. The continued centrality of faith is encouraged in part by the fact that Christian NGOs are often directly associated with a particular religious congregation or ministry, which is then attached to a larger Christian sect, connecting the organization directly to the greater religious community even outside the nation's borders in a way that is often beyond the capabilities of Muslim and Hindu charitable groups. In partial consequence of this, the vast majority of Christian organizations appear to be led by ministers and to be much more focused on direct action to spread the faith than similar organizations associated with the Muslim and Hindu communities. For example, the Gospel Echoing Missionary Society (GEMS), a large organization that works primarily in northern and eastern India, demonstrates a typical prioritization of activities for Christian groups when it explains: "The activities of the society are primarily church planting evangelism. Later educational services, medical services and social services were added in order to cater to the needs of people" (see "Know Us" at http://www.gemsbihar.org/index.asp).

Even though they are only a secondary emphasis for the organization, the social service activities of GEMS are extensive. It runs primary schools, a hospital and nursing school, health clinics, orphanages and rehabilitation homes for children, an HIV care center, a clean water program, and a polio rehabilitation center and also conducts occasional disaster relief work. The organization actively recruits volunteers to work in its hospital, schools, and children's homes to help with missionary work and to get involved in Internet and other computer-related projects.

GEMS's Reverend D. Augustine Jebakumar reports "an encounter with the Lord through a vision" (see "Jebakumar's Messages" at http://www.gemsbihar.org/index.asp) led him to abandon his job and take up missionary work. This is a common pattern among the leaders of Christian organizations in India who often report a direct experience with Christ that led them to their present work, sometimes following a period of degenerate living. Another example of this is Reverend Dr Mera Jesudass, head of the Loving Hands Ministries of Hyderabad, who was the son of a "pioneer gospel preacher," but became a "violent communist" before returning to his father's calling after experiencing a "dramatic encounter with Jesus Christ." The Ministry's youth director is also represented as having previously lived a "worldly" and "sinful" life before he had an "encounter with God" after his father was in an accident (see "About Us" at http://www.lovinghandsministries.com). In this way, the service of the leaders to the organization is directly linked to service to God and even the Ministry's mundane goals are given with a sort of spiritual urgency.

Dr Jesudass's Loving Hands Ministry is largely focused on preaching and education, running 150 congregations, a Christian school, and a Bible college and theological seminary. However, it also runs an orphanage and widows' home and conducts youth seminars and HIV awareness programs, an income-generating program for women, and a drinking water program. The organization actively recruits volunteers through its Web site to help with its work. Interestingly, the Ministry suggests that financial donors may want to physically participate in the work they are supporting monetarily and notes that arrangements can be made for them to volunteer in the projects they are funding.

An exception to the model of the Christian group leader being compelled to serve humanity through an encounter with God is Reverend P. K. Joshua of the Eternal Hope Charity Mission. Reverend Joshua was inspired to act by the social conditions around him rather than by any direct message from God. Although he was already participating in the work of Christian organizations, the "dying and the destitute" ultimately led him to quit his "secular" job and devote his life to serving the poor through the founding of the Mission in 1992 (see http://www.ehcmission.org/e/about.htm). The Mission has built day-care centers and drinking water lines, runs medical aid and community development projects, and provides financial support to elderly abandoned people. Volunteers are used for a number of tasks. For example, when the organization hears of a destitute person who needs their help, volunteers are sent to assess the physical and mental condition of the person and to help them find shelter. They also recruit volunteer nurses, doctors, teachers, social workers, and counselors to help with their projects.

Islamic Voluntary Organizations

As discussed earlier in this chapter, it is difficult to give an accurate estimate as to the number of NGOs operating in India with a religious affiliation. However, S. Ubaidur Rahman's *Directory of Muslim NGOs in India* (2006) lists approximately 1,200 "important" Muslim NGOs operating throughout the country. Muslim charitable organizations operating in India appear to be more often focused primarily on social service in their own community than Hindu and Christian organizations. There are a number of possible reasons for this.

First, Muslims in India are generally more economically and socially disadvantaged than other communities. Educational attainment and literacy rates are well below the national average, and the poverty rate of the Muslim community is only slightly less than that of the Scheduled Castes (i.e., dalits or "untouchables") and the Scheduled Tribes (Planning Commission, 2006). Many Muslims also feel that they are discriminated against by the majority community and that they have fewer opportunities available to them for economic advancement. For this reason, efforts to target the Muslim community specifically with development and charitable activities may be argued to be need based rather than strictly communal. This need is seen as all the more acute because other types of NGOs often ignore the Muslim community or address it only in the context of promoting inter-communal harmony while ignoring the serious economic and social problems facing the population (Sikand, 2006).

In addition, Muslim-managed organizations may have difficulty securing donations from the majority community and are often much less connected to foreign donors than similar Christian organizations. Moreover, they are generally financially dependent on *zakat* funds (religiously obligatory alms) from their own community, which must be earmarked for Muslim recipients only.

Although their obligatory nature means that the reliability of *zakat* offerings may make such funds theoretically capable of providing a basis for the development of strong voluntary organizations with an Islamic orientation, the use of *zakat* as a funding source is not unproblematic. The aforementioned stipulation that these donations should be used for the benefit of Muslim recipients makes it difficult to work in mixed communities and, in turn, to reap the benefits of tax-exempt status. *Zakat* donations may come with other strings attached as well. For example, many argue that *zakat* should never be used to cover an organization's administrative costs. In addition, such offerings are often seasonal, with many Muslims preferring to pay *zakat* during Ramadan. Many Muslims also prefer to donate *zakat* for activities with a spiritual rather than worldly focus, such as the building of Islamic schools and mosques. The requirement that organizations report donations received also acts as a disincentive to many wealthy Muslims because Muslims are enjoined not to make their charitable giving widely known and because the correlation between *zakat* and net worth means that publishing their donations allows others to calculate their wealth (Harper et al., 2008, pp. 125–126).

Danyal A. Kazi, chairman of the Pain Relief and You (PRAY) Foundation Trust in Bangalore discussed how some of these issues have affected his organization in an interview published on the group's Web site. The PRAY Foundation provides financial assistance to poor patients in need of expensive surgeries. It is dependent almost entirely upon *sadaqa* and *zakat* for its organizational expenses; however, it receives many requests for financial assistance from non-Muslims as well. Although the organization strives to be nonsectarian and to help all those in need, the generally accepted prohibition on the use of *zakat* funds to help non-Muslims has meant that it is difficult for them meet these requests. The only funding sources at the group's disposal for non-Muslim patients are *sadaqa* (i.e., voluntary charitable donations from the Muslim community as opposed to the obligatory *zakat*) and donations from non-Muslims, which are rare and that when received, must thus always be set aside for such patients.

The organization has appealed to Muslim donors to donate more non-*zakat* funds, such as money generated as interest on their deposits, so that the resources can be used to help non-Muslim patients; but Kazi (2004) notes that the response to such requests has been "very weak." It is clear that the issue has caused the organization considerable stress and that it has made it much more challenging for them to meet the needs of the community in which they are working.

Although most Islamic charitable organizations seem to be highly dependent upon religious funding, they vary in the degree of aggressiveness with which Islamic ideals are taught and used to justify their work. There is a wide spectrum in the degree of religious versus secular associations among the groups; however, it is generally possible to loosely divide Muslim NGOs in two categories along these lines by observing the background of the group's founder or president.

On the one hand, there are a number of organizations that work largely in the Muslim community and are managed exclusively by Muslims, but these are headed by individuals with a reputation based on their success in the secular world rather than on any religious credentials. These leaders tend to be doctors and businessmen who decide to use their wealth to give back to their community. For example, the aforementioned Dr Kazi, a retired business professional, could be comfortably placed in this group. Other examples of such leaders include Dr Mumtaz Ahmed Khan, founder of the Al-Ameen Movement, who gave up his profession as a doctor to found a group of medical, educational, and cooperative banking institutions in and around Bangalore (*The Hindu*, 2004) and Irfan Merchant, president and founder of the Rahat Welfare Trust, a Muslim women and children's welfare agency, who comes from a family of cloth merchants (Wajihuddin, 2008). Although these organizations are more likely to refer to themselves as "secular" and to make some effort to show that non-Muslims also benefit from their work, they often remain largely dependent upon the Muslim community for their support and may even consult religious figures regarding the appropriate manner in which to operate when the necessity arises.[3] Such organizations use volunteers for a number of activities. For example, the PRAY Foundation actively recruits volunteer doctors and others willing to help with interviews, surveys, and monthly meetings (PRAY, 2008), whereas the Rahat Welfare trust has a team of 21 volunteers to assist its seven staff members (see http://rahatwelfaretrust.org) in activities such as such as identifying and verifying candidates for assistance (Wajihuddin, 2008).

The second major archetype of Muslim charitable groups in India is organizations headed by a figure with a reputation for religious learning. Such leaders appear to be less common among Muslim organizations than among Christian and Hindu organizations and their role is generally deemphasized, particularly relative to that of the gurus leading many Hindu religious NGOs. One example of this pattern among Muslim NGOs is the Markazul Ma'arif welfare association in Assam, headed by Maulana Badruddin Ajmal Al-Qasmi, which claims to be the largest Muslim NGO in northeast India (*Milli Gazette*, 2005). In explaining how the organization came into existence, Al-Qasmi describes his own spiritual quest to find a way to ameliorate the lives of the poor and notes that the organization ultimately came about through the support and encouragement of many other religious scholars (Al-Qasmi, n.d.)

The Markazul Ma'arif welfare association is involved in a wide variety of social work activities, including the awarding of scholarships to the needy, vocational training, establishment of schools, orchestration of a drinking water scheme, health care and sanitation. However, in line with its more outwardly religious leadership, the association's Web site is much clearer in its Islamic orientation, citing sections of the Qur'an and sayings of the Prophet Muhammad to establish the religious virtue of social service (Al-Qasmi, n.d.), offering free Islamic books for download, providing advice on a wide variety of religious matters, and emphasizing that the organization's primary schools are religious in nature and meant

---

[3]For example, Dr Kazi discusses having consulted with Muslim scholars for an opinion on whether it is permissible to use *zakat* money to help non-Muslim patients (Kazi, 2004).

to "safeguard the believers against the onslaught of *kufr* [disbelief] and *ilhad* [infidelity]" (see "Department of Islamiat" at http://www.markazul-maarif.org/home_in.asp).

Sikand (2006) has expressed concern about such *ulama*-run Muslim NGOs, which he believes thrive due to the small size of the Muslim middle class. He notes that their leaders' "insular" backgrounds often narrow the scope of the activities pursued by such organizations, disproportionately emphasizing Islamic education and making it difficult for them to work toward positive relationships with other communities. However, organizations such as the Markazul Ma'arif demonstrate that it is possible for organizations of this type to have a much broader vision of welfare and development while maintaining a commitment to Islamic education as well.

There has recently been some effort on the part of Muslim NGOs to strengthen their influence and effectiveness by coordinating their efforts with one another. In July 2003, a conference on the networking of NGOs in India met in Mumbai with the intention of sharing experiences and ideas for future coordination among the Muslim NGOs of India. Seventy-five Muslim NGOs from 13 states were invited to the conference, with 58 representatives of 45 NGOs from nine different states attending. The conference identified a number of common problems that the organizations were facing, most of which were not unlike the types of problems that secular organizations might face, but that also included concerns about the casual attitude toward the use and institutionalization of religious charities and the lack of serious involvement of Muslim intelligentsia and philanthropists in NGO activities.

The primary product of the conference appears to have been a proposal by a number of its members to form a Community Council of India (CCI) for networking, counseling, training, and evaluation between and among Muslim NGOs. This council would also take responsibility for linking the organizations to government schemes and for targeting underserved areas of the country (Institute of Microfinance and Development, 2003). Along these lines, a central coordinating committee was initiated at a 2006 workshop for Muslim NGOs in New Delhi. The workshop included 325 delegates from Muslim nonprofit organizations in 19 states, who put forth a joint declaration containing a number of political and developmental goals for the Muslim community (*Milli Gazette*, 2007). The workshop was convened by the Movement for Empowerment of Muslim Indians (MOEMIN) (Asif, 2006), a group made up of representatives of various Islamic sects in

India. Although it is as yet unclear what impact these initiatives will have on the organizations involved or on the Muslim community generally, such efforts directly link the Muslim NGOs with the greater Islamic community, potentially intensifying the religious aspect of their work while encouraging the groups' greater politicization and cooperation.

Conclusions

It is interesting to note the interplay of secular and spiritual impetuses to the activities of all of the organizations explored here. The relative dominance of spiritual or secular programs and leadership seen among the groups appears to result from a number of factors, both internal and external to the organizations. For example, Christian NGOs are often tied to a wider church hierarchy that likely encourages the prominent focus on spreading the faith. Direct efforts at proselytizing do not appear to be as common among Muslim and Hindu groups, although all three religious affiliations include many associated organizations that promote religious publications as part of their agenda. And although all religious NGOs with a charitable focus are no doubt responding to a combination of worldly and religious incentives, some emphasize that they are responding to a direct call from God to serve, some that they are responding to humanitarian impulses, and still others suggest that they have taken up worldly causes in the hope of purifying themselves spiritually through service.

Legal and funding incentives often serve as encouragement to undertake more secular service activities. For example, an excessively religious or communal focus may cost the NGOs their tax exemptions and engaging in the types of secular development programs popular with international donor nations and multilateral organizations may win valuable financial support for an organization with primarily spiritual goals. Funding from individual donors may also be influential in determining the types of programs undertaken. For example, the trends of private overseas Christian patrons greatly influence the type of work that missionary organizations take up; restrictions stemming from Islamic law often limit the freedom of Muslim organizations to administer their programs in the manner they feel is most appropriate.

Leadership types also vary widely across Indian religious charitable organizations, with group leaders often serving as a bridge between their

respective organizations' religious inspirations and their mundane service activities. For example, a Hindu guru with divine knowledge may serve to directly link the spiritual and material goals of her organization, whereas a Christian minister, who presents himself as having encountered God personally and being directly called by Him, may serve a similar purpose of providing religious legitimatization for the secular causes of his organization. However, there are also leaders in all three types of organizations who are simply respected men of religious or secular learning and pious intention, who guide their organizations according to their interpretations of God's desires and humankind's needs. The degree of diversity among religious NGOs operating in India is perhaps not surprising, given the variety exhibited in more secular organizations. In the wide-ranging and important field of charitable and developmental services in India, religious organizations of all types play a valuable role, allowing those with a spiritual inclination to devote themselves both to God and mankind in a spirit of selfless service.

Narratives

Organizational Narrative: Eternal Hope Charity Mission

Reverend Joshua, who runs Eternal Hope Charity Mission (EHCM), an interdenominational Christian organization that he founded on the outskirts of Mumbai, had already decided by the age of 22 that he would like to devote his life to Jesus. Because Jesus had always tended to the downtrodden of society, young Joshua decided to follow in his footsteps. Reverend Joshua recalls the time he spent with Mother Theresa, picking up the homeless on the streets on Mumbai and trying to feed them and tend to their needs. It was then that he realized the immense need for help; "we are but a drop in the ocean," he remarks. He married a young woman who had been brought up in an American mission in nearby Pune and who shared his enthusiasm for reaching out to the needy. Together they began working in the slums of Mumbai.

When asked how his religion plays out in his work, Reverend Joshua stressed that "it is important to see each person as a human in urgent need regardless of caste." When the immediate practical

need is met, and if the human seeks help for the soul, then the person is told about the teachings of Christ. However, Reverend Joshua was quick to assert that religion is primarily about being good to others regardless of their caste or creed.

Soon after Joshua was ordained, and after overcoming the many bureaucratic hurdles, the husband-and-wife team started EHCM. Joshua had graduated from Wilson College in Mumbai, and he decided to approach several of the senior administrators and faculty there for support. A number of them readily joined the Board of Directors and some contributed as much as ₹50,000 to enable the organization to have the ₹450,000 required to begin working toward its mission. Because EHCM is registered as a charity mission, they are allowed to solicit funds, and the NGO does this through door-to-door campaigns, informational talks at schools and other venues, and directly through their Web site.

When EHCM started their first day-care center in a slum in order to take care of the many young children running around the streets, they were regarded with great suspicion by those who lived there. The slum dwellers tore down the construction four times before they realized that the strange missionaries only wanted to feed and take care of their children. This was the first of many day-care centers run by the organizations in different slums. Sometime later, EHCM won the Mahatma Gandhi Award for looking after the downtrodden. Once word got out about the good work EHMC was doing, they received many donations. The Mafatlal Group donated six acres of land to start a children's home in the tribal areas outside of Mumbai. The idea of starting a children's home in these areas occurred to Joshua once he became aware of the great need to house the many orphans and homeless children living there. He approached the government for land, but to no avail. Frustrated with the bureaucracy and the insidious means often required to get things done, he turned to praying—and now he has the land he had prayed for.

EHCM has had many donors. Some are consistent in regular payments paced through time, whereas others give a one-time donation. Representatives of the Swiss government have visited the EHCM sites and the government is now a regular donor. Sometimes, EHCM receives help from the Catholic Relief Service as well,

with donations of dry foods or visits from volunteer doctors and teachers or youth groups who come in for a special project. Other times, some people see the ECHM Web site and send money. All these resources help keep the organization's projects going: the children's education nurseries that provide children with meals, medical care, and education; the children's homes that cater to orphans and children in need of residential facilities; and the sponsorship of girls' education complete with books, school fees, uniforms, and anything required to keep them healthy and educated.

Reverend Joshua has a dream: one day he hopes to have a residential school in Panvel (an area just outside of Mumbai), as well as a technical school where young people can take courses in nursing, teaching, computer studies, sewing, and other career-oriented fields. In the meantime, Reverend Joshua continues to work with his assistants and volunteers on EHCM's expanding range of charitable projects. At present, the organization has 27 paid workers and seven volunteers in Mumbai, along with nine volunteers in Latur, a district outside of Mumbai. The volunteers include a doctor who volunteers her services twice a week, two nurses, two retired teachers, two dentists, and other administrative staff who volunteer their time on a regular basis. They volunteer with EHCM because they believe in the work that is being done and want to contribute. Interestingly, the group's volunteers are not all the Christian but are drawn from a number of faith groups.

Though EHCM focuses on helping people to meet their immediate practical needs, it is also involved in programs focused on long-term goals, such as helping people obtain an education, gain employment skills, and understand their rights. Recently, EHCM was involved with six other neighboring NGOs in a campaign to help the local rural community to understand and safeguard their basic water access rights.

EHCMs action plans are decided by a group of committee members who meet four times a year to review the NGO's progress and to chart out an action plan for the next few months. The EHCM staff gathers once a week to work out the plans for the following week, and Reverend Joshua works with his wife and other team members to implement those plans in the hope that their efforts will spread hope for a better future among the disillusioned.

Individual Narrative: Pravin

Pravin was introduced to the world of Christian volunteering early in life. He grew up in a devout Christian household where his father, who was a doctor, worked with the missionaries of the Church of Scotland and did not charge the poor for visits or their medications. His mother was a teacher who encouraged "giving" as well as working with the poor. Upon completing his Masters of Commerce in accounting, he worked as an accountant with the diocese of the Church of North India. While working there, Pravin was exposed to the community development work that the Church was involved in. He realized that he was drawn to such work and also became aware of Christian NGOs that offered work opportunities.

In order to facilitate involvement in the Church's initiatives, Pravin changed jobs and became a financial coordinator with Wilson College in Mumbai. The college works with nine schools and two colleges and is involved in rural development activities. At the same time, he began his own school, known as "Robertson Convent," for the poor in the rural district of his home in Nagpur. The school has grown and now houses 150 students who study there until the seventh grade. This school has attracted volunteer teachers as well as groups of people who send in donations.

Sometime later, Pravin became aware of EHCM because of Reverend Joshua's connections with Wilson College. He visited the organization and was impressed by the projects it was involved in and the sense of camaraderie among the workers. He decided to devote some of his time to the organization and quickly found that he enjoyed the work.

Today, he divides his time between a week of paid consulting work at Wilson College and two weeks at his own organization in Nagpur where he focuses on the school as well as evangelical work. The last week of the month is devoted to EHCM where he focuses on field work. He stays with the children at the day-care centers and spends his time telling stories, singing songs, and making the children feel cared for. He also provides guidance with education and accounting matters as needed. However, he enjoys his fieldwork most. His eyes light up when he talks about his time with the children whom he likes "very, very much" to visit. He believes that the work EHCM does is worthwhile and that, if there were more volunteers, they could spread the program further afield and help more people advance in life.

Pravin emphasizes that the villages he works in are mainly non-Christian. What matters is that they are people who are in need, and he feels good that he is able to be a part of an organization that caters to their needs. He believes that such work is necessary, and he is glad that he has had the opportunity to be a part of it.

Individual Narrative: Vasant

Vasant came to religious volunteering dramatically and he smiles as he tells his tale. His parents died when he was very young so he was placed in a hostel run by missionaries. When he was in the eighth grade, he happened to walk through a shallow stream in which an electric pole had fallen. The live current threw him out and he landed some distance away. He was initially presumed dead but slowly he struggled back to life. At that time he vowed that if he lived he would devote the rest of his life to doing God's work. He is propelled by this promise and believes that God is instrumental in urging his involvement in social service. He believes that God exists in all human beings, and when he sees a person in need he sees *Prabhu ka roop* (the face of God) in them. He humbly shrugs away any publicity or accolades that he receives for his work and laments that life is too short to do all that he would like to do to improve the lives of others. Vasant is also quick to note that helping others ultimately results in lessening of one's own personal burdens.

When Vasant finished school, he studied to become a teacher, completing his Bachelor of Education as well as his Masters of Art in education. He got a job as a teacher in Aurangabad and then married a nurse who worked at an eye hospital. Both believed in social work and spent every weekend and holiday helping the poor. They pursued this life in Aurangabad until Vasant learned of the work that Reverend Joshua was doing to uplift the poor and the needy. He had met the Reverend when he was a young man at his hostel, but had since lost touch with him. He decided to begin volunteering for EHCM, and for the last five years, he has been coming in to help the organization every time he has a holiday or four to five days each month. He stays at the project in the village of Panvel in the outskirts of Mumbai. He likes the environment of many fruit trees and the "lovely people" who work there. He does whatever Reverend Joshua asks of him: helping children with their education, guiding teachers, taking an elderly woman to hospital, or visiting the slum areas. He has found a kindred spirit with those who work at EHCM and appreciates their sincerity and devotion.

Vasant is also involved in several committees that attempt to ameliorate the lives of the needy and spread peace and goodwill. These include the Peace Committee, which works with the local police to help the destitute, a committee that deals with the *nasha-bandis* (alcoholics), and a group that is trying to end the dowry system which, although outlawed, continues to drive many into deep debt and to encourage the perception of daughters as a burden to families. One of the groups that Vasant enjoys is the Sarvodharma Sambao, an interfaith group that celebrates all religious holidays through an interchange of ideas and group celebration. Vasant likes to sing devotional songs, be they related to the Gospel, the Holy Qu'ran, or the Hindu scriptures. His friends are likeminded people who often spend their holidays driving around and helping those in need.

Individual Narrative: John

John was born into a poor family and he recalls that he never had proper clothes while growing up. He used to help his mother around the house cooking, cleaning, and looking after the many children who never seemed to have enough of anything. In his preuniversity year, he had to drop out of school in order to work and help support his family. This background gave him a heightened understanding of the problems that many poor families encounter in simply obtaining the necessities of life. The experience also instilled in him empathy for the poor and needy and the hope that one day he could help others who were likewise mired in poverty.

To help support his family, John went to Saudi Arabia and worked as a custodial supervisor of a school, where he was responsible for the cleaning of premises and the gardening. He remained in Saudi Arabia for 12 years, sending back remittances to his family. During his time off, he took computer courses. Eventually, he received a computer certificate, and when he returned to India, he found a job as a computer instructor. He had heard about EHCM through friends and wished that he could work with them; however, he was aware that financial necessity precluded him from doing charitable work full-time. John visited Reverend Joshua and told him about his wish to work at the NGO as a volunteer, as well as to help out with the social work whenever he was not working at his office.

John was hired as a coordinator and has been helping with office administration, e-mails, making budgets and proposals, and researching and publicizing information via the Internet. Recently, he sent out an article on how people could donate their organs. He lives near the office and is on call to help out whenever Reverend Joshua requires assistance. He feels deeply drawn to the downtrodden, sick, and destitute and plans to continue helping as long as he is able to.

When asked how religion plays out in his work, John is adamant that he is motivated simply by the desire to help others and does not take into account any other characteristics; in fact, he believes that this is what religion is all about. He derives great peace from the way in which he lives his life and insists that he is lucky to have the opportunity to blend his need to earn a living with his desire to help others. He believes that all the money in the world could not have bought a lifestyle more satisfying than the one he leads.

Toward the end of the interview, John shared with us a disturbing incident of a problem that is, unfortunately, commonly faced by NGOs in India. He had been allotted the task of distributing quilts that had been sent to EHCM from a charitable foundation outside of India. He went out and gathered 50 of the neediest people on the street and brought them to receive their quilts. It was then that he became aware of one of the requirements of some donor NGOs as well as the Government of India that is meant to promote transparency: he was required to list the names and addresses of the recipients or state their ration card numbers.[4] However, the people that he had brought together were utterly destitute and, therefore, had no home addresses or ration cards. This requirement meant that he ultimately had to replace them with a less needy group of

---

[4] Ration cards allow Indians to buy certain foods and other basic goods at varying prices on the basic of their economic condition and also serve as a form of identification.

beneficiaries who had homes and the necessary addresses or ration card numbers. Unfortunately, although such rules may be deemed necessary to establish that the NGOs are legitimate and that the donated goods are being distributed to the poor, as John remarks, they may also prevent the NGOs from reaching out to the poorest people who are most desperately in need of assistance.

Organizational Narrative: Rahat

For some time Irfan Merchant ran his family's garment store. He also worked in an honorary capacity for a Muslim NGO whenever he could find the time, later joining the same NGO as an executive officer and working there for four years. However, he found the organization too structured for his liking. What really bothered him was that though the NGO sponsored children's education, they would not help the children who did not do well in their studies. Irfan left the NGO and started his own nonprofit organization, Rahat, in 1992.

Irfan's initial inspiration for starting an NGO was simply the immense need that he saw around him. In addition to the issue of helping struggling students, he was particularly aware of the plight of young widows who, without any source of support, were struggling to fend for their families. Irfan registered the NGO from his home address. Although he had the necessary work experience for taking on such an endeavor, he did not have sufficient financial resources to start the organization. He sent a letter out to all his friends informing them that he was starting a center for widows and soliciting financial help, and soon he was joined in his project by four likeminded people. The focus was on helping the families of widows who lacked a bread winner, and the group undertook activities such as sponsoring the education of children and helping students to buy books. The Rahat team went door to door in search of potential needy students, convincing families with young daughters that the girls should have an equal chance at being educated and offering to help with the fees. Although they did meet with some resistance, overall, they were fairly successful in their endeavors.

He remembers two incidents vividly. He met a woman in the slums who told him about a young lady who lived in the neighborhood and wanted to become a doctor. Irfan visited the young lady, Rabia, and found her to be earnest and intelligent. He encouraged Rabia to apply for admission to a private medical college and get her documentation ready. Rabia passed the entrance exam and received ₹20,000 to pay her fees. Because her grades were not sufficient to qualify among the highest achievers, she was not able to take advantage of the Indian government's scheme for admitting such students into government medical colleges for only ₹500. However, even after the ₹20,000 donation, Rabia fell short of the required sum to get into the private medical college. Irfan was confident that Rahat would have the required extra money in a month's time, but Rabia's college was about to begin, and there was no time to wait. Irfan took Rabia to see the principal of the college and explained Rabia's predicament. The principal was so impressed that people had been willing to pay Rabia's fees that he accepted her despite her lack of all the required funds.

Rabia had been given the fees with the proviso that she should pay back the money when she was able to and involve herself in voluntary work. However, once Rabia graduated she disappeared. A few years later Rahat received some money from her brother, but still heard no word from Rabia. It was some years later that she visited Rahat as Dr Rabia. She had married and was a practicing doctor in the Middle East. She inquired about the amount spent on her education and then wrote out a check for the amount and much more (₹90,000).

Irfan also remembers a young woman called Tasneem who wanted to become a doctor. Her parents were not in favor of her studying any further and were keen on getting her married. Irfan and his colleagues were able to convince her parents to let her study and then provided her with the practical incentive of ₹35,000. However, she was still short of the required funds. Tasneem searched diligently for funds and was ultimately favored in a ruling that extended the categories falling into the Other Backward Classes (OBC) categorization. When Tasneem's ethnic group was accepted as OBC, she was able to avail herself of government subsidies that enabled her to enter a private medical college. Today, Tasneem is a doctor and is married to another doctor. She sends donations regularly to Rahat.

Irfan has established a humane approach in dealing with families and looks at each family holistically. In this way, the problems the families face with errant children also become Rahat's problems. Rather than dismissing a child who is not doing well in school, Rahat attempts to resolve the problem with extra tutoring as well as attention to nutrition. Irfan remembers the time when someone approached and told him about a young boy who had just lost his father and was destitute. Irfan did not look at the boy's academic standing. All he knew was that here was a boy who needed help, and Irfan was determined to give him this help. Rahat helped fund his education and also paid for him to go to university and get his Bachelor of Commerce degree. Today, the young man is married; he has a good job, an apartment, and a car. He never forgets the people who helped him get to where he is and sends funds regularly to the NGO.

Occasionally, Rahat receives a large donation from an individual donor, but most of the organization's funding comes from a core group that collects ₹15,000–20,000 annually. This funding largely comes from the *zakat* donations of the Muslim community. Irfan does not consult with any religious leaders regarding the operations of the organization and makes every attempt he can to address the needs of members of other communities as well, even starting an organization, Sangam, to help bridge the gap between Hindus and Muslims. However, such a reliance on *zakat* does serve to limit the ability of organizations to address the needs of non-Muslims. Irfan recognizes this problem but notes that many Muslims are scraping the last rungs of the social ladder and that there is an enormous need for help in the community. Sometimes Rahat coordinates with other religious NGOs to work on large projects, but ordinarily, such help is slow in coming, if it comes at all. Irfan thinks that most NGOs are unaware of the dire plight of many Muslim families.

Irfan helped to start a school known as Shaheen Girl's Urdu School, which is now a municipal school. Urdu is a language closely related to Hindi, which is written in a script derived from Arabic and is used primarily in the Muslim community. If left to his own devices, Irfan would have preferred to start an English school as he believes that this medium offers more opportunities for students. However, because the municipal school in the area they live in is an Urdu-medium school that runs up to grade seventh, Shaheen Urdu School was created to provide a continuity from grades eight through ten. The teachers are paid by the Indian government. The students pay the low fees when they are able to and when they cannot afford the fees, Rahat pitches in and helps.

Rahat focuses its help on certain categories of distressed people. These are NYD—needy families where the income earned is small; WID—widowed families where there is no male breadwinner; DIV—divorcees; MSG—when the husband is classified as missing; and DST—when the husband has deserted the family. Most of these families are in dire need of help. Volunteers from Rahat assist the often uneducated clients in obtaining their identity cards, which are prerequisite to getting any help from the government. Their needs are assessed and the volunteers are assigned tasks. In general, the NGO pays for schooling, uniforms, and tutoring. They also cover any urgent medical needs and help with the provision of basic foods.

Volunteers meet every Sunday at the hall of Shaheen High School. Ten to twelve volunteers show up each week and assess the needs of clients who are also invited. Forms are filled out, money is distributed, and tasks are assigned, which helps Rahat to continue to live up to its name—"relief," by serving the many needy people who approach it.

Individual Narrative: Kamar and Farheen

Through its humane assistance of those in need, Rahat seems to have attracted a special breed of donors and volunteers who feel compelled to help others in the manner in which they have been helped. Rabia, Tasneem, and the aforementioned young man, who was helped through school and college, are cases in point. Kamar and Farheen are young women who received help from Rahat and have come back to the organization to serve. Though they both hold jobs with Rahat, they are also key volunteers who help out regularly and who have attracted other volunteers through their enthusiasm for their work.

Kamar completed her Bachelor of Commerce from a college in Mumbai. She was able to do so because of the help she received from

Rahat. She had completed high school and wished to study further, but did not have the means to pay her university fees. She was referred to Rahat by one of her teachers, who knew that the NGO helped out students in need. Kamar received the help she was looking for and completed her degree. She then joined the organization and works as a clerk at Shaheen Urdu School. However, she devotes her Sundays to volunteering with Rahat and helping out whenever she can.

As to why she continues to volunteer with Rahat, Kamar has a simple and straightforward answer: "Without Rahat I would not be here." Rahat has helped her and she would like to help back. Moreover, she enjoys her work and appreciates the guidance she receives from Irfan. She also believes that the work experience she has received from Rahat will provide a springboard for a better future. She does not believe in distinguishing between people by their religious background, arguing that "needy people are simply needy people regardless of their religion."

When Farheen was asked why she joined Rahat as a paid staff member, she was not shy in admitting that a strong element of self-interest was involved. For one thing, the fact that she comes from a large family meant that there was not enough money to go around and she needed the income. Second, she needed the work experience. However, she also likes to volunteer in addition to her work because it makes her feel good to help others and because she is happy to be working with such good people and learning new things. She also asserts that one day she wants to be "somebody" and that she believes that working with Rahat is one of the ways to achieve that goal.

Farheen is no stranger to Rahat. In fact, Rahat has been a part of Farheen's life since she was in grade six. When she was in school, Rahat's volunteers helped Farheen and her family with books and uniforms. Nine years later, Farheen is working part-time for Rahat. She is studying for a degree in mass communication and hopes to graduate within a year. She gets a nominal fee for her work as well as a lot of guidance from Irfan about how to build good work habits. She also spends her Sundays volunteering for Rahat. Farheen's friends have joined her in the volunteering, and they "hang out" together, working and enjoying themselves. Her mother is her biggest supporter and expresses great joy that her daughter has had the opportunity to advance herself.

Organizational Narrative: CORD (Sidhabari, Himachal Pradesh)

CORD is an offshoot of the Chinmaya Mission. It was founded by Swami Chinmayananda, a revered Hindu spiritual leader. Swami Chinmayananda chose one of the most depressed areas of the Himachal Pradesh to found a religious center as well as an NGO that would promote sustainable development in the region. Such development, he believed, was only possible if the local women, generally belonging to lower castes and tribes, were able to take charge of their own lives and progress. Dr Kshama Metre, a follower, associated with his religious center and a practicing pediatrician in New Delhi, agreed to take over the leadership of this NGO in 1985.

Starting in a relatively small way with the donation of a few sewing machines, Dr Metre single-mindedly pursued the vision of empowering the women of the area. From this humble beginning, her energy and vision made this organization into a large, well-funded NGO. The organization currently serves over 27,000 clients in 900 villages and offers a variety of programs that range from literacy and health services to sanitation, micro-finance, and legal aid. Though women are the primary focus of the NGO's activities, by extending their services to include the families of these women where relevant, CORD serves the entire village community.

Dr Metre regularly receives volunteers from all over the world who come to spend a few months with the organization, often in combination with a vacation in India. Some come for a few days, whereas others stay for months. Most volunteers are connected to the Chinmaya Missions that can be found across the globe. Some are doctors, others are teachers, and many are students who come to experience India experientially by volunteering. Kshama Didi ("Didi" is an affectionate name-suffix meaning "sister") assigns them work according to their capabilities. Most go back fulfilled and feeling that they have experienced the joy of helping others (Handy & Kassam, 2007).

Individual Narrative: Ravi

Ravi Danesh appears to be one of the many ambitious young men one encounters in the area of technology. He works in the IT division of a bank in Canada. However, Ravi is more than just another young IT professional devoted to his work. He has been connected to the Chinmaya Mission in Toronto most of his life. This is because his mother is a devoted member who has frequented the Mission and offered her accounting services from the early days when it began under the aegis of the charismatic founder, Swami Chinmayananda, up until today when it operates under the leadership of Swami Tejomayanada. Although Ravi has a tenuous connection to India through the links of the Mission as well as by virtue of the fact that Ravi is of Indian origin, he had never been to India and did not speak any Indian languages. In April 2000, Ravi decided to visit India. This was largely meant to be a "roots" trip to see the land of his ancestors, although he was also motivated by his enthusiasm for the activities of the Chinmaya Mission. He had heard about the great work that Kshama Didi was doing in Sidhabari, with the goal of transforming the lives of villagers and helping them to find sustainable means of livelihood. Curious, he decided to visit the place and see what was happening firsthand.

Ravi took pains to clarify that he "was not your typical volunteer" from Toronto. Some of the youth of the Chinmaya Mission in Toronto applied to spend their summer holidays interning as volunteers for CORD. Ravi did not intend to make this sort of formal commitment and simply planned to drop in to observe the rural development schemes in action.

After arriving in India and touring several other places, Ravi visited Sidhabari as planned. He stayed there for a few days and observed the many income-generating schemes being implemented. He noticed that micro-banking had helped many of the women as well as the elders of the community to meet their needs. However, he also noticed that many of the youth were unemployed. Because Ravi was a "dot-com" man, he began thinking about ways to get the youth involved in technology, and when Kshama Didi visited Toronto the following year, he talked to her about bringing used computers to Sidhabari. After obtaining Kshama Didi's approval, Ravi managed to collect 10 used computers as donations. He planned to pay for their shipment to Sidhabari before setting off on his upcoming travels, which included a trip to the project site in India. When he reached Sidhbari toward the end of this trip, he would help set them up.

It seemed like a simple, straightforward plan. He did not anticipate the bureaucratic battles that would ensue with the customs people in India. At that time, the NGOs did not command the respect that they do today. They were not seen as worthy of receiving their donations duty-free. Ravi argued with the customs people who eventually lowered the cost but did not waive it altogether. Ravi found their attitude upsetting. Instead of facilitating a shipment of free computers, which were going to a certified charity, the customs officials were imposing prohibitively high duties that almost made the whole enterprise futile. Eventually, however, the computers were shipped off to Sidhabari.

Over time, Ravi made it back to Sidhabari himself, where he found that Kshama Didi had allocated some CORD staff to help him set up the computers. He also discovered a group of young children, ranging in age from 11 years to the late teens, all anxious to be a part of his team. A garage in the village had been reserved for Ravi's work. There, with the CORD staff and his group of young children, Ravi began teaching them how to assemble computers from scratch. Once the computers were assembled, they set about making the place presentable. Swami Tejomayananda, the spiritual leader of the Chinmaya Organization, inaugurated the computer center.

Ravi remembers the frantic preparations in the little garage in the village where, initially, nothing seemed to go right. The electricity was simply not geared to power computers and, in the process of setting them up, Ravi and his team managed to blow out all the fuses. Now they had to rely on local resources, such as batteries and makeshift electronic outlets, which they managed to put to good use. Somehow, they managed to get the place in working order by the planned date of October 13, when all of the villagers came out for the grand opening of the computer center, and Ravi was asked to say a few words. He still remembers how he sincerely emphasized that he was glad he could be of some help, insisting that he had benefited from his volunteering because he felt so good that he could be of benefit to others.

Once the computer center was running well, the youth decided to form an organization called Yuva se Yuva (Youth to Youth). The idea was that the youth of the village would run the computer lab. They would charge people for using the computers and they would offer computer classes to the other villagers and charge a nominal fee for this. Soon, the youth were learning how to run the computer center like a business and were setting up a schedule for computer use: the elders would use the computer in the day time, the children would follow after school, whereas the disabled would get the computers for part of the weekend. Ravi believes that his role was limited to teaching the children everything he knew about computers. After this, the youth simply took over and ran the place.

Ravi reflects on how much his first trip to India in 2000 opened his eyes to the extent of want and poverty faced by many in the country. He remembers how poor women would tap his shoulder and ask for some money. He saw the children running around the streets with little to wear, looking to scavenge whatever they could find. Ravi was moved and wanted to do something. He believes that his reaction stemmed from a natural human tendency: if you feel you can do something to help, then you "must" do it. For Ravi, this is the essence of volunteerism.

Although Ravi's first trip to India was more of an exploratory trip, his next trip had a defined purpose. Although he went for only a week and a half and did not speak the local language, this time he had a mission, and he was able to teach the youth and the staff how binary numbers work using pictures. The young people learned quickly and soon figured out how computers talk to each others in 1s and 0s. They also soon understood the different parts of the computers. Ravi was pleased that he could connect with these people despite language barriers. He remembers how one young girl could not afford the nominal fees for the classes. Instead, she drew a beautiful picture and offered it in place of the fee. Her gratitude was immense when she was accepted in the class.

Two things that have stayed with Ravi from his trip to India are the appreciation of the village people for the help they received and the young people's quick intelligence while learning things that were foreign to them. They remain strong motivating factors that propel Ravi into wanting to do more for the village people and to stay involved in fundraising through walkathons and other events. Ravi thinks that he might replicate his efforts at another CORD project in Orissa, a state in east India. Or he may simply enhance what he had already done in Sidhabari. He is not sure where he will go next. However, he is sure of one thing: he will continue volunteering his services in fundraising and will venture out to teach other groups of underprivileged youth how to put computers together so that they can earn their own livelihood.

Commentary

All three of the voluntary organizations profiled profess to be secular in their outlook. This is due both to practical concerns and to a clearly genuine belief that the disadvantaged of all communities are worthy of help and attention. Despite this, religious identity and religious teachings both serve to varying degrees as important elements in framing the mission of the organizations and in encouraging many of the volunteers and donors attracted to such groups to donate their time and money to them over other potential rivals. For example, CORD is an extension of the Chinmaya Mission, which has the aim of explaining Vedanta (the teachings of the ancient Hindu scriptures, the Vedas) to the general public. CORD volunteers are generally members of the Chinmaya Mission who are following the prescripts of *seva*. Likewise, although EHCM helps people of all castes and creeds, it is a headed by Reverend Joshua who is an ordained priest and most of the main actors are Christians and motivated to some degree by Christian teachings. Rahat seems the most distanced from religion; however, its main source of funding is *zakat*, the religious nature of which is a reflection of the motivation of its donors, and the direct beneficiaries of its programs are largely Muslim. On the other hand, it is worth noting that it is not always the case that organizations such as those profiled are served only by volunteers from the community with which the organization is most associated with. For example, we find Hindu and Parsi doctors and teachers volunteering their time to helping the poor and the needy clients of EHCM, despite its explicit association with Christianity.

Although this is not a complaint one often hears in reference to Muslim and Hindu voluntary organizations, it is not uncommon to hear accusations that Christian voluntary groups often tie their services to an implicit condition requiring conversion to Christianity. Organizations such as GEMS, discussed earlier in the chapter, which state a prioritization of "church planting" over social services, no doubt encourage this perspective. However, in our interviews, EHCM took great pains to emphasize that their main goal was not to spread Christianity but to help those in need. Only once these worldly needs are fulfilled and then only if there is a demand for spiritual fulfillment, are beneficiaries told about the teachings of Jesus Christ. Perhaps it is because of this prioritization that the organization has been able to secure volunteers of other faiths and the support of others, like Vasant, who profess an inclination toward interfaith teachings and celebrate all religious festivities.

It is interesting to note that most of the volunteers we talked with in the three NGOs professed to volunteer for the same reasons that many volunteers for secular organization serve: because it makes them feel good. However, this general "feel-good factor" is sometimes identified with a sense of satisfaction in serving God through service to His creatures. The volunteers also commented on the feeling of belonging that comes from being a part of a larger community, which is an important motivating factor for many individuals who volunteer with secular organizations as well. In the end, perhaps it does not matter if the impetus to create a nonprofit organization or to volunteer for one is based on religious convictions or an enlightened humanism. What does matter is that such actions lead to the benefit of the less fortunate and, ultimately, of society as a whole.

7

The Value of Volunteering: What Is It Worth?

Introduction

One may assume, given the ubiquitous nature of volunteering, that it has some social or personal value. However, the questions of what this value is, who gets the benefits, and who incurs the costs are more complex. A number of scholars have estimated the value of volunteering in different countries. The most recent of these efforts comes from the Johns Hopkins University's Comparative Nonprofit Sector Project, which provides valuations of volunteering for a number of countries at the aggregate level. Country estimates range from US$109,012.6 million for the United States to US$7.3 million for Slovakia. In this scheme, the value of volunteer work in India is estimated to be US$1,355.9 million. Although these aggregate values help us understand the comparative picture globally, the study lacks information at the organizational level, which would be useful for management practices (Salamon, Sokolowski, & Associates, 2004).

In this chapter, we elaborate on the methods for assessing the value of volunteerism. In doing so, several questions arise: Who benefits from volunteering? Do benefits primarily accrue to the volunteers themselves, in terms of improved self-image or reputation or to the recipients? Should it be considered a leisure activity for the volunteer, albeit one that may sometimes provide marginal benefits to others? Should we be concerned with volunteers' motives or should we focus only on measuring the potential value of their work to the public good? And why is it important to put a monetary value on volunteering? Perhaps we should simply view volunteer contributions as a gift. Before addressing these questions, we will discuss why it is important to consider this issue. Then we will explore the competing theories and methodologies that attempt to estimate the value of the volunteer hour.

Making the Case for Valuing the Volunteer Hour

It is common for the NGOs to exclude the contribution of volunteers from their financial statements due to the absence of a financial exchange component for volunteer labor. Scholars of social accounting have made cogent arguments suggesting that the NGOs that allow the contribution of volunteers to remain invisible are doing their organizations a disservice in the long run (Mook, Quarter, & Richmond, 2007). These scholars have provided a critique of conventional accounting practices, charging that they miss what is of value to society by focusing solely on those exchanges that have market value, while ignoring the social and environmental impacts of such exchanges. If volunteers create value, the authors argue, then it must be made visible to everyone with an interest in the NGO's activities, including the volunteers themselves, the organization, the funders who can then see how their monetary donations go much further when coupled with the donated time of volunteers, and the general public who often clamor to know what NGOs are doing for public betterment. To address this problem, they have devised a method of social accounting that expands the traditional financial statements of organizations to take account of volunteer labor.

It is especially important that volunteer contributions to the NGOs are not ignored because volunteer labor is such a ubiquitous and important resource. Salamon et al. (2004) documented the importance of volunteer labor to the NGOs in a 2004 study and found that in the 36 countries studied, volunteer labor represented, in terms of hours, the equivalent of 20.2 million full-time jobs, valued at US$316 billion.

The Corporation for National and Community Service (CNCS) (2010) in the United States found that in 2009, 63.4 million volunteers contributed 8.1 billion hours of volunteer service (CNCS, 2010) or the equivalent of 3.9 million full-time equivalent positions. Such resources, thus, represent a valuable contribution that sustains NGOs and their local communities, despite the fact that it is completely absent from the usual accounting statements.

Moreover, despite the scale of their contributions, few countries include volunteer contributions in their national accounts, even though many encourage their populations to engage in volunteering. (Canada is one of the few countries that includes volunteers in the national accounts.) At the organizational level, many NGOs relying on volunteers acknowledge their contribution by way of a footnote in annual reports with few estimating their value in financial terms. This leads not only to inaccurate accounting, but to a lack of information upon which to base decisions affecting the NGOs and the communities they serve.

It is also important that some attempt be made to determine the value of volunteer labor because utilizing volunteers is often done at some cost to an organization. As part of the growing pressure for accountability and transparency in the voluntary sector and reflecting the increasing demands on its limited resources, more and more volunteer program coordinators are being asked to explain their program expenditures and justify their program budget requests. It is often assumed that there is a positive return on volunteer involvement, justified with the reasoning that if volunteers were not a net gain to the organization, organizations would not use them. However, it is rare that any attempt is made to test this assumption. Although volunteers provide free labor, they also represent a cost to their organizations through recruitment, screening, training, and other expenses that come with the use of volunteers. They may also divert the time and attention of paid staff from other activities they could be engaging in. This impact increases as the number of volunteers in an organization grows and their use is professionalized, with the bureaucracy restructured to meet their needs and paid staff hired to supervise them. These costs are even more significant when volunteers engage in episodic volunteering, which is increasing in popularity. All of this makes it imperative that organizations consider carefully the net benefits or costs that their volunteers represent. Recognizing this, an increasing number of organizations are starting to count volunteer hours and to consider the costs and benefits involved in their use (Handy & Srinivasan, 2005; Mook et al., 2007).

Valuing Volunteer Time: Methods and Debates

It is generally assumed that the individual volunteer acts rationally, making the decision to begin or to stop volunteering based on his or her perceived benefits and costs (Wolff, Weisbrod, & Bird, 1993). Organizations using volunteers are also assumed to be rational; they assess the contribution of volunteer labor and balance it with the costs involved. Ideally speaking, the NGOs should seek to input volunteer labor until the marginal benefits to the NGO are equal to the marginal costs of volunteer labor. However, there are many factors that complicate the achievement of this idealistic equilibrium. For example, as previously mentioned, calculations are hard to make in the absence of an accounting method that allows the NGOs to measure all of the costs entailed in the use of volunteer labor. Furthermore, organizational constraints may limit the use of volunteers even where they may be cost effective (e.g., union regulations, which prevent volunteers from encroaching upon work done by paid labor). Another complicating factor is that many of the benefits of volunteer labor, such as spillover effects to the community (i.e., volunteers acting as goodwill ambassadors for the organization in the community), may be difficult, if not impossible, to measure accurately.

One method that may be used in attempts to measure the value of the volunteer hour is setting this value to the amount it would cost the organization to replace the volunteer with a paid staff member. This is known as the "replacement cost method." It is an intuitively attractive method of valuing volunteer labor and one often used by the NGOs. Another approach, which is the most commonly used technique in western countries, is the "industry wage method." This method uses the average wages (plus benefits) of a worker in the paid sector of the industry as a unit of comparison. For example, if the NGO is involved in providing health care, then the value per hour of volunteer work at the NGO would be the average hourly wages of a health-care worker in the economy.

Both of these wage-based methods of determining the value of volunteer labor are problematic in an important way. The simple example of a volunteer coffee server may be used to illustrate this potential difficulty. The aforementioned methods suggest that the value of the time of a volunteer who serves coffee should be equal to an estimate of the cost of hiring a professional coffee server. Both methods assume that the NGO would continue to provide the same level of services if they did not have access to volunteer labor. However, it is possible that if the NGO were to face real costs of providing such a service, it might choose to have a self-serve coffee bar rather than employ an individual to serve coffee, which would likely represent a much lower expense in the long run. Thus, because the NGOs facing budgetary pressures would not necessarily take advantage of all the services being provided at relatively no cost by volunteers if they only had access to paid labor, these methods would likely overestimate the value of the benefits received by the NGO.

In contrast, some scholars have argued that these economic methods of valuing volunteer time are not useful in the context of the NGOs because they "underestimate" rather than overestimate the value of such contributions. Linda Graff asks:

> What is a park worth?
>
> What is a police department worth?
>
> To answer either of these questions, one would not take the number of hours worked by the park workers/police officers, multiply their hours by their average wage, and claim that to be the worth of the park or the police department. It is clear that that calculation is what it costs to generate the value of the park/police department, not its actual value. (Graff, 2010)

Graff suggests caution in using the replacement wage method because, according to her, this type of valuation actually serves to "mask" the real value of volunteer involvement. She asks the reader how they might assign the value of the volunteer hours spent in certain scenarios. We offer some as food for thought (Graff, 2010, p. 19):

- "A volunteer who spends time at the bedside of a dying child?"
- "400 citizens who turn out to find a little girl lost in the swamp (and they are successful!)?"
- "Environmentalists collaborating to clean up a stream bed, preserve the watershed, rehabilitate the sport fishery, and thereby revive the previously failing tourist industry in the surrounding area?"
- "The money collected by volunteers of the arthritis society, which is largely responsible for funding research on successful joint replacement."

Thus, Graff argues that when one considers the multiple beneficiaries of volunteer work (the organization, its clients, the volunteers, and the public at large), the wage replacement method does not capture all the benefits and, thereby, underestimates the real value of volunteer work.

Although we accept that the estimated monetary value of a volunteer's time alone is not a sufficient measure of the value, we also acknowledge that some estimation of volunteer labor is required in order to give a better picture of the value added to the NGO's services in a community. The relevant question is: if paid labor was used to substitute for volunteer labor in the scenarios proposed by Graff above, then would the impact or valuation of the services be different? Clearly, wages—to the hospice worker, search and rescue teams, environmental and sanitation workers, and professional fundraiser—would be a fair representation of value under our current accounting systems, although we agree that this may not represent the true total value to society of acts such as giving emotional support to a dying child or finding a lost little girl.

Expanded Value Statement

Although it suffers from some of the potential problems discussed before, the Expanded Value Added Statement (EVAS) developed by Mook et al. (2007) may be the best tool available for capturing the value created by NGOs and understanding the contribution of its multiple stakeholders. It recognizes the uniqueness of the NGO contribution by focusing on both economic and social impacts instead of just the "bottom line" of financial surpluses or deficits. The EVAS is able to identify key aspects of an NGO's functioning that are not apparent from conventional financial statements alone. The EVAS, they argue, must document the value of unpaid labor, i.e., the labor that is generally provided by volunteers. Mook et al. (2007), although acknowledging the problems with using this method, suggest that unpaid labor is best valued at what it would cost the organization to replace its volunteers with paid staff and continue the services currently provided by a volunteer. For this estimation, they rely on the volunteer value published by the Independent Sector (2008) or on the actual wages for the area in which the NGO is located, if available.[1]

The EVAS builds on the progressive, although still marginal, practice of mainstream accounting called the Value Added Statement. As Burchell, Clubb, and Hopwood (1985, p. 388) state:

> Value added has the property of revealing (or representing) something about the social character of production, something which is occluded by traditional profit and loss accounting. Value added reveals that the wealth created in production is the consequence of the combined effort of a number of agents who together form the co-operating team.

For example, the value added created by a cake-making company is calculated by taking the difference between the price the cake is sold for and the cost of the materials that went into making the cake. Therefore, if

---

[1]In the United States, where Mook et al.'s examples are based, these values may be obtained from the United States Bureau of Labor Statistics National Compensation Survey (Bureau of Labor Statistics, 2008).

a cake sold for ₹100 and the materials cost ₹45, the value added would be ₹100 minus ₹45 = ₹55. That value added is then distributed to the workers, owners, and government (i.e., through taxes).

However, one drawback of the Value Added Statement is that it concentrates on those items that have established market values and does not include those items that have no clear market value, such as social and environmental services. Organizations have social impacts as well as economic ones. The EVAS considers all impacts that have occurred as a result of making the cake. Thus, the EVAS takes the Value Added Statement and adapts it. For example, in the case of the NGOs, the EVAS statement will include the nonmarket value of using volunteers.

The EVAS is not intended to replace existing financial statements, but rather to be presented alongside them. By synthesizing traditional financial data with other data, the EVAS is another instrument for integrating the dynamics of an organization and one that shows great potential for focusing attention on value creation and use.

Creating an EVAS

There are two parts to an EVAS: *(a)* the calculation of value added by an organization and *(b)* its distribution to stakeholders. Determining the market value of the outputs of a for-profit firm is relatively uncomplicated—it is simply the amount of revenues received through sales. However, NGOs' revenues are typically seen as inputs, whereas the term "outputs" is generally used to mean the direct products of its activities—e.g., the services it provides, such as "free" tutoring for 50 children. Determining the market value for the outputs of an NGO is challenging because the service is given for free. In order to assign a comparative market value to the volunteers of nonprofit organizations, we look to the market to find a comparative market value for similar activities.

The adoption of new accounting models such as the EVAS is a complex process; before implementing such a model, an NGO would need to consider realities, such as what resources are available to keep track of volunteer tasks and hours as well as creating an accounting policy for the organization. There is no doubt that such a methodology might be challenging for many NGOs, in part, because of the costs involved in tracking hours and tasks. Moreover, the dearth of published values of volunteer time or easily available market replacement values makes such calculations difficult. However, acknowledging volunteers to be important assets by accounting for their contributed hours in financial statements will go a long way toward producing more accurate statements for NGOs utilizing volunteer labor. It would also be a positive step toward giving the volunteer contribution the respect it deserves.

Narratives

Organizational Narrative: Hypothetical Case Study

We illustrate here the social accounts of a hypothetical NGO to give the reader a flavor of how volunteer contributions can be included in an accounting statement. Please note that all numbers and the organization itself are fictional and used for illustrative purposes only. The hypothetical NGO we discuss is READ (Reading English for Adults with Disabilities), which is a professional volunteer-based organization that assists functionally literate adults with handicaps who want to learn English language skills. READ is located in Mumbai and has the mission of targeting physically handicapped adults who suffer due to their disability and cannot easily access traditional language classes to learn English. The organization teaches English because of the linguistic diversity of Mumbai and because English is the working language among many of the middle and upper classes in the city. Fluency in English is helpful in securing jobs, especially those linked to the growth of the IT sector as well as the business process outsourcing industry.

People with physical disabilities often face difficulties to find affordable individually tailored opportunities that accommodate their disabilities. READ offers its language services free of charge to people with physical disabilities who are residents of Mumbai. It engages volunteers to provide one-on-one or small group tutoring to adults with disabilities who lack English language skills. Completely run by volunteers for nearly seven years, READ hired its first staff person in 1987. By the time of their 20th anniversary in 2000, READ had received contributions of time from 700 volunteers who had served over 2,500 students. Currently, READ has one full-time paid staff member and 204 volunteers. Volunteers logged in over 18,000 hours and taught 162 students during the last fiscal year. Tutors and students meet at mutually convenient locations throughout the area, such as libraries, cafés, churches, schools, community centers, and other public buildings.

The program began in 1980 and was created by three female friends as a project for disabled adults in the Colaba area where they lived. In 1987, it was registered as an NGO with the Maharashtra government. It has a board of seven members who meet three times a year and has four working committees that deal with:

1. resources: fundraising and volunteer recruitment,
2. preparation of literacy materials and training,
3. purchase of books, and
4. oversight on financial matters.

The working committees meet as required, generally 6 to 12 times a year depending on the issues that arise, and work closely with the staff member. All board and committee members are volunteers.

The paid staff member deals with assigning volunteers to students, taking care of the logistics, fielding phone call and e-mails, finding grant opportunities, and other day-to-day business as it arises. The staff person ensures the smooth running of the daily tutoring schedules, making sure that students and volunteers meet up, and arrange for transportation for the students who need it. READ has been successful in raising the required funds for teaching basic English reading and writing skills to adults with disabilities.

READ gets referrals from many hospitals and doctors' offices as well as by word of mouth. The impact that READ makes on the lives of people by offering them English language skills cannot be totally captured in a financial statement, regardless of the sophistication of the measures employed. There are certain side products or positive externalities in the production of language skills that cannot be captured or measured with numbers and that manifest themselves in the self-esteem and confidence that project beneficiaries gain by becoming literate in English. However, using a replacement cost method of analysis as a best estimate for volunteer value, the financial statements of READ provide a more accurate picture of the value added created by the organization than traditional accounting statements.

One way of looking at the significance of volunteer contributions is to examine the proportion of volunteers to the overall human resources of the organization. Based on the estimate of 18,360 volunteer hours contributed by the tutors and a work week of 40 hours (2,080 per year), volunteers contributed almost 8.8 full-time equivalent (FTE) positions for the fiscal year ending June 30, 2007. Volunteer activities account for nearly 90 percent of READ's human resources (Figure 7.1). This means that, including volunteer contributions, READ has the equivalent of 8.8 FTE unpaid staff members working alongside its one paid staff member. In other words, almost nine times more labor is required in the production of READ's goods and services than the traditional accounting statement (that references only the one full-time staff person) shows.

Figure 7.1: Proportion of Total Hours by Volunteer Tutors and Paid Staff for READ

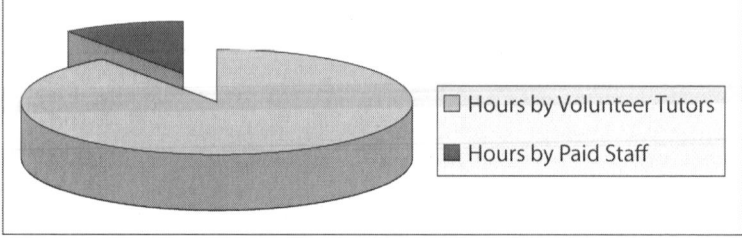

Source: Authors.

Estimating the Value Added by Volunteers

In Table 7.1, we employ a replacement cost method that uses a value of volunteer time based on the average hourly fees for tutoring in Mumbai (using ₹300 per hour as a conservative estimate) to estimate volunteer contribution. The rates for board and committee meetings are estimated at ₹500 per hour, which is the going rate for professional time of board meetings.

READ Community Contributions: Tutoring occurs in public places, including libraries, churches, schools, and community centers. The groups or organizations, which own these buildings in the community, thus, provide resources in the way of space for these interactions at no charge to the NGO. In the fiscal year represented

Table 7.1: Estimated Replacement Cost of Volunteer Hours by Job Classification[2]

		Hours	Rate (in ₹)	Total
Board and Committees	Meetings	805	500	402,500
Board and Committees	Preparations	310	500	155,000
204 tutors, 3 hours a week, 30 weeks per year	Tutoring	18,360	300	55,080,000
Tutors	Preparations			
204 tutors, 0.5 hours a week, 30 weeks per year		3,060	300	918,000
Total		**187,535**		**56,555,500**

by this case, tutors met with learners for a total of 18,360 hours. If READ had to rent space for these interactions, using a conservative rate of ₹25 per hour, they would have to expend additional financial resources of ₹459,000.

READ Financial Resources: READ has been successful in receiving financial assistance from a variety of sources, including donations from board members and the fruits of fundraising efforts. In total, the organization received ₹33,890,100 of which 51 percent came from a government grant, 12 percent from the Mumbai Women's Club Trust, 16 percent from fundraising events by the volunteers, and another 21 percent from a wealthy patron who chose to donate anonymously (see Figure 7.2a).

When considering the financial and nonfinancial resources of the organization, volunteer hours account for 63 percent of the total (Figure 7.2b). This figure shows that volunteer contributions provide the organization with a significant resource that should be counted in its overall performance. Using a traditional accounting method, which

[2]The number of volunteer hours by board and committee members as well as other volunteers would be provided by the NGO. In this example, they are fictional numbers used for exposition purposes only.

Figure 7.2: Resources of READ

a. Financial Resources

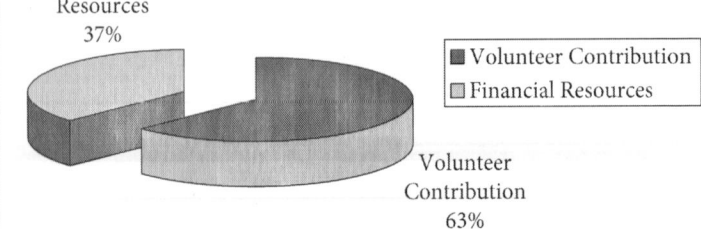

Fundraizing
16%

Donations
12%

Donations
Government
Anonymous gift
Fundraizing

Anonymous gift
21%

Government
51%

b. Financial and Volunteer Resources

Financial
Resources
37%

Volunteer Contribution
Financial Resources

Volunteer
Contribution
63%

Source: Authors.

does not recognize the value of the contribution of these volunteers, yields a very different picture of the resources of the organization.

Putting Together the EVAS

In the case of READ, the amount paid for employee wages and benefits of ₹375,000, depreciation of ₹3,556, and the estimated comparative market value of volunteer hours ₹56,555,500 are added together to come up with a total expanded value added of ₹56,934,056 (shown in the column labeled "Combined;" see Table 7.2). Externally purchased goods and services are calculated by taking the total expenses for the period and subtracting wages, benefits, and depreciation. Using the figures derived for expanded value added and externally acquired

Table 7.2: Expanded Value Accounting Statement (Partial)*

Expanded Value Added Statement (Partial*)	July 1, 2006 to June 30, 2007		
	Financial	Social	Combined
Outputs	33,890,100	57,014,500	90,904,600
Less external goods and services	33,511,544	459,000	33,970,544
Total Value Added	**378,556**	**56,555,500**	**56,934,056**
Wages and benefits	375,000		375,000
Society volunteer contributions		56,555,500	56,555,500
Organization depreciation	3,556		3,556
Value Added Distributed	**378,556**	**56,555,500**	**56,934,056**

Note: *The statement is partial in that not all of the impacts/outputs of the organization are reflected here; this is illustrative to show the impact of volunteers in an NGO.

goods and services, we can then get a value for the organization's out puts by adding these two amounts together, which equals ₹56,934,056 (shown in the "Combined" column).

As is shown in the EVAS for READ in Table 7.2, traditional accounting significantly underreports the resources going into the organization and the value added it creates. In the EVAS, the value added reported is ₹56,934,056, a significant increase compared to ₹378,556 using traditional methods.

The EVAS accounting system also highlights that there are more resources contributing to READ's activities than merely financial. Traditional financial statements would only show financial resources totaling ₹33,890,100. The EVAS also includes volunteer contributions of ₹56,555,500 and community contributions of ₹459,000.

Regarding the percentages, financial contributions are only 37 percent of the total resources, volunteers contributed 63 percent, and the community contributed less than 1 percent.

Discussion

Using the case study of READ, this chapter has shown the usefulness of the EVAS in understanding the impact of a voluntary organization on its community. Social goods and services that are not given a monetary value are often a large part of an NGO's operations. Only by taking these goods and services, including volunteer services, into account do we get an accurate picture of the true value of the performance of organizations like READ and of the contributions made by their volunteers and board members. In our example, the EVAS helps various stakeholders, particularly volunteers, see what value they have added to READ—over 90 percent of the value added! It is important to make this contribution visible as it helps all the stakeholders understand the value created by the organization. Volunteers, e.g., benefit from seeing a clear record of their impact on the outcome of the organization. Other stakeholders can also appreciate and understand the substantial volunteer input without which READ and organizations like it could not provide anywhere near the same level of service at current funding levels.

Difficulties regarding the assignment of monetary values to volunteer time and other unpaid resources do pose challenges in the use of the EVAS. However, such limitations are not unique to the EVAS. Similar problems occur whenever accountants and economists attempt to accurately identify, measure, and quantify social and environmental indicators in the context of sustainable performance (Ranganathan, 1999; White & Zinkl, 1999). Although it is relatively easy to capture the equivalent market value of nonmarket inputs, it is more difficult to capture the outcomes.

Despite the ubiquitous presence of NGOS, policy makers, in general, pay less attention to them than for-profit organizations when making policy decisions. The value added to the economy of NGOs is generally not reflected in macro-level economic data such as Gross Domestic Product (GDP). Social accounting methods generally, and the EVAS in particular, make visible some of this otherwise ignored value and allow policy makers to see a clearer return on their investment in nonprofits.

8

Old and New Trends in Volunteering: Virtual Volunteers, What Next?

Introduction

In the previous chapters, we discussed volunteering by different groups of people in different contexts and offered some theoretical insights into conceptualizing what it means to be a volunteer. Although we have seen great variety in the manifestations of volunteerism, our discussion, by no means, covers the kaleidoscopic nature of volunteering in India. Indeed, the word "voluntary" suggests that individuals are free to be creative in conceptualizing the way in which they will offer their labor to an organization and that the organization can define the nature of the volunteer work to suit the volunteer and the organizational need.

The nature of volunteer work changes along with people and organizations to reflect the changing societies and technologies. In this chapter, we first consider a 1975 study (the only one of its kind to date) that focused on understanding the nature of volunteering in India nearly 34 years ago. We then turn our attention to the changing patterns of volunteerism, which involve both an intensification of old forms of volunteering, such as service clubs and the introduction of new forms of volunteering based on changing lifestyles and the opportunities created by new technologies.

Traditional Patterns

Many NGOs rely on volunteers for labor in order to provide their goods and services to their clients and the public at large. The willingness of volunteers to work without monetary reward makes them an increasingly valuable resource for cash-strapped NGOs with ambitious visions. It also poses some unique challenges because volunteers, unlike paid staff, can vote with their feet at little personal cost. If not engaged or motivated to volunteer at an NGO, they can leave at a moment's notice without financial penalty. Because the demand almost always exceeds the supply of volunteers, volunteers can be as choosy as they wish. This provides the NGOs with real challenges in recruiting, managing, and retaining their volunteers. Volunteers, as we noted earlier, are not without cost to the organization either. Real resources need to be spent to recruit, manage, and retain them. So the NGOs also have to be careful in using volunteer labor: even free labor is not always useful to an NGO.

One of the few examples of earlier research on Indian volunteering is a study of the country's human service volunteers that was conducted in 1975. This study explored many aspects of volunteering, which we discuss in this section. Lalitha (1975) examined the nature of volunteer work in social service agencies and the reciprocal relationship between the volunteer and the agency staff. Each party in the transaction comes to the table with his or her own needs and expectations, and these must be reconciled with those of the other parties involved.

We look at her findings from interviews conducted with 856 volunteers in 390 agencies in nine major cities in India. Most agencies used few volunteers; the average ratio between paid staff and volunteers was 3:1, and a quarter of the agencies surveyed did not have any volunteers. Although the study is somewhat dated, the picture it paints of the Indian volunteer is interesting. It dispels myths that were common at the time, and that are still repeated today regarding who volunteers and why.

For example, Lalitha (1975) writes: "Contrary to common belief and some extent our own expectations, there were an equal number of men and women volunteers in our sample" (p. 50) and that "generally there is not much difference among men and women in the choice of service" (p. 51). There were few elderly volunteers (16 percent were over the age of 55) and nearly half of them (49 percent) were between 25 and 44 years of age. Youth represented a somewhat smaller percentage (14 percent), which was nonetheless higher than what the author expected, given the prevailing norms of volunteering in the mid-1970s. Even at this time, there were about 31 individuals who were volunteering under "volunteer abroad schemes." Perhaps this was a foreshadowing of the "voluntourism" we write about later in this chapter.

The study suggests that the social profile of a volunteer in India is not much different than that of volunteers found in other places. The respondents were, compared to the general population in the country, more educated and were predominantly of the middle- and upper- income groups. Most volunteers surveyed had been volunteering for their agencies for extended periods of time. The majority of them had participated in volunteer work for more than five years (58 percent). They volunteered anywhere from 5 to 20 hours a month, with 10 percent of them volunteering on a full-time basis. About 40 percent offered their services daily and an equal number came weekly. This trend surprised Lalitha (1975), who writes: "This again does not agree with the common belief that volunteers are not regular in their work" (p. 71).

When the respondents were asked why they volunteer, they gave mixed motives; however, the primary motives were altruistic in nature (34 percent), self-interested (25 percent), or work related (17 percent). This picture is not unlike what we find among the motives to volunteer in studies of other countries around the world.

Turning to the agencies, their response to the utilization and management of volunteers is interesting. Over two-thirds reported that their volunteers could substitute for their paid staff on either a permanent or temporary basis, suggesting that the volunteers were providing valuable services to the agencies. This is not surprising because many of the volunteers (48 percent) were highly trained professionals who worked as social workers, teachers, librarians, medical doctors, and nurses. Volunteers (85 percent) and agency personnel (70 percent) agreed that volunteer contributions had improved the delivery of services.

This is a snapshot of volunteers almost 30 years ago in human service agencies across India. We note that although there are many new trends in volunteering today (see ahead), the basic profile of volunteers has not changed much in the last few decades. The typical socioeconomic status of a volunteer remains higher than average, and volunteers continue to be primarily motivated by altruism. Moreover, although changing times may influence the type of work volunteers do, they continue to make a contribution to the organizations they serve. This is particularly true when both the organization and the volunteer make efforts to adapt volunteer assignments to reflect the resources available as well as the needs of the organization and the public at large.

Service Clubs

Lions and Rotary Clubs are service clubs that were founded in the United States in the early 1900s to promote business and social interests by providing services for the betterment of communities. Their service role later grew to meet the needs of the poor and needy within and outside their communities and, with this focus, they went international and began opening chapters in Europe, Asia, and Africa in the 1950s and 1960s. Although the focus of the clubs was service and fellowship, in the beginning, they primarily attracted local businessmen and independent professionals, bringing them together for lunches or dinners and often helping them to build their social and personal networks. This role was later downplayed, and most club members now prefer to see themselves as getting together to promote the collective good and doing charitable services for their communities (Charles, 1993).

Three clubs, Lions, Rotary, and Kiwanis, constitute the majority of service clubs that were exported to India, with a greater presence of Lions and Rotary Clubs and only a handful of Kiwanis Clubs (Charles, 1993). Although the clubs are distinct from one another and have minor differences in their structures and in what they do, one common feature of these service clubs is the many volunteer services performed by their members to help the needy and the vulnerable. In India, such services include initiating and participating in a variety of charitable programs, such as providing eyeglasses and cataract surgery, offering computer education classes, building village schools, and helping communities with projects, such as tree plantation, promoting traffic awareness to reduce accidents, and pollution control. These programs are generally funded through membership contributions and fundraising efforts. In some cases, the parent international club provides grants or matching funds to help the local service clubs with their volunteer service.

Service clubs in India have a long-standing presence in many communities, and their membership is often made up of well-respected and relatively affluent businessmen or other independent professionals and their spouses. Many of the charitable initiatives in urban centers receive their impetus from the proposals and actions of these service clubs. The growth in Rotary Clubs in India provides insight into the popularity of this genre of service volunteering, which is becoming ubiquitous in India.[1] In 1920, Calcutta became the home for the first Rotary Club on the Asian mainland. The growth of Rotary Clubs in India was slow for many years, and the presence it had, was largely due to the efforts of foreigners rather than of Indians (with a few exceptions). By 1947, when India obtained its

---

[1]The history of the Rotary Clubs in India was provided by Rotary Global History Committee member Florence Hui, March 24, 2006 (see RGHF, n.d.).

independence, there were 71 Rotary Clubs with a total membership of 3,121 members.

Following the British departure from India, the growth of Rotary Clubs continued to be slow, with only 54 clubs added in the first seven years following Independence. From the 1970s, however, the growth of Rotary Clubs in India gained momentum, and by the early 1980s, there were 899 Clubs in India with a membership of 35,172 Rotarians. In the late 1980s, there was an explosive growth in Rotary Clubs and another 362 were added. By the mid 1990s, India had 1,654 Rotary Clubs with a membership of 58,777 and by the late 1990s, there were 1,791 clubs in India with a total membership of 68,043.

The growth of Rotary Clubs in India in the last two decades has actually outstripped the growth of Rotary Clubs elsewhere in the world. Although world membership, which stood at 853,000 in 1980, had only climbed to 1,193,000 by 1998, the Rotary's strength in India grew from 35,000 to 68,000. In other words, when the world growth was about 40 percent, India recorded an astonishing 95 percent increase. At the present time, the number of Rotary Clubs in India is 2,896, with a membership of over 1,200,000 (RGHF, n.d.).

Some of this growth has been fueled by aging baby boomers, who have now matured and settled into financially comfortable careers or retirement, and are looking for ways in which to give back to their communities in the company of their peers. However, younger generations of businessmen and independent professionals have also been joining in order to make service commitments and social connections with successful baby boomers as they launch their own careers and businesses.

Umbrella Organizations Promoting Volunteering in NGOs

Volunteer Action Network India

National associations of NGOs play increasingly important roles in civil society. These umbrella groups seek to strengthen civil society through networking and mobilizing voluntary organizations to work toward common interests. Perhaps the largest and most significant of these organizations are Volunteer Action Network India (VANI) and Karmayog.

VANI was founded in 1988 and became a registered society in 1990. The organization's primary objectives are to build the capacity of the voluntary organizations of India and to set an agenda for the sector around which all such organizations can unite. The founders of the organization felt strongly that voluntarism represented "the power of sustainability and security" of the new democratic nation of India and a reminder of the society's pluralistic roots (VANI n.d.). Like the early Gandhian organizations (discussed in Chapter 2), VANI has encouraged the development of community self-sufficiency at the local level and has long advocated for a decentralization of government power. For example, it successfully lobbied the government to set apart sufficient funds for strengthening the local Panchayat Raj Institutions (PRIs) though training sessions for PRI representatives, and has since used these local government institutions to politically empower marginalized citizens. However, as was the case with the early Gandhian groups, this local focus in no way involved a toleration of narrow or communal outlooks, and VANI has had a leadership role in demonstrations advocating communal harmony at critical junctures, such as the period following the demolition of the Babri Masjid.

Recognizing the potentially vast implications, both positive and negative, of government policies on the functioning of the voluntary sector, VANI has also devoted considerable energy to encouraging NGO–government interaction, influencing relevant government policies, and helping the organizations in the voluntary sector respond to shifts in these policies. VANI's efforts to encourage more NGO–government interaction in India included the publication of *To Bring about Collaborative Relationship between Government and Voluntary Organisations* (Planning Commission, 1994), which was later adopted by the prime minister's office. The organization has also exerted pressure on the government to modify policies and laws viewed as detrimental to the functioning of India's voluntary sector, pushing for a softening of the FCRA (discussed in Chapter 2), which regulates foreign contributions to individuals and organizations in India, along with reevaluations of the Income Tax Act and the Societies Registration Act. Likewise, when the government initiated a structural adjustment program in India under pressure from the World Bank and the International Monetary Fund, VANI worked to increase awareness among voluntary organizations regarding its implications and also campaigned with the government to reconsider its budget.

VANI's efforts are not only focused on advocacy with the government, however, and the organization also expends considerable energy on encouraging the reform of voluntary organizations from within. For example, as early as the late 1980s, it participated in a Commonwealth Foundation project aimed at drafting guidelines for good practices by the NGOs. It has continued to participate in similar efforts by promoting the initiation of a Credibility Alliance in 2001, which advanced a set of norms for voluntary organizations.

The other major umbrella organization we profile, Karmayog, is an excellent example of how rapid changes in technology have impacted volunteering in a positive way. Karmayog (the organization translates its name as "selfless-service with love gives bliss") uses the Internet to broker volunteering among interested individuals and the NGOs. Established in 2004, Karmayog describes itself as "a unique free platform for concerned citizens—for social and civic issues" (see http://karmayog.org/). The organization connects citizens, NGOs, corporations, media, and government through online (and offline) methods. Its Web site has over 60,000 pages of information available in modules that represent hundreds of ongoing civic and social causes as well as a directory of the NGOs in India. The Web site also hosts online discussion groups in which over 40,000 people provide inputs on their experiences, concerns, opinions, ideas, news, and other matters dealing with the NGOs, volunteering, and civic and social causes. It includes links of resources for NGOs, including free materials, services, and advice for those running their own NGO or seeking to start one and even a list of potential donors. Karmayog's interests extend to the corporate sector as well, where it works with corporations to promote volunteering among their employees. Karmayog also conducts an annual evaluation of the CSR efforts of the 500 largest companies in India (discussed in Chapter 5).

Most significant for our purposes, Karmayog's Web site provides a wonderful online platform for individuals seeking volunteer opportunities and NGOs seeking volunteers. The NGOs registered with Karmayog are looking for volunteers in fields, such as software and Web development, fundraising, writing, publicity, networking, event management, investment advice, financial planning, Internet research, filing and office work, accounts, phoning, meeting people, fieldwork, translations, developing marketing materials, designing business plans, handling calls, responding to letters, computerizing data base, managing volunteers, and legal advice. Currently, 189 NGOs are registered with this service as are more than 2,100 volunteers in the Mumbai area alone. Although this brokering was initially limited to Mumbai and surrounding areas, the organization has now broadened its scope to meet growing demand. Along with the NGOs registered through its brokering service, Karmayog maintains an online list of over 18,500 NGOs across the country by geographical location and category of service (see http://karmayog.org/).

The organization also acts as a direct catalyst in initiating volunteer activity through its promotion of "59 Dream Community Projects for Mumbai." Karmayog suggests that several of Mumbai's problems have reached such "daunting levels" that they can only be resolved through concerted citizen initiative involving volunteerism. It goes on to list the 59 dream projects in various categories such as education and awareness, health and cleanliness, and hygiene, to name just a few. In each category are listed ways in which these projects can be initiated. For example, teaching poor children via volunteers is a suggested action under the education and awareness category. Volunteers are invited to send in their ideas to start new projects or to join any of the projects in their area by contacting Karmayog via e-mail.

The Internet and Virtual Volunteering

As Karmayog demonstrates, the Internet is an excellent resource for connecting potential volunteers with work opportunities. The Internet has also enabled many individuals to assist organizations without being physically present at the office or project site. Information and communication technologies (ICTs) and the Web 2.0, in particular, have radically changed the way both NGOs and their volunteer programs operate. There has been a rapid development of a new type of volunteering known as "Virtual Volunteering," which is attracting technologically savvy youth to participate in volunteer projects in India and to collaborate with others globally to make a difference. Although still a relatively new phenomenon, NGOs across the globe often now rely on virtual volunteers for many tasks that are easily done over the Internet such as translating, managing online Web site content, organizing campaigns, sending out information and communications to members, conducting online research, providing online mentoring, and facilitating the signing of petitions.

Virtual volunteering involves the provision of services via the Internet by volunteers using home or work computers. These services may include translating documents, sending out information and communications to members, conducting online research, providing online mentoring, fundraising and running campaigns, or the signing of petitions. The birth of this form of volunteering is dependent entirely on the Internet, which allows people to connect in ways not possible in the days of telephone and fax communication. According to Cravens (2000), the Internet is a vehicle for effective volunteer recruitment that can target different audiences. The opportunity that online volunteering provides for "volunteering in your pajamas" significantly widens the scope of volunteer opportunities available and offers particular benefits to those NGOs that provide 24-hour services, due to the prospect it offers of attracting volunteers from different time zones.

Cyberactivism has also grown and efforts of virtual volunteers to mobilize hundreds and thousands of individuals in campaigns to add signatures to petitions, send letters of protest, and turn out the vote have been immensely successful. The "Jaago Re! One Billion Votes" campaign is focused on encouraging the 18–30 age group to participate in elections and provides a Web site that helps individuals register to vote. The campaign was able to register over 340,000 in the five months of their operation and to lay the foundations of participatory democracy using virtual volunteers and the Internet. More recently, in February 2009, the successful "Pink Chaddi" campaign, mentioned in our introduction, was mounted by virtual volunteers against right-wing groups. The use of blogs and Facebook mobilized over 39,000 people within 10 days. Cyberactivism works rapidly and connects thousands of like-minded people easily, giving rise to successful Web-based activism. The YP foundation, a group targeted toward and founded by youth, has successfully used virtual volunteers to extend their reach to areas outside the city where they are based, in part through the use of Facebook as a social and political networking site (Mehta & Kumar, 2009).

Although cyberactivism may rely on individuals volunteering for a specific cause over the Internet for a project period, which can range from a short to an extended period of time, this type of volunteerism is generally episodic in nature and often single-issue based. Other forms of virtual volunteering that involve organizations with ongoing needs may rely on their volunteers to participate more consistently over an extended period of time. In this case, virtual volunteers, like traditional volunteers, need to be not only recruited, but managed and rewarded in order to keep them volunteering effectively. This may be a real challenge; however, as NGOs struggle to meet the growing demands of their members and clients with limited resources, virtual volunteering is particularly beneficial because it can bring many specialized services to the organization at reduced costs.

For many NGOs, the Internet has been a successful way of attracting volunteers who have not responded to the usual recruitment methods of volunteering, particularly introverted individuals who may hesitate to get involved because of social anxiety about going to new places and working among strangers (Handy & Cnaan, 2007). Volunteering over the Internet has also presented many opportunities to people of all age groups who simply find it appealing to volunteer without having to leave the comfort of their homes and who prefer great flexibility in their volunteer hours.

Modernity and the Episodic Volunteer

Some of the literature on volunteerism reflect on the ways in which volunteer labor supply shifts in response to broader processes of modernization, secularization, and individualization. This shift is commonly viewed as representing a transition from "traditional" or "collective" to "modern" or "individualized" types of involvement (Hustinx & Lammertyn, 2003; Lorentzen & Hustinx, 2007). As discussed in Chapter 2, modern volunteers often prefer short-term volunteering assignments or discrete task-specific volunteering projects that commit them to particular tasks or time periods rather than traditional long-term assignments that involve a greater commitment to the organization itself. Such volunteering, termed "episodic volunteering," has been increasing in popularity significantly in recent years (Handy, Brodeur, & Cnaan, 2006; MacDuff, 2004). In India and elsewhere, several factors are likely to be contributing to this change: increasing numbers of women joining the paid labor force, people changing jobs with greater frequency, mass media and culture becoming increasingly international, and the rapid erosion of barriers to accessing information and meeting people from outside one's social sphere.

Examples of episodic volunteers include someone who volunteers at a food bank for one day over Christmas, and someone who works at the same food bank and other seasonal charities for many days throughout the holiday season. It is likely that many organizations that rely on volunteers have a base of episodic volunteers who coexist alongside a base of long-term traditional volunteers. Brudney (2005) attempted to assess the scope of episodic volunteering in the United States based on data from the Independent Sector. He found that 31 percent of all volunteers can be defined as episodic volunteers. Although the existence of episodic volunteering is now well-acknowledged in the literature in the United States and certain other Western countries, there are no comprehensive studies or statistics relating to episodic volunteering in India. We have come across a number of examples of such volunteers in our research on women-led NGOs, however, and all of the aforementioned factors that encourage episodic volunteering are also relevant in the Indian context (Handy et al., 2006).

Young Indian professionals, whether working in IT or in other professions, are operating in an increasingly competitive marketplace, and they often find themselves short on time to pursue volunteering activities that put consistent demands on their free time. Thus, those who are interested in helping their communities and the vulnerable members of society, will often prefer to do so in the form of short-term or informal assignments.

This reluctance to commit to a long-term volunteer assignment is a response to lifestyle changes; if the NGOs want to take advantage of the services such individuals have to offer, they must find ways to enable them to volunteer on their own terms, such as organizing short-term projects that would allow volunteers to see a beginning and end to their commitment. This is perhaps particularly relevant for corporate volunteering, as employers often demand that employee volunteers juggle their volunteering tasks with other work-related demands on their time.

Tourism and Volunteering

The Voluntourists

A growing trend in international volunteering involves individuals serving not only outside their communities but outside of their countries as well. Such "voluntourism" brings foreigners to India (and other countries) for a period of anywhere from a week to a few years. Volunteer assignments vary depending upon the interests of the volunteer and the needs of the host organization, but commonly include projects related to ecological preservation or social and economic development (Sherraden et al., 2006). Voluntourism may be viewed not only as an interesting trend in volunteering, but also as a significant part of contemporary tourism (Mustonen, 2006). As travelers of all ages seek opportunities for unique, personal travel experiences, the popularity of volunteer tourism continues to grow.

In the past, volunteer travel typically meant a significant investment of time with volunteers often required to spend several weeks, months, or even years supporting a project. The volunteer projects were generally organized by religious congregations or through the outreach programs of government-supported initiatives such as the Peace Corps (the United

States of America) and CUSO (Canada). The new trend of voluntourism is beginning to take new forms, however, reflecting many of the same concerns that have led to episodic volunteering. In particular, voluntourism is increasingly structured in such a way as to allow individuals to combine their vacation time with service activities while still holding full-time employment in their countries of residence.

There exist a multitude of options for such "voluntourists" that mix small doses of volunteering in with their holiday travel. With such a wide variety of options, the question for many would-be voluntourists becomes, "How can I find a good volunteer travel program?" Although, as mentioned previously, this new trend is partly a response to lifestyle changes that imply diminished long-term loyalty to any one organization or cause, some voluntourists maintain their connection to their volunteer projects by raising money in their home countries and remitting these funds to the projects or organizations with which they volunteered.

Novelli's (2005) study of volunteer tourism opportunities showed that many of the top 10 destinations are Asian, African, Central, and South American countries with India being the top destination in terms of total number of volunteer tourism projects. Although no official statistics exist, the number of sites promoting volunteer opportunities combined with travel to India number in the millions. A recent Google search for sites catering to "volunteer in India" resulted in over 11 million results!

This is an example of one voluntourism opportunity offered by a company called Intrepid as described on the Web:[2]

Trip Valid: 01/01/2009 to 31/12/2009, Duration: 14 days (ex Chennai)

Highlights: Build infrastructure to support the community's needs, Teach in a rural school, Explore the Tamil Nadu region, Experience Indian village life, Make local friends, Join like-minded travellers to work as a team, Make a difference

Guarantee: Departure is guaranteed, subject to 4 people travelling

Group Size: Minimum 4, Maximum 16, Price: Prices from USD $1245

The following was posted as a blog to describe the trip:[3]

---

[2]From http://www.intrepidtravel.com/trips/HMA/brillianttrips, accessed March 21, 2009.

[3]From http://blog.brillianttrips.com/2009/02/volunteer-in-india-this-summer/, accessed August 14, 2010.

This summer, Intrepid is offering a 14 day volunteer project near Chennai, India, that allows participants to experience real Indian village life. Based in Tamil Nadu on the south-east coast of the Indian subcontinent, participants volunteer at a rural project among some of the poorest rural communities in the country. Time on this 14 day project is split between a building project and teaching at a local school. By working alongside local builders, staying in the community and spending time with the kids, participants will become an essential part of the community. Taking part in this unique experience will truly make a difference to an Indian community.

The project begins and ends in Chennai where visitors can get acquainted with the narrow streets and colorful bazaars or maybe stroll through historic George Town, home to the city's fort and India's oldest surviving British church. After a group meeting, participants leave the city behind and head along the coastline to the project village. Watch the waters of the Indian Ocean pound against the sand on this scenic journey, then enjoy a warm welcome from locals upon arrival. Settling in to the shared accommodation where facilities are basic, including cold-water showers and little or no electricity is all part of the adventure. Living like the locals is the best way to understand village life.

Days typically start early and participants will soon settle into a daily routine of rotating teaching and building. It's not all hard work and there is also plenty of free time to learn the language, play games with the kids, and get to know the villages. Perhaps you will even head off on weekend adventures further afield to discover secluded beaches, rural villages and little known corners of southern India that have barely been explored.

If you're interested in experiencing Indian village life this summer, start dates are May 9 and July 4. All meals are included while on the project site and participants stay in a multi-share group house. To book this experience, simply follow the Intrepid 5 step booking process that concludes by downloading your travel documents. Participants who complete this experience will not only make a difference; they will come back different.

This sort of project has an appeal that resonates with tourists of all ages who are seeking a deeper understanding of the places they visit and the opportunity to experience life in less widely travelled regions. In a recent study of individuals, who had participated in a volunteer vacation, participants were asked their main motive for participating in each of their volunteer tourism trips. Although respondents gave more than one motive for going on their trips, the primary and most often quoted motive was that "Participants desired a new experience" (Carter, 2008). It is often true that individuals who participate in volunteer tourism have had considerable experience traveling abroad.

It is not surprising that the Euro Monitor International has projected that voluntourism will be one of the fastest growing travel segments in the next three to four years. MSNBC and *Condé Nast Traveller* have shared preliminary results from their 2008 Voluntourism Survey in which they find that, of the more than 1,600 respondents surveyed, approximately one in five had taken at least one volunteer vacation. Of those who had not taken such a trip, nearly two-thirds said they would be very or somewhat likely to take one (Lovitt, 2008).

A 2008 study done by University of California at San Diego finds that the popularity of voluntourism is growing among the United States population. About 40 percent of Americans surveyed expressed openness to the idea of spending several weeks on a voluntourism project with 13 percent willing to make a commitment of one year. Although people in all stages of life may consider becoming "voluntourists," members of Generation X and Baby Boomers appear to prefer shorter assignments, whereas the Retiree Generation and Generation Y would like to help out for many weeks or an entire summer. This is likely a reflection of the greater amount of leisure time generally available to the latter groups.

Tourism-oriented NGOs are becoming increasingly relevant as an alternative and legitimate source of aid to many developing countries. The NGOs are now encouraging voluntourists to come from rich countries to help them meet their goals of poverty reduction and increasing social welfare among the poor. Such partnerships ensure direct community involvement for volunteers looking for experiential learning and also promise benefits to the communities in which the facilitating the NGOs and their volunteer helpers work. The NGOs participating in these partnerships are often involved in education and advocacy, areas where voluntourists can get involved easily without much training or loss of time.

Although trends in volunteering have shifted over the years, both in terms of the types of projects and organizations served and in terms of the degree of time and commitment involved, the essential nature of volunteerism, which involves the desire to be involved in social service for reasons other than monetary gain, remains constant. Although it is generally assumed that such activities benefit the organizations involved and society at large, measuring the extent of this benefit may be a tricky proposition, as we discussed in Chapter 7.

Volunteering in the Global Context: How Does India Compare Internationally?

Although we have focused on volunteering within India, it is worth considering how volunteering in India compares in a global context. As our voluntourism discussion suggests, volunteers are showing increasingly little regard for political borders. Volunteering is becoming a global activity, with volunteering trends in one country often significantly affecting those in other countries. There are, of course, cultural and historical factors unique to countries as well that also affect the direction in which voluntary action has developed. Few empirical studies have done comparative work on volunteering in different countries as thoroughly as that undertaken by Anheir and Salamon (1999) at the Johns Hopkins University. The University's Center for Civil Society Studies is actively engaged in documenting nonprofit sector and civil society issues across the world. As part of this effort, the Center has produced the first comprehensive comparative assessment of the size, structure, financing, and role of the nonprofit sector at the global level. This analysis includes a discussion of the scope of volunteering relative to the total work force in each country. This project, entitled "The Comparative Nonprofit Sector Project" (CNP), is the largest organized research project documenting and analyzing the scope and structure of nonprofit activity throughout the world. Currently, the findings are available for 36 countries across the world, including India. We use the study's findings to report on how India compares in the domain of volunteering relative to the other 35 countries in the project.

The work by Salamon and his colleagues at the CNP shows that volunteering is an important activity worldwide, with citizen participation averaging 10 percent of the adult population in the countries studied. Volunteer participation rates range from a high of 54 percent in Norway to a low of 0.1 percent in Mexico. Developed countries such as Australia, the United States, Belgium, France, Germany, Ireland, Netherland, Poland, and Sweden report an average rate of participation of 15 percent. Developing and transitional countries, such as Argentina, Brazil, Egypt, India, Peru, Romania, and Uganda report a lower average rate of participation of 6 percent. Table 8.1 illustrates these comparative rates. We see that the participation rate in India is 2 percent of the adult population. Nearly 20 million people, or 3.4 percent of the adult population, work on a paid or volunteer basis in nonprofits. The rate of participation also

Table 8.1: Volunteering in 36 Countries

Country	Value of Volunteer Work (Million US$)	People Volunteering* Number (Thousand)	People Volunteering* Percentage of Adult Population
Argentina	2,693.2	1,913	8
Australia	4,484.8	1,832	13
Austria	1,380.4	550	8
Belgium	4,197.7	809	10
Brazil	754.1	6,483	6
Colombia	229.1	1,149	5
Czech Rep.	196.4	381	5
Egypt	22.1	233	1
Finland	2,657.5	326	8
France	41,929.6	6,536	14
Germany	48,433.0	7,071	10
Hungary	49.7	277	3
India	1,355.9	16,490	2
Ireland	715.6	293	1 1
Israel	894.7	235	6
Italy	8,290.7	2,048	4
Japan	23,354.8	485	0.5
Kenya	52.0	955	6
Mexico	219.6	30	0.1
Morocco	98.4	699	4
The Netherlands	16,991.6	1,962	16
Norway	4,255.3	1,847	52
Pakistan	68.1	133	0.2
Peru	38.2	729	5
The Philippines	775.9	2,833	6
Poland	150.8	3,614	12

(Table 8.1 Contd)

(Table 8.1 Contd)

| | | People Volunteering* | |
Country	Value of Volunteer Work (Million US$)	Number (Thousand)	Percentage of Adult Population
Romania	155.0	325	2
Slovakia	7.3	149	4
South Africa	960.5	2,659	9
South Korea	2,433.2	1,204	3
Spain	7,055.1	1,681	5
Sweden	10,206.1	2,009	28
Tanzania	289.5	2,092	11
Uganda	30.5	2,606	23
United Kingdom	21,976.2	14,357	30
United States	109,012.6	44,564	22
Total	**316,415.6**	**131,557**	–
Developing/transitional country average		–	6
Developed country average		–	15
All-country average		–	10

Source: Salamon, Wojciech Sokolowski & Associates, 2004.
Notes: *See Methodological Appendix for estimating procedures.
Reference years: 1995–2000.

appears to vary from region to region within India, and according to a related study, 90 percent of all the persons working in nonprofit organizations in West Bengal are volunteers. Nationwide, volunteers represent nearly five-and-a-half times more staff than paid employees in nonprofits (Tandon & Srivastava, 2003).

Using another comparative perspective, Table 8.2 shows volunteering as a share of GDP by country. We see that in India this is fairly low; however, it is important to note that this analysis excluded volunteering in religious worship organizations, and a significant amount of volunteering may take place in such organizations. Indeed, many studies focused on other countries have shown that religious organizations are often highly dependent upon volunteers for their functioning (Cnaan et al., 2002).

Table 8.2: Volunteering across the World

Country	Volunteering (in Percentage)**
The Netherlands	4.70
Sweden*	4.03
Tanzania	3.30
Norway	3.18
France	2.98
United Kingdom	2.97
Germany	2.49
United States	2.18
Finland	2.12
Belgium	1.59
Australia	1.51
Argentina	1.30
Canada	1.26
Spain*	1.25
Ireland	1.20
Israel	1.05
The Philippines	0.96
South Africa	0.83
Italy	0.80
Korea, Rep. of	0.78
Austria	0.61
Japan	0.61
Portugal	0.53
Kenya	0.49
Uganda	0.48
Romania	0.45
Czech Republic	0.43
India*	0.31

(Table 8.2 Contd)

(Table 8.2 Contd)

Country	Volunteering (in Percentage)**
Colombia*	0.28
Brazil	0.21
Pakistan	0.13
Hungary	0.12
Poland	0.11
Mexico*	0.08
Peru*	0.06
Slovakia	0.04

Source: Salamon, Wojciech Sokolowski & Associates, 2004.

Notes: The data are presented as a percent of the GDP for the base year, which varies by country.

*Data on volunteering to religious worship organizations not available.

**GDP total adjusted to account for unrecognized value of volunteer work in these calculations.

Narratives

Individual Narrative: Ashish, a Cyberspace Volunteer

Ashish is a classic cyberspace volunteer. He is a member of Dream-India 2020, a group of young professionals with chapters all over India. These volunteers are driven to work for the social development of India, and share a dream of helping India achieve the living standards of a developed country by 2020. Ashish is one of the 20 member professionals of the Pune chapter of DreamIndia. The organization has no offices, no funding, no physical structure—it exists only as an informal network of volunteers tied together by cyberspace. Ashish's story is interesting because it shows how the flexibility of the modern volunteering network allows volunteers working outside of the structures of an existing NGO to respond to community needs as they arise.

Ashish grew up in the small town of Ujjain, and after finishing his engineering degree, came to Pune to do his MBA. He completed his MBA at Symbiosis International University. Ashish first started volunteering as a graduate student, when he joined a group that made visits to Sandhya, an old age home. He soon realized that volunteering had become an integral part of his life and that it had helped to replace the void of not having his family nearby. To Ashish, spending time and exerting effort to help the elderly was "more like a hobby" than social service. When he joined Persistent Systems Ltd, he was happy to find people there who worked on projects such as Aple Ghar (Our House, an orphanage) and Manavya (a home for children with HIV), with the NGO DreamIndia 2020. He soon became an enthusiastic volunteer for all of these projects.

Ashish had many dreams about what he would accomplish in the future. Like a number of his friends who were a part of DreamIndia 2020, he had long desired to work for the education of those children who, because of poverty, lacked the opportunity or ability to attend traditional schools. This dream began to take form in response to an accidental interaction on the street between a couple of Ashish's friends and a young boy. The two friends had been wondering aloud about the proper directions to a certain place when a poor child, who looked as if he lived on the street, overheard their conversation and gave them perfect directions in English. They were so surprised at the boy's English skills that they began talking to him about his background. They found out that the eight-year-old was called Vijay and that he earned his living polishing shoes on the street. His family lived in the slums and could not afford to send him to school as they needed his earnings. Vijay had learned English by simply listening to others on the street. The two friends were so impressed that they encouraged their volunteer colleagues to join in the cause and try and bring some schooling to the children in the slums. Every Saturday a group of volunteers would visit the slums for a couple of hours. A hut would be emptied for their "school" and they would teach the 17 children basic Mathematics, English, and Hindi.

The volunteer buddies soon realized that their efforts were not enough. They encouraged the children to enroll in government schools. Many of the slum children were from the tribal areas of northern India and lacked the necessary documentation required for admission. Nevertheless, the volunteers worked around the system and managed to get a number of their birth certificates

made. Eventually, many of the children were admitted to the local government schools. The satisfaction that the volunteers felt
was short-lived when they found out that most of the children
had dropped out of school a week later. When the volunteers took
their case to the children's parents, they discovered, much to their
chagrin, that the parents were mired in their own problems, the
chief of which was alcoholism, and that they did not care whether
their children went to school. In fact, they were happy that their
children brought home considerable earnings from begging on
the streets. When talking with the young drop-outs, they found
out that the children did not like being taught in Marathi, the medium used in most local government schools, because they were
more familiar with Hindi, a widely used north Indian language.

The volunteers then approached a local NGO that specialized in
child welfare. With the help of the NGO, they built a small dwelling
within the slum community. They called this little school Masti ka
Patshallah (house of mischief). A teacher conversant in Hindi and
Marathi taught the children there for four hours a day. The parents
were happy that the children remained within the community and
did not have to travel great distances. On weekends, the volunteers
visited the school to teach the children computers and help them
with their studies.

As for young Vijay, the volunteers had charted a wonderful future
for him. They had explained his case to a successful executive who
was willing to underwrite his education. One of the good residential schools at the hill station nearby had been approached and had
agreed to accept Vijay into their school. The executive was going to
pay for Vijay to complete his high school education at a reputable
school. The future looked bright for Vijay and the volunteers felt
good about themselves for having helped. However, Vijay's parents
backed out of the plan just a few days before school was to start.
They claimed that they could not survive without the earnings he
brought in. The executive sponsor was unperturbed. When he made
arrangements with a local grocery store to supply Vijay's parents
with all their needs, they agreed to let Vijay go to school. Then the
saga of Vijay's schooling took an unexpected and tragic turn. At the
last minute, Vijay's parents again refused to let him go, this time using the excuse that they would miss him too much. The frustrated

executive manager threw up his hands and gave up on Vijay. He then left for the United States, closing the chapter.

The bewildered volunteers went back to pursuing their various volunteer projects and Vijay went back to working on the streets. Many weeks later, Ashish spotted Vijay and his cohorts. By now they were all like old friends as they had spent so much time together, and they began talking. The children told them their success stories of getting money from people because of the way they talked. One of the young men was boasting about the new cricket bat that Vijay had bought for ₹600. Another young boy was showing off about how he so impressed a gentleman on the street with his English, that the gentleman just gave him ₹150. They also heard the story of a woman who had just bought two of the children a carom board when she heard them shouting to each other in English. Ashish and his friends looked at each other in horror. They realized that instead of encouraging a love for learning or helping the children to gain the skills necessary to pursue productive work, the schooling had simply made them better beggars by increasing their English proficiency. The children had no intention of continuing their education. Their hope was simply to become more articulate beggars. They also found out that the boys had found ways to gamble with their street earnings.

Ashish and his friends were disturbed to find how triumphantly each boy brandished his prize-earnings from begging and charming members of the public. Polishing shoes was simply a ruse to engage the public and try to cajole money out of them. They got together and assessed their situation. They realized that they could only volunteer their weekends to the street kids. They could not monitor them all the time. And as long as it was far more profitable to earn money from begging, the street children had no incentive to give up their easily won earnings in order to go to school. The parents were also not willing to let their children give up their short-term begging money for a long-term gain from education. The future was a nebulous concept and could not compete with the present.

One of the authors of this book encountered Vijay on the same infamous street corner asking politely in English: "Could you please give me some money so that I can buy myself a case of boot polish and earn my living?" One may argue that parents are basing their decision to keep their children from school on a rational, cost-benefit analysis, as, on average, children net close to ₹200 each day—well above ₹80, the daily wages of a laborer. However, their decision dramatically prioritizes short-term over long-term interests, because the children's earnings from begging will certainly decrease dramatically as they age, falling well short of what is necessary to cover their medical and other needs. The prospects for their future are grim, and they do not understand the rationale of investing in this future because they do not see themselves as part of the forward-moving "India shining" proclaimed by politicians.

Ashish and his friends have now changed their tactics. They have started an Anti-Child Begging Campaign (ACBC) to expose the consequences and the reality of begging. Through road shows and informative posters, they are hoping to convince members of the public that they are not helping a child by giving money when he or she begs. Instead, they are keeping the child mired in a life of begging and away from school and a better future. Along with increasing the availability of quality schooling to educate impoverished children, they view campaigns such as theirs as necessary for fulfilling their dreams of an India in which all children can get a good education. Ashish is adamant that it is not the children who are at fault, nor their parents, but a system in which begging and giving money to beggars are encouraged. This charitable impulse is exploited by parents, whose lack of education encourages them to push their children toward begging as a quick cure to their present-day penury instead of focusing on long-term benefits. Ashish and his colleagues are optimistic that they will reach their goal despite the detours—so long as they keep working and setting new goals that are grounded in the everyday realities facing the poor.

Individual Narrative: Dilbur, Founder of Aseema (Mumbai)

Volunteers are the lifeblood of NGOs, which are a major driving force of development in India. They have proliferated in Maharashtra where we located our earlier study, *Grass-Roots NGOs by Women for Women* (2006). Here, we found that many of the NGOs were started by women with little financial capital. In most cases, volunteer labor was the most important resource, and usually required, for recruiting friends and family members (Handy, Mook, & Quarter, 2006, p. 42). Dilbur, responsible for founding an NGO in Maharashtra, is one such remarkable individual. Dilbur is a courageous lawyer, who worked with the International Commission of Jurists in Geneva for five years as their legal officer for Asia and the Pacific. She gave up her job and returned to India where she started Aseema in Mumbai, an NGO providing quality education to underprivileged street children.

Dilbur's decision to abandon her plush surroundings in Switzerland to face an uncertain future working with the Indian poor was not based upon any consciously rational process of weighing costs and benefits. She simply followed her instincts, which compelled her to work toward providing street children with a basic education. Her case does not represent the newer trends in volunteering, such as technology facilitated or episodic volunteerism, but demonstrates the continuation of the traditional pattern of a well-to-do woman who dramatically reorients her life to focus on helping the less fortunate.

When Dilbur first began her work in 1997, she had little in the way of financial resources. She could afford only one teacher and was largely dependent on volunteers. She recruited eight volunteers who came in at fixed times during the week: some came just once a week, others twice, and some every day. Dilbur emphasizes that "their help was invaluable those first few years and still is."

Today, Aseema has adopted a municipal school that is now regarded as a paradigm for state-run schools. Here, children are taught in the Montessori method alongside enriching activities, such as art, music, yoga, judo, and sports. Dilbur reports proudly that today Aseema has a paid staff today of 45, which includes teachers, helpers, and office staff working full-time and part-time shifts. However, Aseema still relies on volunteers as well, who have grown to form a support staff of 30. Dilbur asserts that for an organization like Aseema, which believes in giving focused attention to children and having a good student–teacher ratio, volunteers are important because children learn better in small groups under their guidance. She reiterated the value that volunteers provide to NGOs such as hers: "Some of our finest teachers have been volunteers who give their all to the children—both in terms of knowledge and developing skills; and through the respect and love they give to the children they bring out the best in the child."

Aseema has been lucky to attract volunteer artists, who give their time to teach children how to draw and paint. The art program has been so successful that the children's paintings are showcased at exhibitions and garner prizes as well as large sums of money from their sale. There are volunteers who teach the children yoga, others who come and sing to them, and still others who teach the children how to sing. Some corporations have made Aseema their partner NGO and have taken the children on trips to educational and other interesting places around Mumbai. One such trip that some of the children enjoyed was an airplane ride over Mumbai and its environs.

More recently, Aseema has been expanding its education programs into the rural areas of Maharashtra. As a first step, a large piece of land has been bought in the tribal areas a few hours outside of Mumbai. There are plans to create nursery and primary classes as well as a middle school. There will be a special space for women where they can take literacy or vocational guidance classes. All of this is possible only because Aseema has been able to attract volunteers to work alongside their paid staff who take special pride in catering to the needs of the underprivileged.

The volunteers have different time commitments and do different tasks: there are those who come once or twice a year in order to teach the children a skill, to take them on an outing, or to simply spend time playing with them. There are others who come on a regular basis to serve meals to the children or to assist the staff in teaching reading or other skills to them. Others help with administrative tasks, either on an episodic or long-term basis. There have been volunteer counselors and child psychologists who work to ensure mental stability of the children as well as sports or martial arts specialists, who teach children their special athletic skills. All of these volunteers have contributed to making the street children, who are educated at Aseema, parallel in ability and performance to children in any exclusive private school. When meeting with these students, attired in their neat uniforms and carrying their loaded knapsacks, and hearing them speak in fluent English, viewing their art work, or seeing the happy glow on their faces, one quickly recognizes the impact that Aseema's volunteers have had on their lives.

Individual Narrative: Rohini and the Roses

Rohini proudly asserts that she is a "secular Indian," who is interested in doing what she can to help sustainable development in the country. Like many other volunteers, she comes from a family with a history of involvement in social work. Her older sister is a professional social worker, and Rohini herself has been engaged in informal volunteering as far back as she can remember, helping her neighbors, friends, and family members in small ways. And she remembers all the other members of her family doing the same.

Professionally, Rohini is a confident and well-educated young lady from an upper middle-class background, who had worked successfully in marketing for several years. However, she later reached a stage when she realized that she wanted to do something more meaningful than selling shampoo. So, she decided to "wash her hands" of marketing bath products and take a year off. Having no liabilities, she decided that she would lose nothing by switching careers. As she surveyed the job market and sent out applications, she found that she received many job offers for resource mobilization and fundraising. However, she realized that this was not quite what she was looking for. She wanted to "get her hands dirty" and to make a difference at the grassroots level. One day while surfing the Internet she came across the iVolunteer Web site and learned of the opportunity to work with Voluntary Service Overseas (VSO).

VSO is an international development agency that employs volunteers to fight global poverty through the sharing of skills and knowledge among communities around the world. Rohini liked the fact that the organization offered training as well as the opportunity to volunteer in underprivileged countries and that placements were based on individual skill sets. Rohini applied and stated her experience. She was accepted and given a placement in Uganda in a project called "Reach Out," which provided holistic care for people with HIV/AIDS at the "Roses of Mbuya," a vocational and tailoring workshop.

Rohini had been assigned the task of managing the "Livelihoods Initiative" for the project.

Rohini remembers that the Roses of Mbuya department was considered a black hole. An investment of 20 million Ugs (approximately US$11,000) in the year 2004 had yielded practically no returns, and the Roses had been operating at a loss consistently during the three years since its inception in 2002. When Rohini observed the entire operation, she was puzzled. The department seemed to be doing excellent work and her predecessor had established an efficient system to track sales and prices. But there were no sales—why? The women had learned to sew flawlessly and were now able to produce a variety of attractive hand-sewn products—but they had no idea how to sell them. It was evident to Rohini that marketing skills were sorely lacking. Her predecessor had advised that the project should be closed down so that the money being wasted in sustaining its operation could be used to better provide those in need with the basics of life.

The coordinator believed in the project, however, and Rohini had been invited to help find a solution to the marketing issue. Even though the NGO was not making any money with the project, it was keeping many women employed who were dependent on the small income they received for their work. Many were isolated because either they had lost their families to HIV or had been abandoned by their families. Work gave them a semblance of normalcy, and it was, therefore, important for them to keep working. Rohini was drawn to the challenge of making the project work in order to help both the women and the organization stay afloat.

Rohini slowly developed contacts in a part of the world that was foreign to her. She began receiving contracts and work began to flow in. As the work orders came, Rohini could see that the women were revitalized and a joyful energy had begun to spread among them. Rohini believes that the success was attributed to more than her marketing skills. The women realized that this was their last chance of independence and they produced beautiful products at record speed. Rohini loved the connection she had established with those "wonderful women." Rohini was in Uganda for only 16 months and had completely turned the project around. She had developed a marketing model that the women could follow up on after she left with an assurance of continued sales. She had also made valuable connections with the women and was inspired in her own life by their hard work, tenacity, and enthusiasm.

Rohini believes that her volunteering was a life-changing experience: "This has been an immensely enriching and satisfying emotional and professional experience for me," she asserts. Today, Rohini appreciates her comfortable lifestyle and is back at work. However, she asserts that she will return to volunteering when the commercialism of life begins to get to her. She knows that volunteering will connect her back to the realities of life and the joys of living.

Individual Narrative: Savant, a Proud Rotarian

Savant is a proud Rotarian. He considers his membership in the Rotary Club to be an integral part of his life. He refuses to talk about himself, insisting that the work the Rotary Club does is far more important because it touches so many lives. He explained that there are 147 Clubs in the state of Maharashtra, and 50 of these are located in the city of Pune. Savant is member of the Rotary Club of Ganeshkhind, which is one of the districts of Pune. He told us about the ways in which the Club makes a difference in people's lives.

One interesting example is the way in which the Rotary Club involves local schools in efforts to spread the word about its polio camps. Several days before the event, a rally is organized with the help of local school teachers and some Rotary members. The school children engage in a form of public relations by carrying banners, distributing flyers, and letting people know about the forthcoming event. The polio camp is conducted by doctors, Rotarians, Rotaractors, and Interactors (young/older children who are trained to disseminate information). The volunteers visit homes and persuade people to bring their children to the camp to receive their polio vaccine. The vaccination is administered by doctors who operate from a mobile van, which is usually parked in the middle of a heavily populated area. The funding for such camps comes from money raised by local Rotarians, who then notify the international Rotarians about the event. Usually an international club is invited to match the funds offered by the local group and this finances the camp.

The Dairy Project started by this Rotary Club is another success story. Forty of the neediest women who owned their own cows and buffaloes were invited to run a Dairy Project. Fourteen of these women were sent to the Department of Husbandry at the Agricultural University to receive training in the mechanics of running a dairy. The dairy was then registered as a cooperative society and housed within an area that could store milk so that the women could now control the production and sales from their dairy.

Phase two of the Dairy Project involved inviting 21 women who could not afford to buy their own cows. They were assigned donated cows and buffaloes and were trained to look after them. The proviso was that they were to milk their cows and keep only a liter of milk for their own family consumption and the rest was to be donated to the Dairy Project. The grant allowed the dairy to be fully computerized with a fat checking machine, water content checking machine, electronic weighing machine, freezers, a computer, and a stock of animal feed. As the output of milk increased, a bigger location was needed. The local Panchayat[4] allocated about 5,000 square feet of land for the dairy and material for the construction of the building was donated by a local hatchery. Two local women who had completed tenth grade were selected to train others on the use of the equipment. Although the project was run by the local women, volunteers from the Rotary Club were responsible for overseeing the project, including its early preparations, its architectural design and engineering, and the general project management. They continue to oversee the project to this day.

Savant is a good story teller and he related some of the stories of his encounters with social issues, replete with the personal anecdotes that bring a story to life. Some of the stories are poignant and interesting because of their human touch and also because they give us an insight into how the awareness of problems may lead to projects that are geared toward their resolution.

One such story relates to the origins of the Water Project, which was a follow-up to the Dairy Project. A woman who worked at the Dairy Project asked for a leave of absence to visit a relative from the

---

[4] Panchayats are local, village-level assemblies.

neighboring village who had just lost her son. She told the Rotarians that the death was attributed to the bad quality of water in the village. Consequently, Savant accompanied the woman to the nearby village and tested three local wells for water quality. The tests suggested that the water was of such bad quality that it endangered the lives of people, particularly pregnant women. This alarmed Savant, who wrote about the problem to a foreign Rotarian. Soon funds were allocated and plans drawn up to start a Water Purification Project, which was then approved by the local Rotarians and the village people. The project was completed in such a manner that clean water became readily available from taps near the houses of the village and people no longer had to walk vast distances to draw water. Today, the members of the village refer to it as "modern" because of the Water Project, which is run by the local Panchayat and is overseen by the local Rotarians.

Savant was also instrumental in starting the local primary health-care center, which houses two incubators and two warmers. He was in the village when he heard that a local woman had delivered a premature baby, and he became involved in a discussion regarding how to get the woman to the hospital, which was 30 kilometers away. Savant offered to pay for the taxi to avoid the rigors of the bus tip and enhance the child's chance of survival. The woman's husband had deserted her when he found out that the new baby was a girl. The woman was apprehensive about taking the trip by herself and, in the midst of the discussions, the baby died. The child had apparently died because of the lack of an incubator in the village, which piqued concern that other deaths could follow. The Rotary Club decided to improve the facilities provided by the local primary health-care center. They had to overcome many bureaucratic hurdles to receive funding grants from their foreign counterparts. Today, the Rotarians are rightly proud of the new facility that they founded in the village, which has all the equipments required to run a good primary health-care center, including a sonography machine. Rotarians oversee this project, which has grown to include services such as ophthalmic, maternity, dental, and small operations. The center also hosts a popular health education program each year.

Savant tells us that the Rotary Club has more recently started dental clinics, camps for the disabled, as well as blood donation camps in the neighboring areas of Pune. Savant is happy with his involvement in the Rotary Club and believes that it has brought meaning to his life. His responsiveness to the needs of the local villages and his diligent efforts to resolve their problems has certainly brought happiness to many others as well. The Rotary Club has provided him with a platform from which he can bring about change in the lives of many through utilizing a large international network of people and resources.

Commentary

The narratives in this chapter represent both long-standing traditions and current trends in volunteering in India. Ashish is a classic cyberspace volunteer who joined an NGO that has no physical office space and exists only as a networking mechanism for volunteers. Rohini, likewise, utilized the Internet to find an opportunity for her to contribute to the public welfare in an area far removed from her own personal connections. Dilbur, on the other hand, closely resembles the model of a traditional volunteer, in that she works from her NGO office, whereas Savant exemplifies the increasing appeal of service clubs in India and the mixture of charitable service and business and social networking they provide.

The volunteers profiled represent a variety of backgrounds; however, as is the case among volunteers across regions, they are disproportionately from the middle and upper classes. Whereas Ashish comes from a poor family and, therefore, is cognizant of the realities and problems that poor people experience, this is not the case for the other volunteers. Dilbur hails from a comfortable background and the same applies to Rohini and Savant. These well-to-do volunteers gave up the security of their careers for a variety of time frames: Dilbur abandoned her career indefinitely to work toward educating the poor, whereas Rohini made a temporary commitment with the partial intention of finding meaning in her life. Savant has not given up his career, either permanently or temporarily, but carries out his volunteer work on a consistent part-time basis in a way that complements rather than competes with his paid employment.

These narratives, thus, reflect the myriad of forms that volunteering now takes in India. Some volunteers come from poor backgrounds and are determined to lend a hand to others once they get to the top. Others are already financially on top but reach out to the poor and the needy out of concern for their welfare. Some work from offices, others from clubs, others venture to foreign lands, and still others network from cyberspace. They come from all castes and creeds and some, like Rohini, assert that they are "secular Indians." All are confident, purposeful, and enjoy helping others in need. They do what they do not only because of altruistic impulses but also because volunteering makes them feel good and makes life meaningful. And in the process of volunteering, they discover a community of like-minded people that gives them a sense of belonging.

Bibliography

Preface

Drèze, J., & Sen, A. (Eds.) (1997). *Indian development: Selected regional perspectives.* New Delhi, India: Oxford University Press.

Gill, P. (February 20, 2009). Trying new roles. *India Today.* Retrieved July 7, 2010, from http://indiatoday.intoday.in/site/Story/29725/SUPPLEMENTS/Trying+new+roles.html

Handy, F., Kassam, M., Feeney, S., & Ranade, B. (2006). *Grass-roots NGOs by women for women: The driving force of development in India.* New Delhi, India: SAGE Publishers.

Mehta, T., & Kumar, S. (February 15, 2009). Online campaigners voice social consciousness. *India Today.* Retrieved June 29, 2010, from http://indiatoday.intoday.in/site/Story/29121/LATEST%20HEADLINES/Online+campaigners+voice+social+consciousness.html

Perry, A. (November 29, 2004). *A tale of two Indias.* Retrieved August 3, 2010, from http://www.time.com/time/asia/covers/501041206/story.html

UNDP (United Nations Development Programme). (2009). *India: Urban poverty report 2009.* Retrieved July 7, 2010, from http://data.undp.org.in/poverty_reduction/IUPR_Summary.pdf

Introduction

Bellah, R., Madsen, R., Sullivan, W., Swidler, A., & Tipton, S. (1985). *Habits of the heart: Individualism and commitment in American life.* Berkeley and Los Angeles: University of California Press.

Clary, E. G., Snyder, M., Ridge, R., Copeland, J., Stukas, A., Haugen, J., Miene, P. (1998). Understanding and assessing the motivations of volunteers: A functional approach. *Journal of Personality and Social Psychology, 74*(6), 1516–1530.

Cnaan, R. A., & Goldberg-Glen, R. S. (1991). Measuring motivation to volunteer in human services. *Journal of Applied Behavioral Sciences, 27*(3), 269–284.

Handy, F., Kassam, M., Feeney, S., & Ranade. B. (2006). *Grass-roots NGOs by women for women: The driving force of development in India.* New Delhi: SAGE Publications.

Immanuel, J. (September 8, 2008). *Bridging the literacy gap in India* (UNV Report). Retrieved July 7, 2010, from http://www.unv.org/en/news-resources/news/doc/bridging-the-literacy-gap.html

Lalitha, N. V. (1975). *Voluntary work in India.* New Delhi, India: National Institute of Public Cooperation and Child Development.

Salamon, L., Sokolowski, S. J., & Associates. (2004). *Global civil society: Dimensions of the nonprofit sector,* Vol. 2, Chapter 1, Overview (pp. 3–60). Bloomfield, CT: Kumarin Press.

Sen, S. (1993). *Defining the non-profit sector: India* (Working Paper). Baltimore, MD: The Johns Hopkins Comparative Nonprofit Sector Project.

Tandon R., & Srivastava, S. S. (2003). *Invisible, yet widespread: The nonprofit sector in India.* New Delhi, India: PRIA.

UNV (United Nations Volunteers). (July 31, 2008). *"Teach India": One of the largest campaigns of its kind* (UNV Report). Retrieved July 5, 2010, from http://www.unv.org/en/news-resources/news/doc/teach-india-one-of.html

Chapter 1

Ariff, M. (Ed.). (1991). *The Islamic voluntary sector in Southeast Asia.* Singapore: Institute of Southeast Asian Studies.

Beckerlegge, G. (2007). Responding to conflict: A test of the limits of neo-Vedântic social activism in the Ramakrishna: Math and mission? *International Journal of Hindu Studies, 11*(1), 1–25.

Chinmayananda (Swami). (n.d.). *The Bhagavad Gita.* Mumbai: Central Chinmaya Mission Trust Publications.

Datta, D. M. (1956). India's debt to the West in philosophy. *Philosophy East and West, 6*(3), 195–212.

Dhesi, A. S. (1996). From centralised to decentralised development in India: The communitarian perspective. *Community Development Journal, 31*(3), 201–213.

Gupta, K. S. (2005). *The philosophy of Rabindranath Tagore.* Burlington, VT: Ashgate.

Harris, I. C. (1987). Sarvodaya in crisis: The Gandhian movement in India today. *Asian Survey, 27*(9), 1036–1052.

Hettne, B. (1976). The vitality of the Gandhian tradition. *Journal of Peace Research, 13*(3), 227–245.

John, A. (April 30, 2007). *Foreign contributions: Do we need amended regulations?* Retrieved May 1, 2007, from http://news.indlaw.com/guest/columns/default.asp?aju6

Kantowsky, D. (1980). *Sarvodaya: The other development.* New Delhi, India: Vikas Publishing House.

Kapoor, A. K., & Singh, D. (1997). *Rural development through NGOs.* Jaipur, India: Rawat Publications.

Lacy, C. (1965). *The conscience of India: Moral traditions in the modern world.* New York: Holt, Rinehart & Winston.

Narottamananda (Swami). (1982). *Home of service: A retrospect* (Rev. ed.). Varanasi, India: Ramakrishna Mission Home of Service.

Natarajan, S. (1962). *A century of social reform in India.* New York: Asia Publishing House.

PRIA (Society for Participatory Research in Asia). (2001). *Historical Background of the Nonprofit Sector in India* (Working Paper No. 1). New Delhi, India: PRIA.

Rajesekhar, D., & Biradar, R. R. (2002). *People, government and the NGOs* (Working Paper No. 114). Nagarabhavi, India: Institute for Social and Economic Change.

Ravichandran, N., Rajashree, S., Sathyapriya, Y., & Jain, A. (2006). Perspectives on non-profit mission and financing in India. *Journal of Health Management, 8*, 207–227.

Riley, J. M. (2002). *Stakeholders in rural development: Critical collaboration in state-NGO relationships.* New Delhi, India: SAGE Publications.

Rothermund, I. (1969). The individual and society in Gandhi's political thought. *Journal of Asian Studies, 28*(2), 313–320.

Sen, S. (1993). *Defining the nonprofit sector: India* (Working Papers of The Johns Hopkins Comparative Nonprofit Sector Project No. 12). Baltimore, MD: The Johns Hopkins Institute for Policy Studies.

———. (1997). India. In L. M. Salamon & H. K. Anheier (Eds.), *Defining the nonprofit sector: A cross-national analysis* (pp. 401–445). The Johns Hopkins Nonprofit Sector Series 4. Manchester, UK: Manchester University Press.

———. (1999). Some aspects of state-NGO relationships in India in the post-independence era. *Development and Change, 30*(2), 327–355.

Sharma, A. (2006). Crossbreeding institutions, breeding struggle: Women's empowerment, neoliberal governmentality, and state (re)formation in India. *Cultural Anthropology, 21*(1), 60–95.

Singh, S. R. (1968). *Nationalism and social reform in India: 1885 to 1920.* New Delhi, India: Ranjit Printers & Publishers.

Sooryamoorthy, R., & Gangrade, K. D. (2001). *NGOs in India: A cross-sectional study.* Westport, CT: Greenwood Press.

Tandon, R., & Srivastava, S. S. (2003). *Invisible, yet widespread: The nonprofit sector in India.* New Delhi, India: PRIA.

Taylor, C. C., Ensminger, D., Johnson, H. W., & Joyce, J. (1965). *India's roots of democracy: A sociological analysis of rural India's experience in planned development since independence.* New York: Frederick A. Praeger.

Thapar, R. (2004). *Early India: From the origins to AD 1300.* Berkeley and Los Angeles: University of California Press.

Tinker, H. (1964). Magnificent failure? The Gandhian ideal in India after sixteen years. *International Affairs, 40*(2), 262–276.

Tripathi, P. M. (1992). *Government-NGO interface in India's development: A country paper.* Association of Voluntary Agencies for Rural Development (AVARD). Presented at the ANGOC-APDC Regional Dialogue on Prospects for GO-NGO Collaboration, Chiang Mai and Bangkok, Thailand.

Weber, T. (1994). The lesson from the disciples: Is there a contradiction in Gandhi's philosophy of action? *Modern Asian Studies, 28*(1), 195–214.

Chapter 2

Cnaan, R. A., Handy, F., & Wadsworth, M. (1996). Defining who is a volunteer: Conceptual and empirical considerations. *Nonprofit and Voluntary Sector Quarterly, 25*(3), 364–383.

Ellis, S. J., & Noyes, K. H. (1990). *By the people.* San Francisco: Jossey-Bass.

Ferraro, P. J., & Taylor, L. O. (2005). Do economists recognize an opportunity cost when they see one? A dismal performance from the dismal science. *Contributions to Economic Analysis & Policy, 4*(1). Retrieved October 17, 2010, from http://www.bepress.com/bejeap/contributions/vol4/iss1/art7

Handy, C., & Day, T. (1988). *Understanding voluntary organizations*. Harmondsworth, UK: Penguin Books.

Handy, F., Cnaan, R. A., Brudney, J. L., Ascoli, U., Meijs, L. C. P. M., & Ranade, S. (2000). Public perception of "Who is a volunteer?" *Voluntas, 11*(1), 45–65.

Lyons, M., Wijkstrom, P., & Clary, G. (1998). Comparative studies of volunteering. *Voluntary Action, 1*(1), 45–54.

McCurley, S. H., & Vesuvio, D. (1985). Brief response: Who is a volunteer. *Voluntary Action Leadership,* (Summer), 14–15.

Meijs, L., Handy, F., Cnaan, R. A., Brudney, J. L., Ascoli, U., Ranade. (2003). All in the eyes of the beholder? Perceptions of volunteering across eight countries. In P. Dekker & L. Halman (Eds.), *The values of volunteering: Cross-cultural perspectives* (pp. 19–34). New York: Kluwer/Plenum.

Salvoza, M. F. (October 23, 2004). On make a difference day, 3 million help hurricane victims, troops abroad. *USA Today*. Retrieved March 7, 2007, from www.usaweekend.com/diffday/2004_articles/04dayof.html

Scheier, I. H. (1980). *Exploring volunteer space*. Boulder, CO: Volunteer: The National Center for Citizen Involvement.

Shure, R. (1991). Volunteering: Continuing expansion of the definition and a practical application of altruistic motivation. *Journal of Volunteer Administration, 9*(Summer), 36–41.

Smith, D. H. (1994). Determinants of voluntary association participation and volunteering: A literature review. *Nonprofit and Voluntary Sector Quarterly, 23*, 243–263.

Stebbins, R. A. (1996). Volunteering: A serious leisure perspective. *Nonprofit and Voluntary Sector Quarterly, 25*(2), 211–224.

The President's Task Force on Private Sector Initiatives. (1982). *Volunteers: A valuable resource*. Washington, DC: United States Government Printing Office.

United States Department of Labor. (1985). Fair Labor Standard Act, 29 U.S.C. SS201–219 & FLSA Regulations, 29CFR S553, 100–106. Retrieved July 2, 2011, from http://www.dol.gov/compliance/laws/comp-flsa.htm

Van Til, J. (1988). *Mapping the third sector*. Washington, DC: Foundation Center.

Wilson, A., & Pimm, G. (1996). The tyranny of the volunteer: The care and feeding of voluntary workforces. *Management Decision, 34*(4), 24–40.

Wymer, W. (2006). Insights from a review of the literature on cause marketing. *Journal International Review on Public and Nonprofit Marketing, 3*(1), 9–15.

Wymer, W. W. (1997). Segmenting volunteers using values, self-esteem, empathy and facilitation as determinant variables. *Journal of Nonprofit and Voluntary Sector Marketing, 5*(2), 3–28.

Yavas, U., & Riecken, G. (1985). Can volunteers be targeted? *Journal of the Academy of Marketing Science, 13*(2), 218–228.

Chapter 3

AIESEC. (2009). *Experience incredible India*. Retrieved August 2, 2010, from http://www.aiesecsa.com/india.html

Astin, A. W. (1998). The changing American college student: Thirty-year trends, 1966–1996. *Review of Higher Education, 21*(2), 115–135.

Astin, A. W., & Sax, L. J. (1998). How undergraduates are affected by service participation. *Journal of College Student Development, 39*(3), 251–263.

Astin, A. W., Sax, L., & Avalos, J. (1999). Long-term effects of volunteerism during the undergraduate years. *Review of Higher Education, 22*(2), 187–202.

Baum, F., Modra, C., Bush, R., Cox, E., Cooke, R., & Potter, R. (1999). Volunteering and social capital: An Adelaide study. *Australian Journal on Volunteering, 4*(1), 13–22.

Cappellari, L., & Turati, G. (2004). Volunteer labour supply: The role of workers' motivations. *Annals of Public & Cooperative Economics, 75*(4), 619–643.

Carlin, P. S. (2001). Evidence on the volunteer labor supply of married women. *Southern Economic Journal, 67*(4), 801–824.

Clary, E. G., Snyder, M., & Stukas, A. A. (1996). Volunteers' motivations: Findings from a national survey. *Nonprofit and Voluntary Sector Quarterly, 25*(4), 485–505.

Clary, E. G., Snyder, M., Ridge, R., Copeland, J., Stukas, A., Haugen, J., & Miene, P. (1998). Understanding and assessing the motivations of volunteers: A functional approach. *Journal of Personality and Social Psychology, 74*(6), 1516–1530.

Cnaan, R. A., & Goldberg-Glen, R. S. (1991). Measuring motivation to volunteer in human services. *Journal of Applied Behavioral Sciences, 27*(3), 269–284.

Davis Smith, J. (1998). *The 1997 national survey of volunteering.* London: National Centre for Volunteering, University of East London.

Day, K. M., & Devlin, R. A. (1998). The payoff to work without pay: Volunteer work as an investment in human capital. *Canadian Journal of Economics, 31*(5), 1179–1191.

Devlin, R. A. (2001). Volunteers and the paid labour market. *Isuma: Canadian Journal of Policy Research, 2*(2), 62–68.

Dickinson, M. J. (1999). Do gooders or do betters? An analysis of the motivation of student tutors. *Educational Research, 41*(2), 221–227.

Freeman, R. B. (1997). Working for nothing: The supply of volunteer labor. *Journal of Labor Economics, 15*(1), S140–S166.

Friedland, L., & Morimoto, S. (2005). *The changing lifeworld of young people: Risk, résumé padding, and civic engagement* (CIRCLE Working Paper 40). Retrieved February 29, 2008, from http://www.civicyouth.org/PopUps/WorkingPapers/WP40Friedland.pdf

Gabard, D. L. (1995). Volunteers in AIDS service organizations: motivations and values. *Journal of Health and Human Services Administration, 17*(3), 317–337.

Gillespie, D. F., & King, A. E. O. (1985). Demographic understanding of volunteerism. *Journal of Sociology & Social Welfare, 12*(4), 798–816.

Hall, M., Lasby, D., Gumulka, G., & Tryon, C. (2006). *Caring Canadians, involved Canadians: Highlights from the 2004 Canada survey of giving, volunteering and participating.* Toronto, Canada: Statistics Canada.

Hall, M., McKeown, L., & Roberts, K. (2001). *Caring Canadians, involved Canadians: Highlights from the 2000 national survey of giving, volunteering, and participating.* Ottawa, Canada: Industry Canada.

Handy, F., & N. Srinivasan. (2004). Improving quality while reducing costs? An economic evaluation of the net benefits of hospital volunteers. *Nonprofit and Voluntary Sector Quarterly, 33*(1), 28–54.

Herzog, A., Kahn, R., & Morgan, J. (1989). Age differences in productive activity. *Journals of Gerontology: Series B: Psychological Sciences and Social Sciences, 44*(4), 129–138.

Independent Sector, Panel on the Nonprofit Sector. (2006). *Strengthening transparency, governance, accountability of charitable organizations.* Retrieved August 3, 2010, from http://www.independentsector.org/uploads/Accountability_Documents/Panel_Supplement_Final.pdf

Jones, F. (1999). Seniors who volunteer. *Perspectives on Labour and Income, 11*(3), 9–17.

———. (2000). Youth volunteering on the rise. *Perspectives on Labour and Income, 12*(1), 36–41.

Katz, E., & Rosenberg, J. (2005). An economic interpretation of institutional volunteering. *European Journal of Political Economy, 21*(2), 429–443.

Knoke, D. (1986). Associations and interest groups. *Annual Review in Sociology, 12*(1), 1–21.

National Cadet Corps. (n.d.) *About us.* Retrieved July 2, 2007, from http://nccindia.nic.in/aboutus.htm

Omoto, A. M., & Snyder, M. (2002). Considerations of community: The context and process of volunteerism. *American Behavioral Scientist, 45*(5), 846–867.

Prouteau, L., & Wolff, F. C. (2006). Does volunteer work pay off in the labor market? *Journal of Socio-Economics, 35*(6), 992–1013.

Reed, P., & Selbee, L. K. (2000). Distinguishing characteristics of active volunteers in Canada. *Nonprofit and Voluntary Sector Quarterly, 29*(4), 571–592.

———. (2001). The civic core in Canada: Disproportionality in charitable giving, volunteering, and civic participation. *Nonprofit and Voluntary Sector Quarterly, 30*(4), 761–780.

Serow, R. C. (1991). Students and voluntarism: Looking into the motives of community service participants. *American Educational Research Journal, 28*(3), 543–556.

Smith, D. H. (1994). Determinants of voluntary association participation and volunteering. *Nonprofit and Voluntary Sector Quarterly, 23*(3), 243–263.

Spence, M. (1973). Job market signaling. *Quarterly Journal of Economics, 87*(3), 355–374.

Sundeen, R., & Raskoff, S. (1994). Volunteering among teenagers in the United States. *Nonprofit and Voluntary Sector Quarterly, 23*(4), 383–403.

Thompson, A. M., III, & Bono, B. A. (1993). Work without wages: The motivation for volunteer firefighters. *American Journal of Economics and Sociology, 52*(3), 323–343.

Wilson, J. (2000). Volunteering. *Annual Review of Sociology, 26*(1), 215–240.

Winniford, J. C., Carpenter, D. S., & Grider, C. (1995). An analysis of the traits and motivations of college students involved in service organizations. *Journal of College Student Development, 36*(1), 27–38.

Web sites

Ministry of Youth Affairs and Sports, Government of India. http://yas.nic.in/index.asp?layid=1

Chapter 4

Agarwal, S., & Dadrawala, N. (2004). Philanthropy and law in India. In M. Sidel & I. Zaman (Eds.), *Philanthropy and Law in South Asia* (pp. 115–181). Quezon City, Philippines: Asia Pacific Philanthropy Consortium.

Arora, B., & Puranik, R. (2004). A review of corporate social responsibility in India. *Development, 47*(3), 93–100.

Canton, N. (2007, July 30). Mumbai's Gennext. *Hindustan Times*, p. 2.

Carnegie, A., & Titchi, C. (1902). *Autobiography of Andrew Carnegie*. Boston: Northeastern University Press.

CSR Digest. (November 2, 2009). *International bank launches new green initiative in Mumbai*. Retrieved July 29, 2010, from http://www.csrdigest.com/2009/11/international-bank-launches-new-green-initiative-in-mumbai

Dandiwalla, N. (2008). Personal interview. October 31.

DevelopedNation. (n.d.). *Interview with Mr. Vijay Gupta*. Retrieved September 27, 2008, from http://www.developednation.org/interviews/vijaygupta.htm

Easwaramoorthy, M., Barr, C., Runte, M., & Basil, D. (2006). *Business support for employee volunteers in Canada: Results of a national survey*. Toronto, Canada: Imagine Canada. Retrieved July 28, 2010, from http://nonprofitscan.imaginecanada.ca/files/kdc-cdc/imagine_business_support_report.pdf

Frankel, F. (2005). *India's political economy: 1947–2004* (2d ed.). New Delhi, India: Oxford University Press.

GE (General Electric). (2010). *Citizenship fact sheet*. Retrieved June 6, 2010, from http://ge.ge.ee/citizenship/priorities_engagement/citizenship_fact_sheet.jsp

Govindarajulu, N., & Daily, B. F. (2004). Motivating employees for environmental improvement. *Industrial Management & Data Systems, 104*(4), 364–372.

Graff, L. (2004). *Making a business case for employer-supported volunteerism*. Ottawa, Canada: Volunteer Canada. Retrieved August 24, 2008, from http://www.volunteer.ca/volunteer/pdf/ESVThinkPiece.pdf

Hall, M., Easwaramoorthy, M., & Sandler, W. (2007). *Business contributions to Canadian communities: Findings for a qualitative study of current practices*: Toronto, Canada: Imagine Canada.

Harita, Pratima. (2009). Personal Interview. February 12.

Hertzber, F, Mausner B. & Snyderman, B. (1959). *The Motivation to Work*. New York: John Wiley and Sons.

Honeywell Hometown Solutions. (n.d.). *Volunteering*. Retrieved July 29, 2010, from http://www51.honeywell.com/hhs/ourprograms-sub/volunteering.html

Honeywell Technology Solutions Lab. (n.d.). *Community service*. Retrieved July 29, 2010, from http://www.honeywell.com/sites/htsl/backgroundmaterials3_CA3OJD6LUP0L-HON1XR72LR5PAQ1WVH6HW_HAIQMZ4RH71KG5P53F3L11MSF2GSW0HYH.htm

HSBC (Hong Kong & Shanghai Banking Corporation). (n.d.). *Employee volunteering*. Retrieved August 8, 2008, from http://www.hsbc.co.in/1/2/miscellaneous/about-hsbc/corporate-sustainability/employee-volunteering

ITC Ltd (2009). *Sustainability Report 2009*. Retrieved July 29, 2010, at http://www.itcportal.com/sustainability-report-2009/index.htm

Kadrolkar, V. M. (2008). Globalization and corporate social responsibility. *Nitte Management Review, 2*(2), 62–71.

Kumar, R., Murphy, D. F., & Balsari, V. (2001). *Altered images: The 2001 state of corporate social responsibility in India poll*. New Delhi, India: Tata Engineering Research Institute.

Maslow, A. (1943). A theory of human motivation. *Psychological Review, 50*(4), 370–396.

McGregor, D. (1960). *The human side of enterprise*. New York: McGraw-Hill.

Menon, N. (2006, July 26). I volunteer. *The Times of India*, p. 39. Retrieved August 8, 2008, from http://www.karmayog.org/library/libartdis.asp?r=152&libid=770

Mullerat, R. (Ed.). (2005). *Corporate social responsibility: The corporate governance of the 21st century*. London: Kluwer Law International.

New Academy of Business. (2004). *Enhancing business-community relations.* New Delhi, India: New Academy of Business. Retrieved March 16, 2009, from http://www.newacademy.ac.uk/research/businesscommunity/unvpages/india/india_report_appendices.pdf

Parashurama K. G., Jafadish, B., & Siddegowda, Y. S. (2008, December). *Corporate social responsibility and emerging areas of participation.* Paper presented at Nitte Conference, Mangalore, India.

Partners in Change. (1997). *Report on corporate involvement in social development in India* (Research supported by ActionAID India and undertaken by Social and Rural Research Institute, New Delhi). New Delhi, India: Partners in Change.

Peloza, J., & Hassay, D. N. (2006). Intra-organizational volunteerism: Good soldiers, good deeds and good politics. *Journal of Business Ethics, 64*(4), 357–379.

Points of Light Foundation. (2005). *Measuring employee volunteering programs: The human resources model.* Volunteer Center National Network & The Center for Corporate Citizenship of Boston College. Retrieved April 2, 2009, from www.pointsoflight.org/networks/business/evp_pdf.cfm

Reed, P., & Selbee, K. (2001). The civic core in Canada: Disproportionality in charitable giving, volunteering, and civic participation. *Nonprofit and Voluntary Sector Quarterly, 30*(4), 761–780.

Rochlin, S., & Christoffer, B. (2000). *Making the business case: Determining the value of corporate community involvement* (Working paper). Boston: Boston College Center for Corporate Citizenship.

Rog, E., Pancer, S. M., & Bactz, M. C. (2004). *Community and corporate perspectives on corporate volunteer programs: A win-win approach to community betterment.* Toronto, Canada: Canadian Center for Philanthropy.

Rolnick, P. J. (1962). Charity, trusteeship, and social change in India: A study of a political ideology. *World Politics, 14*(3), 439–460.

Sharma, S. (2005a). A model for corporate development: A holistic approach. *Vilakshan, XIMB Journal of Management, 2*(2), 71–78.

———. (2005b). A Vedic integration of transitions in management thought: Towards transcendental management. *Gurukul Business Review, 1,* Spring, 4–12.

Shrivastava, H., & Venkateswaran, S. (2000). *The business of social responsibility in India.* New Delhi, India: Partners in Change.

SCB (Standard Chartered Bank). (2009). *Employee volunteering.* Retrieved May 6, 2010, from http://www.standardchartered.com/sustainability/community-investment/employee-volunteering/en/

Sudip, M., & Kumar, V. (2005). *Emerging trends in corporate social responsibility: Perspective and experiences from post-liberalized India* (Report). Hyderabad, India: National Academy of Legal Studies & Research, Nalsar University of Law.

Zutshi, A. & Sohal, A. (2003). Stakeholder involvement in the EMS adoption process. *Business Process Management Journal, 9*(2), 133–148.

Web sites

Karmayog. http://www.karmayog.org
Tata. http://www.tata.com/

Chapter 5

Abruzzese, S. (November 25, 2007). U.S. Peace Corps recruiting older volunteers, *New York Times*. Retrieved July 28, 2010, from http://www.nytimes.com/2007/11/25/world/americas/25iht-peace.1.8466588.html?_r=1

Baldock, C. V. (1999). Seniors as volunteers: An international perspective on policy. *Ageing & Society, 1*(5), 581–602.

Baruah, T. (December 2004). Service with a smile. *Harmony Magazine*. Retrieved April 1, 2009, from http://www.harmonyindia.org/hportal/VirtualPageView.jsp?page_id=981

Bass, S. A., & Caro, F. G. (1995). Older people as researchers: Benefits to research and the community. *Educational Gerontology, 2*(5), 467–478.

Butrica, B. A., Johnson, R. W., & Zedlewski, S. R. (2007). *Volunteer transitions among older Americans*. Washington, DC: Urban Institute.

Corporation for National and Community Service. (2010). *Volunteering in America: Information of volunteering and civic engagement*. Retrieved July 2, 2010, from http://www.volunteeringinamerica.gov/special/Older-Adults-(age-65-and-over)

Cnaan, R. A., Boddie, S. C., Handy, F., Yancey, G., & Schneider, R. (2002). *The invisible caring hand: American congregations and the provision of welfare*. New York: New York University Press.

Developments. (2008). *India: Facing an ageing population*. Retrieved July 28, 2010, from http://www.developments.org.uk/articles/india-facing-an-ageing-population

Ezine, Sattva. (September 22, 2008). *Tech firms chip in: Citizen matters in Bangalore*. Retrieved January 1, 2009, from http://bangalore.citizenmatters.in/articles/view/453-infosys-aol-csr

Herzog, A. R., House, J. S., & Morgan, J. N. (1991). Relation of work and retirement to health and well-being in older age. *Psychology and Aging, 6*(2), 202–211.

Kim, J., Lee, J., Lee, M-A., & Lee, Y. (2007). Volunteering among older people in Korea. *Journals of Gerontology: Series B: Psychological Sciences and Social Sciences, 62*(1), S69–S73.

Kreutzbruck, V. von. (May 31, 2007). Germany's army of senior volunteers: A graying population gives back to society. *Spiegel Online*. Retrieved July 28, 2010, from http://www.spiegel.de/international/germany/0,1518,485097,00.html

Kutner, G., & Love, J. (2003). *Time and money: An in-depth look at 45+ volunteers and donors. Multicultural Study*. Washington, DC: American Association of Retired Persons.

Lehr, U. (2003). Psychologie des Alterns [Psychology of Aging] (1st ed. 1972 ; 10 rev. eds). Wiesbaden.

Li, Y., & Ferraro, K. F. (2006). Volunteering in middle and later life: Is health a benefit, barrier, or both? *Social Forces, 85*(1), 497–519.

Lum, T. Y., & Lightfoot, E. (2005). The effects of volunteering on the physical and mental health of older people. *Research on Aging, 27*(1), 31–55.

Mehta, K., & Yunong, H. (2004). Across-national study of senior volunteerism in two nongovernmental organizations in Singapore and P.R. China. *Hallym International Journal of Aging, 6*(2), 157–173.

Mitra, A., & Van Delinder, J. (2007). Elite women's roles in empowering oppressed women: Volunteer work in NGOs in Kolkata, India. In K. L. Misra & J. H. Lowry (Eds.), *Recent studies on Indian women* (pp. 355–380). New Delhi, India: Rawat Publications.

Morrow-Howell, N. (2006). Civic engagement at the 2005 White House Conference on Aging. *Public Policy and Aging Report, 15*(1), 13–17.

Morrow-Howell, N., Hinterlong, J., Rozario, P. A., & Tang, F. (2003). Effects of volunteering on the well-being of older adults. *Journals of Gerontology: Series B: Psychological Sciences and Social Sciences, 53B*(3), S137–S145.

Narushima, M. (2005). "Payback time": Community volunteering among older adults as a transformative mechanism. *Ageing & Society, 25*(4), 567–584.

NSSO (National Sample Survey Organization). (March 2006). *Morbidity, health care and the condition of the aged* [Report No. 507, (60/25.0/1)]. New Delhi, India: Ministry of Statistics and Programme Implementation, Government of India.

———. (November 1998). *The aged in India: A socio-economic profile* [Report No. 446 (52/25.0/3)]. New Delhi, India: Ministry of Statistics and Programme Implementation, Government of India.

Piliavin, J. A., & Siegel, E. (2007). Health benefits of volunteering in the Wisconsin Longitudinal Study. *Journal of Health & Social Behavior, 48*(4), 450–464.

Polanki, P. (February 20, 2004). "Retired" yes; yet full of zest. *The Times of India*. Retrieved July 28, 2010, from http://timesofindia.indiatimes.com/city/pune/Retired-yes-yet-full-of-zest/articleshow/507574.cms

Registrar General of India. (1996). *Provisional population totals, Chapter 4: Population projections*. Retrieved July 29, 2010, from http://censusindia.gov.in/Data_Products/Library/Provisional_Population_Total_link/PDF_Links/chapter4.pdf

Savishinsky, J. (2004). The volunteer and the sannyasin: Archetypes of retirement in America and India. *International Journal of Aging & Human Development, 59*(1), 25–41.

Saxon-Harrold, S., McCormack, M., & Hume, K. (June 2000). America's senior volunteers. *Independent Sector*. Retrieved March 14, 2006, from http://www.independentsector.org/uploads/Resources/americas_senior_volunteers.pdf

Schlesinger, R. (March 1, 2006). Giving peace a chance: A growing number of older Americans are signing up for the Peace Corps. *AARP Bulletin*. Retrieved February 9, 2009, from http://bulletin.aarp.org/yourworld/reinventing/articles/giving_peace_a_chance.html

Sengupta, N. (2004). *Home work time*. Retrieved December 2, 2009, http://www.harmony-india.org/hportal/VirtualPageView.jsp?page_id=777

Van Willigen, M. (2000). Differential benefits of volunteering across the life course. *Journals of Gerontology: Series B: Psychological Sciences and Social Sciences, 55*(5), S308–S318.

Visaria, P. (2001). Demographics of ageing in India. *Economic and Political Weekly, 36*(22), 1967–1975.

Wilson, J., & Musick, M. (1999). The effects of volunteering on the volunteer. *Law and Contemporary Problems, 62*(4), 141–168.

Chapter 6

Agarwal, S., & Dadrawala, N. (2004). Philanthropy and law in India. In M. Sidel & I. Zaman (Eds.), *Philanthropy and law in South Asia* (pp. 115–181). Quezon City, Philippines: Asia Pacific Philanthropy Consortium.

Al-Qasmi, M. B. A. (n.d.). *How the long journey began*. Retrieved January 18, 2009, from http://www.markazulmaarif.org/home_in.asp

Asif, A. U. (2006). National Workshop of Muslim NGOs. *Fana Watch*. Retrieved July 28, 2010, from http://fanawatch.com/index.php?do=news_view&id=195

AVARD (Association of Voluntary Agencies for Rural Development). (1992). *Government-NGO interface in India's development: A country paper*. Presented to the AN-GOC-APDC Regional Dialogue on Prospects for GO-NGO Collaboration, Bangkok, Thailand.

Berger, M. S. (2006). *Religion and development aid: The special case of Islam*. Retrieved November 30, 2008, from http://www.clingendael.nl/publications/2006/20061000_cdsp_pap_berger.pdf

Copal Partners Research. (2006, June 19). *India's charity sector: An overview and analytical approach*. Retrieved October 1, 2008, from http://www.copalpartners.com/Copal_Partners_Charity_Sector_Report_060619.pdf

D'Souza, A. L. (2000). The Church and social service. In S. Arokiasamy & J. Chathanatt (Eds.), *Songs of silence: Christians in nation building*. New Delhi, India: Media House. pp. 32–34, 46.

Handy, F., & Kassam, M. (2007). Practice what you preach? The role of rural NGOs in women's empowerment. *Journal of Community Practice, 14*(3), 69–91.

Harper, M., Rao, D. S. K., & Sahu, A. K. (2008). *Development, divinity and dharma: The role of religion in development and microfinance institutions*. Warwickshire, UK: Practical Action Publishing.

Kazi, D. (2004). *Interview with Danyal Kazi, Chairman, PRAY Foundation Trust*. Retrieved July 28, 2010, from http://www.painreliefandyou.org/views.html

Krishnan, M. (December 3, 2001). The Trojan Horse act. *Outlook India*. Retrieved October 5, 2008, from http://www.outlookindia.com/fullprint.asp?choice=1&fodname=200112 03&fname=NGO+Funding+(F)&sId=1

Lobo, L. (1999). Social vision and concern in Christianity: A historical perspective. In C. Patel (Ed.), *Social work practice: Religio-philosophical foundations* (pp. 57–71). Jaipur, India: Rawat Publishing.

Milli Gazette. (August 10, 2005) *Padma river opens hell on Murshidabad in Bengal, Markazul Ma'arif reaches to the rescue of 1200 families*. Retrieved July 29, 2010, from http://www.milligazette.com/IndMusStat/2005a/027-mmerc-10aug05.htm

———. (May 23, 2007). *Brief Report of the National Workshop of Muslim NGOs held in New Delhi*. Retrieved November 30, 2008, from http://www.milligazette.com/dailyupdate/2007/200705232_indian_muslims_islam_upliftment_NGO_islamic.htm

Institute of Microfinance and Development. (July 2003). *Report of the first conference on networking of NGOs of India*, Mumbai. Retrieved July 28, 2009, from http://imad.in/report1.pdf

PRAY (Pain Relief and You). (August 2008). *PRAY organizational PowerPoint presentation*. Received through personal e-mail.

Planning Commission. (2002). *Report of the steering committee on voluntary sector for the tenth five-year plan (2002–07)*. New Delhi: Government of India. Retrieved September 20, 2008, from http://planningcommission.nic.in/aboutus/committee/strgrp/stgp_vol.pdf

———. (November 2006). *Social, Economic and Educational Status of the Muslim Community of India: A Report* (Sachar Report, Prime Minister's High Level Committee, Cabinet Secretariat, Government of India). New Delhi: Government of India. Retrieved July 23, 2009, from http://www.imc-usa.org/reports/2006/pmhlc.muslims.pdf

Rahman, S. U. (Ed.) (2006). *Directory of Muslim NGOs in India*. New Delhi: Global Media Publications.

Riley, J. M. (2002). *Stakeholders in rural development: Critical collaboration in state-NGO relationships.* New Delhi, India: SAGE Publications.

Sen, S. (1993). *Defining the nonprofit sector: India* [Working Papers of The Johns Hopkins Comparative Nonprofit Sector Project No. 12. L. M. Salamon & H. K. Anheier (Eds.)]. Baltimore, MD: The Johns Hopkins Institute for Policy Studies.

Sikand, Y. (September 8, 2006). Being Muslim in India today: Some reflections. *Milli Gazette.* Retrieved November 30, 2008, from http://www.milligazette.com/dailyupdate/2006/20060908_Muslim_india_reality_reflections.htm

Tandon, R., & Srivastava, S. S. (2003). *Invisible, yet widespread: The nonprofit sector in India.* New Delhi, India: PRIA.

The Hindu. (February 14, 2004). Man with a Mission. Retrieved July 28, 2010, from http://www.hinduonnet.com/thehindu/mp/2004/02/19/stories/2004021900230400.htm

Wajihuddin, M. (October 19, 2008). He helps orphans take confident strides in life. *The Times of India.* Retrieved November 30, 2008, from http://timesofindia.indiatimes.com/articleshow/msid-3613557,prtpage-1.cms

Web sites

AIM for Seva. http://www.aimforseva.org

Amma. http://www.amma.org

Arpana. http://www.arpana.org

Bochasanwasi Shri Akshar Purushottam Swaminarayan Sanstha (BAPS). http://www.swaminarayan.org

Chinmaya Mission. http://www.chinmayamission.com

Eternal Hope Charity Mission. http://www.ehcmission.org/e/about.htm

Gospel Echoing Missionary Society. http://www.gemsbihar.org/index.asp

Loving Hands Ministries. http://www.lovinghandsministries.com

Maharishi Ved Vigyan Vishwa Vidyapeetham. http://www.maharishi-india.org

Markazul Ma'arif. http://www.markazulmaarif.org/home/default.asp

Rahat Foundation Trust. http://rahatwelfaretrust.org

Chapter 7

Burchell, S., Clubb, C., & Hopwood, A. G. (1985). Accounting in its social context: Towards a history of value added in the United Kingdom. *Accounting, Organizations and Society, 10*(4), 381–413.

Bureau of Labor Statistics. (2008). *Occupational employment statistics.* Retrieved March 14, 2008, from http://www.bls.gov/oes/current/oes_40380.htm

CNCS (Corporation for National and Community Service). (2010). *Volunteering in America 2010: Fact Sheet.* Retrieved August 15, 2010 from http://www.volunteeringinamerica.gov/assets/resources/FactSheetFinal.pdf

Graff, Linda. (2010). *A note on assessing value from BEST OF ALL: The quick reference guide to effective volunteer involvement.* Retrieved August 15, 2010 from http://www.energizeinc.com/art/abeso.html

Handy, F., & Srinivasan, N. (2005). The demand for volunteer labor: A study of hospital volunteers. *Nonprofit and Voluntary Sector Quarterly, 34*(4), 491–509.

Independent Sector. (2008). *Value of volunteer time.* Retrieved March 14, 2008, from http://www.independentsector.org/programs/research/volunteer_time.html

Mook, L., Quarter, J., & Richmond, B. J. (2007). *What counts: Social accounting for nonprofits and cooperatives* (2d ed.). London: Sigel Press.

Ranganathan, J. (1999). Signs of sustainability: Measuring corporate environmental and social performance. In M. Bennett & P. James (Eds.), *Sustainable measures: Evaluation and reporting of environmental and social performance* (pp. 475–495). Sheffield, UK: Greenleaf Publishing.

Salamon, L. M., Sokolowski, S. W., & Associates. (2004). *Global civil society: Dimensions of the nonprofit sector.* Vol. 2. Bloomfield, CT: Kumarian Press.

White, A., & Zinkl, D. (1999). Standardisation: The next chapter in corporate environmental performance evaluation and reporting. In M. Bennett & P. James (Eds.), *Sustainable measures: Evaluation and reporting of environmental and social performance* (pp. 117–131). Sheffield, UK: Greenleaf Publishing.

Wolff, N., Weisbrod, B. A., & Bird, E. J. (1993). The supply of volunteer labor: The case of hospitals. *Nonprofit Management and Leadership, 4*(1), 23–45.

Chapter 8

Anheier , Helmut & Salamon, Lester. (1999). Volunteering in cross-national perspective: Initial comparisons. *Law and Contemporary Problems, 6*(4), 43–65.

Brudney, J. L. (2005). Designing and managing volunteer programs. In R. D. Herman (Ed.), *The Jossey-Bass Handbook of Nonprofit Leadership and Management* (pp. 310–345). Jossey-Bass: San Francisco.

Carter, K. A. (2008). Volunteer tourism: An exploration of the perceptions and experiences of volunteer tourists and the role of authenticity in those experiences. (Master of Applied Science dissertation, Lincoln University, Canterbury, New Zealand).

Charles, J. A. (1993). *Service clubs in American society: Rotary, Kiwanis, and Lions.* Urbana: University of Illinois Press.

Cnaan, R. A., Boddie, S. C., Handy, F., Yancey, G., & Schneider, R. (2002). *The invisible caring hand: American congregations and the provision of welfare.* New York: New York University Press.

Cravens, J. (2000). Virtual volunteering: Online volunteers providing assistance to human service agencies. *Journal of Technology in Human Services, 17*(2/3), 119–136.

Handy, F., Brodeur, N., & Cnaan, R. A. (2006). Summer in the island: Episodic volunteering. *Voluntary Action, 7*(3), 31–46.

Handy, F., & Cnaan, R. A. (2007). The role of social anxiety in volunteering. *Nonprofit Management and Leadership, 18*(1), 41–58.

Handy, F., Kassam, M., Feeney, S., & Ranade. B. (2006). *Grass-roots NGOs by women for women: The driving force of development in India.* New Delhi: SAGE Publications.

Handy, F., Mook, L., & Quarter, J. (2006). Organizational perspectives on the value of volunteer labour. *Australian Journal of Volunteering, 11*(1), 28–37.

Hustinx, L., & Lammertyn, F. (2003). Collective and reflexive styles of volunteering: A sociological modernization perspective. *Voluntas, 14*(2), 167–187.

Lalitha, N. V. (1975). *Voluntary work in India*. New Delhi, India: National Institute of Public Cooperation and Child Development.

Lorentzen, H., & Hustinx, L. (2007). Civic involvement and modernization. *Journal of Civil Society, 3*(2), 101–118.

Lovitt, R. (2008). *The value of voluntourism: Msnbc.com-Condé Nast survey explores emerging travel trend*. Retrieved July 26, 2010, from http://www.msnbc.msn.com/id/23262573

MacDuff, N. (2004). *Episodic volunteering: Organizing and managing the short-term volunteer program*. Walla Walla, WA: MBA Publishing.

Mehta, N. T., & Kumar, S. (February 15, 2009). Online campaigners voice social consciousness. *India Today*. Retrieved March 14, 2009, from http://indiatoday.intoday.in/index.php?option=com_content&task=view&id=29121&sectionid=4&issueid=93&Itemid=1

Mustonen, P. (2006). Volunteer tourism: Postmodern pilgrimage? *Journal of Tourism and Cultural Change, 3*(3), 160–177.

Novelli, M. (Ed.). (2005). *Niche tourism: Contemporary issues, trends and cases*. Oxford: Elsevier.

Planning Commission. (1994). *Action plan to bring about a collaborative relationship between voluntary organisations and government* (Hindi and English). New Delhi: VANI. Available for purchase at http://www.vaniindia.org/vanipublication.php

RGHF (Rotary Global History Fellowship). (n.d.). *History of Rotary in India*. Retrieved March 14, 2009, from http://www.rotaryfirst100.org/global/regions/india.htm

Salamon, Lester M., Wojciech Sokolowski, S., & Associates. (2004). *Global civil society: Dimensions of the nonprofit sector, Vol. 2*. Bloomfield, CT: Kumarian Press.

Sherraden, M. S., Stringham, J., Sow, S. C., & McBride, A. M. (2006). Forms of international voluntary service: A sector of global civil society. *Voluntas, 17*(2), 156–173.

Tandon R., and Srivastava, S. S. (2003). *Invisible, yet widespread: The nonprofit sector in India*. New Delhi, India: PRIA.

Voluntary Action Network India (VANI). (n.d.) *History*. Retrieved July 8, 2010, from http://www.vaniindia.org/history.asp

Web sites

Karmayog. http://www.karmayog.org/

Voluntary Action Network India (VANI). http://www.vaniindia.org

Index

About the Authors

Femida Handy is Professor at the School of Social Policy and Practice at the University of Pennsylvania in Philadelphia (United States of America) and Senior Scholar at the Faculty of Environmental Studies at York University in Toronto (Canada). She specializes in the study of nonprofit organizations and volunteers, and international NGOs, and is the Editor-in-Chief of *Nonprofit and Voluntary Sector Quarterly*. Her articles have appeared in many journals and received numerous awards.

Meenaz Kassam is Assistant Professor of Sociology and is currently teaching at the Department of International Studies at the American University of Sharjah (United Arab Emirates). She is on the Board of Directors of the NGO Aseema whose mandate is to promote and protect the rights of underprivileged children and women. Her articles have appeared in the *Journal of Community Practice, Social Development Issues, Nonprofit Management and Leadership,* the *Journal of Women's Studies,* and the *Canadian Journal of Sociology.*

Jillian Ingold is a PhD candidate of South Asia Studies at the University of Pennsylvania (Philadelphia, United States of America). Her interests are in politics, nonprofit regulation, and Muslim minority issues in modern India. She has lived in India and Bangladesh and speaks Hindi, Urdu, and Bengali.

Bhagyashree Ranade is CEO, Marketing and Market Research Consultants and Discovery and Transition. She is also a trustee for the Institute for Women Entrepreneurial Development and Animal Life in Pune (India). Her publications have appeared in the *Journal of Community Practice, Nonprofit Management and Leadership, Nonprofit and Voluntary Sector Quarterly,* and *Social Development Issues.* She has coauthored the book, *Grass-roots NGOs by Women for Women: The Driving Force of Development in India* (SAGE, 2006) along with F. Handy, M. Kassam, and S. Feeney.